CIVILIZATION
AND BARBARISM

CIVILIZATION AND BARBARISM

Punishing Criminals in the Twenty-First Century

Graeme R. Newman

SUNY
PRESS

Published by State University of New York Press, Albany

For information, contact State University of New York Press, Albany, NY
www.sunypress.edu

Library of Congress Cataloging-in-Publication Data

Names: Newman, Graeme R., author.
Title: Civilization and barbarism : punishing criminals in the twenty-first century / Graeme R. Newman.
Description: Albany : State University of New York Press, [2020] | Includes bibliographical references and index.
Identifiers: LCCN 2019027837 | ISBN 9781438478111 (hardcover : alk. paper) | ISBN 9781438478128 (pbk. : alk. paper) | ISBN 9781438478135 (ebook)
Subjects: LCSH: Punishment. | Imprisonment. | Alternatives to imprisonment. | Corporal punishment. | Criminal justice, Administration of.
Classification: LCC HV8693 .N479 2020 | DDC 364.6/7—dc23
LC record available at https://lccn.loc.gov/2019027837

10 9 8 7 6 5 4 3 2 1

Contents

Acknowledgment

For several decades I have enjoyed the wonderful service and resources of the University at Albany Libraries. There has never been a book, article, or other item they could not find. It's like having my own personal library. This book, more than any other, would probably never have been written without this amazing resource. My sincere thanks to the many library professionals who have helped me over several decades. I have always said that their work is mostly unseen and too often unappreciated. But to me, they are the heart of the University.

Introduction

A Humane Solution to a Barbaric Situation

This book challenges the nature, justice, and morality of criminal punishment in Western civilization. It questions the received history of criminal punishment; so, of necessity, it focuses on corporal punishment, because the history of criminal punishment is largely a history of corporal punishment (and its extreme form, the death penalty), its transformation into prison, and eventually the transformation of prison into mass incarceration. It uncovers the barbaric effects and practices of mass incarceration, and identifies credible, humane alternatives to the often violent punishments inflicted on today's offenders. The overall aim is to bring back a sense of moderation to criminal punishment, to eliminate punishments of excess (mass incarceration and the extensive penal and societal harm that it inflicts) and replace them with moderate and limited punishments.

Trying to reform criminal punishment is nothing new. For the last hundred years many reformers have advocated alternatives to incarceration: rehabilitation, probation, parole, fines, restorative justice, community service, and on and on. But as these alternatives have been introduced, the more incarceration has increased. So, regardless of their claimed success or beneficial effects, none of these can be taken seriously as having served as an alternative to prison. In fact, they may have even contributed to mass incarceration, since the idea of rehabilitating offenders through prison offers a ready justification for its existence, and more of it.

I offer two alternatives as a way to rid us of mass incarceration: (1) for the majority of offenders moderate corporal punishment (MCP), that is, the precise, limited, temporary, application of pain to the body, carefully controlled and administered according to specific guidelines; and (2) for the very serious and worst of the worst offenders, open incapacitation (OI), carefully monitored physical incapacitation *without incarceration.*

Now, before you slam this book shut or switch off your Kindle, bear with me. I have come to these alternatives with much trepidation. But I have concluded that the immediate and long-term penal harm of prison (even a tiny bit of prison) is so destructive of individual, family, and community life that we must try something new, even if at first blush it seems distasteful, cruel, or even immoral. I have come to these two punishment alternatives to prison after comparing the outcomes of all alternative punishments according to available scientific data, cutting through the bias against corporal punishment that pervades the research and penal policy.

It might be argued that if a punishment is even a little bit immoral (or if you prefer, evil) it should be rejected and surely that is why we discarded the horrendous corporal and capital punishments of the past. But if that were the case, we could not punish at all, especially with prison, for as I will show, all punishment has an evil side to it, and that includes very well-meaning punishments such as rehabilitation.

The fact is that punishment is a very complicated concept, idea, or practice. All punishment, even the mildest, is a destructive act, always violent or surreptitiously aggressive. At its extreme, it destroys people's lives so that it can restore them. It may create remorse in the punisher as much as, or more than, in the punished. It is irresistible, always searching for ways to spread its evil wings.

Three Justifications

Punishment is universally resented, but universally applied. Though it takes on different forms in different cultures, there are basically three justifications for its use.

The first is obedience, better known in the criminal justice world as deterrence—a forward looking justification that seeks to ensure that the infraction will not happen again.

> Little Johnny, a four-year-old, lives in center city Philadelphia. On his way to day care, he breaks away from his mommy and runs across Lombard Street without looking. A car screeches to a halt, almost running him over. His mom rushes to him and

gives him a sharp slap on the legs. In tears, she cries, "Don't you ever do that again! You could have been killed!" Johnny winces, and cries.

If little Johnny repeats his offense, he will get a harder slap. One must be cruel to be kind, which is why mommies everywhere sometimes cry after they punish their child, though "Tiger moms" are said to develop a steely disposition. This natural response by a parent to her child's infraction, a practice as old as families have existed, gives credence to what is called the utilitarian philosophy, a wide-ranging approach to understanding society and human behavior, popularized and systematized by the English thinkers of the eighteenth century, Jeremy Bentham its greatest proponent. The hope that Johnny will not repeat his disobedience is called in the criminal justice world, individual deterrence. However, not only is it for his own good, it is for ours too. Had his siblings or friends been watching the slap, his punishment would also be called general deterrence, based on the hope that those witnessing the punishment will also be deterred. The moral basis of this philosophy is summed up simply: the end justifies the means.[1] That is, we want a secure, ordered society (family or community), and a punishment for disobedience is a means to get it.

The second is deserts, payback, "it serves you right," or "he asked for it." This view of punishment is commonly referred to in criminal justice as retribution, its more primitive version, revenge or vengeance.

In Singapore Anuar, a nine-year-old, uses an f-bomb at the dinner table. His father takes him firmly by the hand to the bathroom. "Give me your toothbrush," he demands. Anuar does as he is told. Dad wets it, rubs it on a bar of soap and says, "You used a very dirty word. Wash your mouth out with soap and water!" Anuar does as he is told. He has done this before. "I'm sorry! I'm sorry! I didn't mean it, I couldn't help it!" he cries.

This is a backward looking justification, necessarily brought on the offender by his own action. It rests on a "categorical imperative" (that is, a blunt moral assertion) that every wrong deed must be punished because it was wrong, and most importantly with a punishment that fits the crime. Often the punishment reflects the offense in some way, hence the punishment of Anuar is washing out his mouth, from whence came the dirty word.

The third is redemption and its many close and distant relatives (restoration, rehabilitation, enlightenment, reform, penitence, community service, and so on).

> In a quiet suburb of San Francisco, three-year-old Billy throws a tantrum because his mommy refuses to give him a second ice cream. "That's it! Time out!" cries mommy. "Go to your corner and face the wall. You can come back when you're ready to say you're sorry!" Billy stands in his corner, sobbing. He turns around. "Face the wall!" calls mommy. But soon she relents, and goes to him. "Are you ready to say you're sorry?" she asks tearfully. "Yes mommy, I'm sorry." Mommy gives him a hug.

This approach, which may also include within it elements of the first two justifications, rests on the assumption that it is through pain and suffering of punishment that the offender learns his lesson and demonstrates to us that he truly understands the error of his ways, the horrible effects of his crime. On the positive side, this justification may have deep religious overtones, the enlightening functions of suffering that are recognized and practiced by most of the major religions of the world, whether through self-flagellation, austere restrictions on bodily movement (the lotus position, for example), or strict diet. The problem, though, is to suffer in such a visible way that one's confession of wrongdoing and expression of remorse are sufficiently convincing. The way we punish can help the punished to overcome a past wrongful act.

When toddlers misbehave, mothers everywhere in the West say, "Time out!" The child is ushered into a selected corner of a room, usually out of our sight, or, if he has been especially naughty, required to turn and face the wall, as described above. The type of punishment here is social ostracism, and its severity gauged by the length of time he is required to remain in the "time out" zone. Mothers of the twentieth century used the most familiar punishment of "go to your room," but in the twenty-first century this punishment doesn't work well because it is not demonstrably painful enough. If the offender is a teenager, it may be very much what she wants, to get away from all adults; and for any age child there is plenty to do in one's room, where most often one finds all the trinkets of the twenty-first century: iPads, tablets, computers, electronic games, Lego, TV, and even books. Like prison for white-collar criminals, it just isn't painful enough. Parents these days are stuck without the good old alternative expressed in the adage "spare the rod and spoil the child," the punishment philosophy expressed to his mother by Hamlet, who was very, very naughty, capable of the cruelest deeds:

I must be cruel only to be kind.
Thus bad begins and worse remains behind.[2]

Until the twentieth century, punishment had a simple solution. You whacked the offender, then felt sorry for him and yourself. If only the offender had not misbehaved, you would not have had to punish. You do not want to punish, but for the good of all you *must*. Translated into eighteenth-century Enlightenment policy, each act of punishment is applied in the name of civil society. It is the righteousness of religious practice that relieves the guilt of cruelty, because it is done in the service of good government. It begins at home, where each child is turned into a good family member and eventually a good citizen. It is for the good of all.

It was during the Enlightenment, as we will see, that the very entrails of punishment, bodily pain intentionally inflicted, were torn from criminal punishment. The direct punishment of the body was abolished in a matter of several decades, and it was replaced, at the societal level, with the confinement of prison, and, within the family and schools, with "time out" and confinements of various kinds.

Except, that is not quite what happened. The violence of punishment of the body continued to be applied haphazardly within prisons, as I will recount often throughout this book. Nor did it go away in families or in schools, or, at least, it persists. Surveys show that the majority of college students report having been slapped or hit by parents when they were children. In the face of active campaigning, corporal punishment in schools still persists in some states of the United States and throughout many countries of the world, especially those less developed.[3]

Two Ways to Punish

There are basically two ways to punish: punish the body directly or confine the offender's body in some location or setting. Johnny and Anuar received bodily punishment. Billy was confined to a place. We should note, though, that Billy went to his place when told. There will be many occasions in which he must be taken by the hand or shepherded to that location. In other words, even confinement in a place requires for the most part direct contact with the body of the offender.

Both methods of punishment may also be adjusted according to severity. Punishments of the body may be swift and temporary (a smack, a flogging, an electric shock) or drawn out, even permanent (the scarlet letter, whether branded on the body or worn on clothing, the cutting off of the hand or testicles, the death penalty).

Confinement may be for long or short terms—in criminal justice, from days to years or life in prison—and may be adjusted according to intensity, such as solitary confinement, hard labor, diet, and so on.

There are also techniques to enhance or aggravate each way of punishing. Direct bodily punishment may be applied in sessions spanning several months and, in practice, is usually combined with imprisonment—the setting most usual for torture, as we will later see. Bodily punishment is directly or indirectly always part of the punishment of imprisonment. It is more difficult to invent a confining punishment of prison that is short, sharp, and temporary, compared to corporal punishment that does not require prison. Shock incarceration, which we will review later, is one such invention. Both types of punishment may also be enhanced by the use of humiliation, again expressed and administered in many different ways, but usually in some kind of public spectacle, or, if in prison, the coercive, physical domination of inmates by guards or their designated surrogates.

The Moral Problem of Punishment

As we saw with Johnny's mom, those who punish are invariably ambivalent about it, the punisher regretting the necessity to do it. This moral ambivalence is reflected in many societies, if not all. The moral problem with punishment is that it requires the intentional infliction of pain or suffering on an individual. As such, it has to be "legitimized," and so we have criminal laws to do just that. Western civilization has also developed a complex, chimerical, self-serving way to punish criminals that allows it to pretend that we do not intentionally inflict pain and suffering on an offender, or, if we do, it is accidental, so not our fault, even justifiable.[4] The isolated and largely secret conditions of prison life provide this moral smokescreen. In other societies that inflict violent punishment in public, such as most Islamic societies, the moral justification comes directly from Allah, via the

Qur'an, interpreted and applied by clerics or mullahs. They therefore do not need prisons as a moral cover, and, generally, their incarceration rates are much lower than those in the West.

Criminal punishment serves the morality of cultures in many ways, as the famed French sociologist Emile Durkheim so well demonstrated one hundred years ago.[5] What he did not quite manage to say, however, was that the enforcement of morality brings with it an inevitable hypocrisy, so well expressed in Judeo-Christian literature: "There but for the grace of God go I." Durkheim argued that punishing criminals reinforced the feeling of community and cohesiveness of society. It brought people together in combined moral condemnation of the criminal. It also established the premise for later scholars such as the great French playwright (and criminal) Jean Genet, who argued that, because criminals bore the brunt of society's morality play, they were sacrificial lambs to the greater morality of society; saints, not sinners. This view of criminal punishment stereotypes criminals as scapegoats and those who punish them as motivated by violence in the name of doing good for society. It is a recipe for excess. It is also why the language of punishment is replete with nonsense and fabrication,[6] such as, for example, the common claim in most textbooks of "corrections," that we send criminals to prison "*as* punishment, not *for* punishment"—that prisoners are being rehabilitated, not punished.

We point to the violent punishments of days gone by to provide the fodder for our moral assumptions today, to justify and dismiss the destructive conditions of prison life. We are fascinated by those ancient punishments because we cannot imagine applying them today, proof that what we do must therefore be more enlightened, civilized. After all, we have replaced them with nonviolent punishments of which we are proud: prison, probation, parole, community service, counseling, rehabilitation, restorative justice, work release.

In sum, we need those sins of our fathers to justify what we do today. We have lost sight of the essential ingredient of punishment, which is pain, without which punishment cannot be just. Given the confusion of our experts about criminal punishment, revealed, as we will see, by sentencing chaos and the fake ambivalence between punishment and treatment, maybe it is time for a civilized society to reconsider the painful possibilities of criminal punishment—all the possibilities, including various ways of inflicting pain that (1) preserve the dignity of both the offender and the punisher, (2) can be kept under control more reliably compared to prison, (3) are fiscally responsible, (4) are more compatible with the retributive and redemptive justification of punishment, and, for the worst offenders who deserve it, (5) can, for our protection, incapacitate the worst offenders who deserve it, without using prison.

Overview of the Book

The book first revisits the received history of criminal punishment, showing how punishment to excess, the essence of human folly, led us to deny the scandal of mass incarceration. It then argues that returning to physically based punishments—moderate corporal punishment (MCP) and open incapacitation (OI), incapacitation without prison—will break open the intellectual wall that shields prison from its many failed critics. The moral superiority of MCP and OI over prison is well demonstrated. Finally, modern technology can be harnessed to control, administer, and—maybe—normalize it by reining in the human excesses of criminal punishment by making it an everyday affair, no longer the spectacular, disruptive, and violent event it has been in the past.

Chapters 1 through 3 deconstruct the language of civilized punishment and examine why corporal punishment's disappearance in Western civilization coincided with the introduction and growth of prison. They compare the assumed barbarity of corporal punishment in the history of penology to that of the civilized punishment that replaced it: prison. They define what corporal punishment is and is not and distinguish it from torture. The overall question is, if corporal punishment were replaced by prison, is there any chance that its reintroduction would replace prison?

In answering this question, I uncover the basic (and necessary) hypocrisy upon which all punishment rests and deconstruct the modern language of punishment, identifying its many distortions and abuses. I show that aggression is the universal element of all punishment, which drives it towards excess, clearly revealed in the history of criminal punishment. Finally, I identify the bureaucratic facilitators of modern criminal punishment: the corrections establishment and the academy that feeds it.

Chapters 4 and 5 examine in more detail the moral justifications of punishment in the context of criminal justice. They dissect the strengths and weaknesses of retribution and deterrence and uncover the bias against corporal punishment that has caused researchers and policymakers to reject corporal punishment in favor of prison. These biases and practices have contributed to a chaotic criminal punishment system that reeks of injustice and inequity, exacerbating the already terrible effects of mass incarceration. Then, in chapter 6, I address the third moral justification for punishment, redemption in the context of incapacitation (the major justification for the incarceration of the very serious offenders and the worst of the worst), and show how they may be incapacitated without prison.

Chapter 7 systematically assesses the range of criminal punishments available today, including moderate corporal and digital punishments, according to a set of criteria that assesses the outcomes of all punishment types. Moderate corporal punishment easily comes out the winner, but then the question is, to what crimes should MCP be applied? Along the way we also see that prison, by comparison, suffers from severe moral and practical defects compared to moderate corporal punishment.

In chapter 8, we look at the tremendous possibilities for refining the application of moderate corporal punishment that the technologies of the twenty-first century offer: in effect, the use of robotics to control and apply both moderate corporal punishment and incapacitation outside of, and instead of, prison. The great advantage of robotic delivery of punishment is that it can be applied equitably much more than other punishments and avoids human error.

Chapter 9 returns to the question of civilized punishment, comparing the punishments of Western civilization with those of Islamic civilizations that use corporal punishments. It asks why is it that the United States has the highest incarceration rate in the world and Islamic countries generally have very low incarceration rates? Perhaps prison is not as civilized a punishment as popularly assumed? I pursue answers to these questions by examining how the two approaches to punishment bear up according to the standards of international human rights and the US Constitution.

In Chapter 10, now freed from the blinders of twentieth-century thinking about punishment, we look at the possibilities, given the rapid changes in technology, of what might be the way forward to the end of punishment as we know it. Wouldn't it be wonderful if we could abolish punishment completely? Of course, that is a human impossibility. But there may be ways to make it more flexible, less severe, and less voracious, especially by first of all getting rid of mass incarceration. In this chapter, I offer a twelve-step guide to reaching that goal, but I also suggest ways to blunt the current destructive effects of criminal punishment:

- "Normalize"—that is, remove the spectacle of—all criminal punishment.

- Remove human error from the administration and control of criminal punishment by conducting trials, sentencing decisions, and administration of punishment robotically.

- Create the facility for individuals to punish themselves, instead of having the state do it, thus eliminating the most invidious role of punisher against punished.

In 1985, in my book *Just and Painful*, I laid out a powerful argument for the limited corporal punishment of some criminals. This book goes well beyond that thesis, shedding light on why that argument was, and still is, viewed with such shock and even outrage, when the logic and evidence in its favor far surpass that for prison, least of all mass incarceration. In the present book, I revisit some of the original arguments, with many additions demanded by the rapid technological changes of the past two decades, but, more importantly, I place them in the historical and philosophical context of the complicated, verging on tragic, role of punishment in Western civilization, of which the United States is the shining beacon.

And for those of you who just can't wait to debunk any of what I have asserted so far, or what you think I may say in the rest of the book, I have included an appendix that recounts the common (misguided) criticisms and my replies that you can refer to at any time.

Chapter One

From Barbaric to Civilized

The Replacement of Corporal Punishment with Prison

Halfway through the twentieth century, we in the West thought we had progressed nicely and had worked out a civilized and humane way to treat criminals. This mutually shared delusion among academic penologists and practitioners of punishment (that is, the prison bureaucratic complex) has fostered the incredible growth of prison as a punishment in the Western world and the convenient failure to notice the continuance of violent punishments in many countries, especially in the south and east of the Mediterranean and much of Southern Asia. Had it not been for the rapid development of the Internet and global media, this ignorance of the amount and extent of punishment practices and their heavy presence in every country of the world would have continued through to the twenty-first century. Of course, we need not even mention the daily horrendous violent punishments and tortures that are a great attraction in cinemas everywhere.[1] The exotic violence of criminal punishments (formal and informal) is very much a part of the cultural life of those who live in the twenty-first century. It is important to acknowledge that, while adults may be shocked by what they see, their children will grow up used to seeing these violent punishments.

What are the implications of this global context for criminal punishments of the West? The daily presence, notoriety even, of the corporal punishments of Islam and mass media has not yet penetrated the moral bubble within which those in the West live in respect to punishing criminals. Possibly, we are witnessing a "clash of civilizations" (Huntington's thesis)[2] and a return to the forms of punishment that Western civilization once condoned, remembering that even then those punishments occurred within a *civilized* society.

A Short History of Civilized Punishment

Of the ancient civilizations of our past, the Romans and the Greeks used corporal punishments extensively. The Romans thought themselves an enlightened and certainly advanced civilization compared to others, such as their mortal enemies the Parthians, Carthaginians, and the Gauls, all considered barbarians because they indulged in human sacrifice. Yet at the same time, the Romans used torture as a matter of course in conducting interrogations, especially of slaves, whose testimony as witnesses was never allowed unless obtained under torture. And, at the height (and imminent demise) of the Roman Republic, the casual use of crucifixion as a death sentence reached its height when in 71 BCE Crassus crucified some six thousand rebellious slaves along a stretch of the Via Appia. Still, the Romans considered themselves civilized. Indeed, theirs was a magnificent civilization, setting the model of government and rule of law for Western civilization as we know it today.[3]

In fact, all major civilizations today have used corporal punishment at one time or another in their long histories. None have totally abolished it, though they may give the appearance that they have, and, indeed, at particular times in history, corporal punishment has ebbed and flowed.[4] Today, in the United States and other Western countries, it is an officially forbidden method of judicial punishment, but has been replaced with an all embracing form of corporal punishment, one that allows for the possibility to pretend that it is not corporal punishment—prison.

It is very hard to defend prison as an enlightened or civilized punishment, particularly as it is slowly coming to light how many lives are destroyed by this blunt, negligent, unenlightened, irresponsible punishment. For every individual locked up in prison (now close to two million in the United States), there are countless relatives and family members deprived of a livelihood; whole neighborhoods are devastated by prison.[5]

It is likely that the rise of prison is the direct result of the abolition of corporal punishment. The detailed history of the demise of corporal punishment in the West is yet to be written, though what happened to corporal punishment is what is now happening to prison: it was used to excess and it came to a point where (powerful) people said enough is enough. It took but a few outrageous cases of cruel and destructive use of corporal punishment to bring about its abolition, and this occurred in different parts of the Western world. Perhaps the most famous was the 250 lashes laid on a Brazilian sailor in 1910 that resulted in the one-week Revolt of the Whip in Rio de Janeiro.[6]

While the maximum number of lashes was originally set at forty in the Bible (Deuteronomy 25:2–3), the number administered far exceeded that biblical limit, especially in venues such as the military and navies of many Western countries, where discipline was brutally enforced.[7] The numbers of lashes had increased enormously by the end of the nineteenth century. General George Washington petitioned the Continental Congress in 1776 to increase the number of allowed lashes to one hundred from its then thirty-nine. And in 1781 he requested authority to impose up to five hundred lashes. The reason, it has been suggested, was that this helped fill the "punishment gap" between one hundred lashes and the death penalty.[8] The campaign against the death penalty led by Charles Dickens probably resulted in an excessive use of corporal punishment in England; it filled the void left by the movement of capital (not corporal) punishment behind prison walls. Furthermore, since many criminals were shipped off to Australia and other British colonies, they became subject to the corporal punishments of the ships they inhabited and of the indentured servitude they served in Australia.

The early forerunner of mass incarceration, solitary confinement, replaced whipping when it was abolished by the US Navy in 1850. Many naval officers argued that solitary confinement was far more brutal and less humane than was whipping. They also argued that it punished the innocent, since the absence of one sailor in solitary placed a higher workload on remaining workers.[9]

Leading up to this climate, the time of the "Enlightenment" in Europe, movements arose to reduce or abolish whipping. This occurred in Russia[10] and throughout Europe, in favor of various forms of incarceration, the punishment of the "soul" rather than the body, as popularized by French philosopher Michel Foucault in his classic *Discipline and Punish*, who was perhaps the first to recognize the insidious governmental value of prison as a punishment and of the parallel asylums for lunatics.[11] There were two main reasons for the movements against corporal punishments: they had been used in excess (a danger of all punishments), and their public nature was too much of a spectacle, an insult to the refined lives of those who lived above the rabble.[12] What better way to cover up the dreadful truth of a civilized society than to hide away in prison the wanton violence done to those who break the laws, hopefully never to be heard of again, and, of course, in a place where corporal punishments have (and do) run riot within the secrecy of prison walls. It is important to understand that corporal punishment was not replaced by prison, a myth promoted by twentieth-century scholars. It was simply moved behind prison walls.[13]

Until the twentieth century, punishment was first and foremost a spectator sport. With few exceptions, depictions of corporal punishment throughout history show large numbers of onlookers. Its central characteristic was to humiliate to the point that the emotions of the crowd would be both piqued and conflicted. Could one not feel sorry for another reduced to the levels of subjection by the lash, blood pouring from the wounds, or constrained to the whipping post in the town square, shackled to the pillory or stocks? But the objects of punishment were, after all, criminals who had committed offenses against others, or, worse, against the society of onlookers. There is an embedded sense of satisfaction and even pleasure out of seeing someone get what they deserve.

Yet it is an uneasy satisfaction, at bottom full of anguish; it is a sentiment poised on top of a persistent, gnawing guilt. The entire edifice of crime and punishment sits precariously on a deep hypocrisy, revealed by Jesus when he said, "Let him who is without sin cast the first stone" (John 8:7). Or, its twenty-first-century cynical version, "Better him than me!" It is the price we pay (well worth it) for the rule of law. The trouble is that historically it has been very difficult to keep the need to punish under control. There is the constant demand for more.

On the surface of it, watching someone receive corporal punishment brings great clarity and simplicity to the arrangements of social life. It is comforting because the subjection of another through punishment is for something special; it is for a guarantee of order. For social order to exist, rules must be obeyed, individuals must of necessity give themselves up to the rule of order. And if they will not willingly do so, they must be forced to do so. The Enlightenment thinkers of the eighteenth century were almost unanimous on this point (though they did go wobbly at times, especially Rousseau), so well expressed by Rousseau's complaint that "man is born free but everywhere is in chains." Thinkers such as Rousseau, Voltaire, and the father of criminal justice, Cesare Beccaria, viewed the intentional infliction of pain by one human on another as an evil in itself that could be justified only by the rule of law.[14] As a justification for criminal punishment, this was not a new idea. It was the ancient Romans who invented the secular justification for punishment based on a constitution (of sorts).[15] Criminal punishment was justified on the basis of the survival of the Roman Republic (and later the Empire), its social order, and, of course, its commerce. As the Enlightenment thinkers all knew, punishment was the price paid for social order; individual liberty (and commerce) was not possible without it. Their ideas grew directly from the Greco-Roman philosophy and law with which they were, to a man, well versed.

It was the *spectacle* of corporal punishment that upset the Enlightenment thinkers. It was why eventually, thanks to Charles Dickens, the administration of the death penalty was removed to behind prison walls—in lieu of its abolition. What better argument against the spectacle of corporal punishment could be made than the famous scene of Madame Defarge sitting beside the platform of the guillotine watching the heads roll, the blood pour off the platform. Depending on whose side one was on, the beheadings were either unjust, well deserved, or both! It was why, in his famous argument against the death penalty almost a century before Dickens, Beccaria made the seemingly unconvincing argument at the time that life in prison was a far more painful substitute for the death penalty, an argument subsequently taken seriously by those who eventually achieved the abolition of the death penalty in England and elsewhere.[16] The monolithic Eastern State Penitentiary in Philadelphia, opened in 1829 marked the abolition of public corporal punishments and the dramatic reduction of the death penalty in America.[17]

All the humiliation accompanying punishment should be enough to convince us that any kind of punishment that is done in public should be forbidden. It is so degrading. But the philosopher Kevin Murtagh defends corporal punishment by arguing that it is not necessarily degrading—mainly, I think, to the one punished, not so much to the person or organization administering the punishment.[18] One might argue that degrading or humiliating an offender through punishment is not necessarily in itself bad, if it can be shown that the offender deserved it. And it may well be the case that it is a good thing if the person or organization administering the punishment is degraded by it; a solid reminder that what is being done to another person is something that we would all rather not do, a necessary evil? The trouble is that modern society has developed ways to avoid taking the responsibility for administering punishment, thus avoiding the degradation of the punisher by hiding punishment away inside the bureaucratic prison complex.

There are many reasons why the demand for punishment can never be fully satisfied. The only twentieth-century historian of corporal punishment, George Ryley Scott, was convinced that it was sex.[19] His *History of Corporal Punishment*, published in 1938, was based on a Freudian view of the close relationship between sex and violence, that there were cases (he never said how many) where whipping excited the sexual desire and that therefore corporal punishment should be abolished. His book was not so much a history of corporal punishment, but a catalogue of horrors, sadism and masochism lavishly mentioned throughout.[20] If he is right, then we have to conclude that Muslims are a sex-driven lot, since corporal punishment occupies an important place in the range of punishments inflicted by Shari'a law.[21] More on this in chapter 9.

Corporal punishments shock the sensibilities of the Western world. Twenty-first-century Shari'a law has come suddenly into view, migrating from the East to the West at a rapid rate via the massive migration to Europe and North America of refugees from North Africa. The growing Muslim immigrant populations in Western countries have also begun to campaign for the introduction of Shari'a law within their adopted countries. In the US elections in November 2015, Hamtramck, Michigan, made history by electing an Islamic majority to its city council. At least one poll in 2015 found that 51 percent of American Muslims preferred Shari'a law over the American Constitution.[22] And, according to media reports, there are over eighty-four Shari'a courts in the United Kingdom, and London now has a Muslim mayor. This may indicate a coming clash—or conjoining—if it is not already here, of punishment cultures, which I will discuss more fully in chapter 9. For the moment, claiming that we do not do corporal punishment in a civilized (Western) society demeans Islam as a civilization in its own right, does it not? Perhaps its use of corporal punishment is not barbaric, but civilized?[23] I will pursue the ideas of civilized and barbaric punishments in further detail in the next chapter.

In sum, prior to the eighteenth century, the history of criminal punishment in Western civilization has been essentially the history of corporal punishment and aggravated forms of the death penalty. Then a transition began where criminals were sentenced to indentured servitude, criminals were transported to the colonies during Western imperialism, and, finally, there was the building of prisons. But the most significant change in punishment practice as prisons gained hold was the shifting behind prison walls of both the death penalty and corporal punishment. The significant change, then, was away from the public display of criminal punishment. The violence committed against criminals inside prison was hidden from public view. Strictly speaking, corporal punishment did not stop, and, some would argue today, has never stopped behind prison walls. In other words, the central *civilizing* feature of criminal punishment was its secrecy not the disuse of violence. And, from the establishment of prisons to this day, this civilized feature of prison has been enabled by the legion of reformers and reforms that never question the existence of prison but offer ways in which it may be made more humanitarian. This is no different than trying to reform how to inflict the death penalty, a more humane way of killing people, or how to torture humanely.

But we are a civilized people, aren't we? We don't want officially to hurt people, unless we absolutely have to. Isn't that the credo of a civilized society? And if we absolutely have to, we should punish as little as possible. Is that not so? Such was the ethic of the eighteenth-century reformers such as Beccaria and Bentham, utilitarian to the core. And did you know that neither was totally against corporal punishment (though they were against cruelty)? So maybe we should reconsider corporal punishment and ask whether there is a way to civilize it that does not depend on prison as a substitute. Maybe we could turn it around and show that, carefully controlled and brought back into public view, corporal punishment would turn out to be more humane and more civilized than prison.

Chapter Two

From Civilized to Barbaric

Prison, the Civilized Punishment,
Violates both Body and Mind

We think of bodily punishments with repugnance because they have been historically linked to the process of torture. But painful punishment is clearly distinguishable from torture, as we will see. And, although severe bodily punishments were used in English criminal justice until less than a couple of hundred years ago, there is very little evidence that the process of torture as it was used in continental Europe ever took hold in England.[1] Therefore, there must be additional reasons for our revulsion. "It is because we are civilized," we say. "We don't do that sort of thing anymore." We are a civilized people, and so we are naturally revolted by barbarities. But what are barbarous acts? And are they the opposite of civilized acts? There are three ingredients of punishments that represent the essence of barbarism: mutilation, excess, and violence.

The Body of Mutilation

The prototype of the barbaric act of mutilation is that of killing and eating another human being, cannibalism.[2] The savagery of our past history cannot be denied, and, indeed, is still recognized on the battlefield. Yes, our history is also full of great altruism and kindness, but we must recognize that there is an underside to our precariously civilized state. Even though we in the West gave up eating each other very early in human history, we were unable to give up mangling the bodies of criminals and prisoners of war until very late indeed—some would say only half a century ago, if we consider the atrocities of the Vietnam War. But perhaps not at all, if we include the atrocities of the war in former Yugoslavia as part of the "progress" of Western civilization. And if we include the "Middle East" as part of the civilized world (Islam, after all, has common roots with the Judeo-Christian civilization), such atrocious attacks on the body are still with us,[3] thanks in part to ISIS.[4]

Our revulsion at mutilations is also conditioned by the fact that we have, in large part, become "disembodied" in our relationships with each other. Much more emphasis is placed today on the person as a "psychological entity" than on a person as a "thing" or "body," as was, perhaps, the perception of people in the days when slavery was considered the normal state of affairs; days not long gone, and, in parts of Africa, still with us, even flaunted by such groups as ISIS.

In the West, the mid–twentieth century gave birth to the culture of "narcissism"—that is, love of one's own body or self,[5] expressed through the extreme view of the body as being inviolable, sacred, private, except for very specific sexual and medical purposes. This change in the perception of the person probably remains true today,[6] though it is expressed through the obsession of youth with social media and other means of interaction that do not require a physical other.[7]

Mutilating punishments are, then, barbaric because they violate the body's integrity, which is a value we have come to respect in our (Western) civilization, and because they seem like a throwback to our cannibalistic past. But the resolution of the problem of barbarity is not that simple, where punishment is concerned. We must recognize that this explanation is culture-centric. The variations in the use of mutilating punishments across cultures, particularly in Islamic culture, should give us pause for thought. We should recognize that to call any punishment barbaric is to apply a blunt value judgment, and certainly to say that we do not use such a punishment is no cause for moral superiority, especially in an age that, by inaction or indifference, fosters mass incarceration—a form of criminal punishment that is universally considered to be civilized.

We say that prison was introduced as a "civilized" punishment if we subscribe to the idea that there is some "progress" from barbaric to civilized in the history of punishment,[8] or if, even putting aside this sticky question, we merely claim that prison took the place of the mutilating punishments of the past. Apart from the fact that prison actually permits the violation of the body by default (violence and rape in prison), one may also argue that it is based on the idea of mutilating the very soul of the prisoner. So one might speculate whether it would be more humane to do less of the mentally and physically mutilating punishment of prison and use a moderate amount of corporal punishment instead, especially of the kind that is less injurious of the body, that leaves no lasting mark at all.

This idea may seem incredible, but there is a variety of corporal punishments available, some of which are much less mutilating, or, indeed, may not be mutilating at all. For example, electric shock ("electronic flogging," not to be confused with electroconvulsive therapy), properly applied, leaves no bodily scars or mutilations, so does not leave behind it the stigmata (physical and mental) that go with bodily mutilation. Most important, as we will see in chapters 7 and 8, it can be administered in a very brief time, seconds if need be, so that the actual period of violation of the individual may be kept at a minimum. All other bodily punishments of history have been unable (or their advocates unwilling) to avoid this violation of body and mind. Electronic flogging avoids that violation—but only if it is not used in excess.

Excess

The punishments of the eighteenth and early nineteenth centuries in England were clearly excessive: people could be hanged just for stealing a loaf of bread! There were two important and illuminating reasons why these punishments were so excessive. One was the ancient idea that the body or parts of the body should be punished by analogy.[9] The other, and the more important, was that the rulers of England callously used the criminal law to terrify the common people into obedience (we call it "deterrence" today). This occurred especially at the end of the eighteenth century, when the rulers were concerned that there might be an uprising of the "dangerous classes," as had occurred in the revolutions of France and America.[10]

Punishment by analogy to the body was common enough throughout Europe. On November 7, 1817, the severed head of Jeremiah Brandreth was held up to the London crowd as the source of the traitor's crime. Sometimes the offender's heart was cut out, transfixed to his open hand, then held before his face with the words, "Here is your heart."[11] These were intricate punishments designed to get to the very depths of the criminal disposition. The seat of the criminal's guilt was wrenched out of her in no uncertain terms. Today, it might be said, we do not do this because we consider that the seat of guilt lies in the mind, not the body.

But these punishments are also aggravated forms of either corporal punishment or capital punishment, and as such they may be said to be unintentionally excessive, because their overriding aim was to punish the crime by analogy to the body, not to administer as much pain as possible. The analogical function of these punishments (that is, trying to reflect the crime in the punishment, essentially retribution), however, also made it easy to pervert their use for other purposes, namely, those of deterrence. The transformation of analogical punishments into deterrent punishments occurred when the punishment was made exemplary: by punishing publicly, by adding words of admonishment, such as, "Behold the head of a traitor," and by graphically communicating the punishment to the populace, such as placing the dismembered limbs of the offender on public display.

The educative function of analogical punishment that is really a basic form of retribution (as we saw in the introduction and will revisit in chapter 4) has been largely lost in our use of punishment today. It has been displaced by a deterrent function, that is, the use of deserved punishments for a utilitarian purpose. In the case of eighteenth-century England, the purpose was to terrorize the populace into submission. Excesses of punishment resulted, by which we mean that the severity of the punishments often was out of proportion to the crime (that is, death for a petty theft, a punishment that did not reflect the crime at all). This is a widely recognized defect in the utilitarian justification for punishment, of which the deterrence principle is a part. It is unable to set limits on particular punishments. That is, provided that one can make an argument that some greater good can be obtained by using some outrageous punishment as an example to others (and this may include the punishment even of an innocent person, if it can be shown that the evil of doing so is overcome by the good achieved by the ultimate goal), one can claim that it is morally defensible. A clear cause of excess, therefore, is the sheer force of the utilitarian ethic that will press for more and more punishment by example. In the era of bodily punishment, this led to excessive use of punishments that we find easy to pronounce as barbaric, and which we have rightly eliminated from our punishment repertoire.

Note that the exemplary punishment of retribution is not intended to set an example of fear to others at all. Rather, it is intended to enlighten or embellish the significance of the crime both to the criminal and society. The idea is not to frighten individuals into submission (although that may happen), but rather for all to learn together about the evil of the offense committed. We shall have more to say about this aspect of retribution shortly, when we consider the important practice of punishing publicly. In sum, it is an error to confuse the excesses of punishment with the types of punishment. Not all corporal punishments mutilate. Not all corporal punishments in and of themselves are excessive (but corporal punishments are widely believed to be "excessive" simply because they are corporal). For example, the paddle has been used since time immemorial, but used with restraint, there are few who would say it is "barbaric" (though one may disapprove of it for other reasons). If we do say that it is barbaric, we are forced to admit that we are not a very civilized people at all, since it is widely used in the United States and many countries of the world as a method of disciplining children.[12] But if it is used to excess, as was whipping, that is another matter.

The reasons whipping became excessive are two: the highly utilitarian purposes to which it has been put (discipline in the navy), and the fact that it is a numerically based punishment—the numerical base, of course, being another product of the "civilizing process." A brief look at the history of whipping demonstrates the interesting relationship between barbarity and what one might call "civilized excess."

Whipping is probably the oldest numerically based punishment we have, making it possible to calculate in an abstract way the proportion of the punishment to the crime. This is what makes whipping and similar temporary corporal punishments "civilized." However, the abstraction of the relation between the crime and the punishment—that is, having to translate the seriousness of the particular crime into the one dimension of whipping—sets the path to excessive punishments. Sentences may be pronounced with little regard for the concrete facts of the punishment, since the abstraction, the numerical sentence, blurs the real differences in severity of the punishment both as administered and as it is felt by the offender. The one punished certainly knows the difference between, say, thirty lashes and fifty lashes. But to the judge or legislator the difference between thirty and fifty lashes is never felt or even comprehended as anything but an abstract number.

In eighteenth- and nineteenth-century England, this is exactly what happened, and it occurred especially in the navies of the imperial nations of the time,[13] where whipping was the sole form of punishment for serious and minor offenses alike, since many of these offenses could be dealt with summarily by the captain of the ship. The use of numbers to define the differences between the seriousness of offenses reached bizarre proportions in the military and navy, where the practice of whipping was much older than in the criminal justice arena. It reached its gravest proportions in the late eighteenth and early nineteenth centuries, when punishments of one or two hundred lashes were common.[14]

The actual number of lashes was always prescribed by the captain or commanding officer; whatever written laws or rules there were did not state the specific number of lashes for a specific offense, though they did in some jurisdictions specify a maximum. The main reason for this was that most offenses were of a summary nature, so that such offenses as "disobedience" or "drunkenness" were commonly punished by severe whippings. Although whipping in general was the prescribed punishment for most offenses, when it came down to giving the order to punish, the commanding officer always specified the number of lashes. Some also claim that the large majority of those punished was not subjected to more than twenty-five lashes, although the records reported in *The Punishment Response* would not suggest this.[15] Fifty or more would seem to have been quite common, and this got worse and worse as the eighteenth century wore on.

During the British Royal Commission on whipping, conducted by the Royal Navy in 1835–1836, a strong argument for its retention was that it was a milder punishment than the death penalty, which was a common punishment for quite minor offenses. There was a famous case of a sailor being sentenced to death for flipping a button at a superior officer.

It is of great interest to note that the actual number of lashes was not prescribed in English criminal law until quite late. Whipping, when it was applied with other punishments, was not prescribed in terms of number of lashes. Sentences typically pronounced that the offender be "whipped at the cart's tail," without reference to the number of strokes. The only suggestion of "how much" was implied in the distance the offender was to be dragged by the horse and cart.[16]

In 1539, under the rule of Henry VIII, the infamous Whipping Act, which was designed to punish vagrants, never stated the number of lashes. It simply ordered that the offenders were to be "tied to the end of the cart naked, and beaten with whips throughout each market town till the body shall be bloody by reason of such whipping." Fifty years later, the cart's tail was eliminated, and the whipping posts erected. This served the purpose of focusing the punishment specifically upon the whipping itself, and it was at this time that the actual number of strokes was legislated. Note that this was introduced as a reform, since it was thought that by using the post, the number of lashes could be counted more easily than if the whipping were administered to a moving body!

We may conclude that for criminal punishment by whipping there was no clear concern with matching the numerical amount of whipping to the particular crime until the end of the sixteenth century. Rather, it was added into the mixture of punishments that often included the pillory, ridicule, branding, being paraded through the streets sitting on a horse facing its tail, and all manner of demonstrative punishments. The focus of the punishments was on making a clear link between the *quality* of the crime and the *quality* of a punishment. There was no attempt to punish in proportion by matching amount for amount as we do today. It was only when whipping posts were erected, focusing the punishment more clearly on a stationary object, that we had the judicial requirement of the number of lashes to be administered. Even here, so long as other punishments were still administered, as were the pillory and the stocks, there was little attention paid to the number of lashes.

While legislating the number of lashes introduced limits to the amount of whipping, there were still effectively no limits with many of its corollary punishments. The pillory, for example, could lead to a death penalty if the offender happened to be unpopular with the street crowds that were likely to pelt him with stones. We do not see clear trends towards the necessity to introduce limits into the amount of punishment until Jeremy Bentham in the eighteenth century, who pronounced the utilitarian dictum that the evil of the pain must be only just enough to outweigh the pleasure of the offense. But this method of arriving at limits also has its difficulties, since it still requires a highly abstract assessment of how serious the particular offense is (or, in Bentham's words, how much pleasure could be derived from it).

With the introduction of the numerical sentencing of offenders—whipping, prison, and transportation to the colonies—the qualitative base for the punishment very quickly disappeared, and led to the horrendous punishments of several hundred strokes of the lash, many years in prison, or many years transportation. The bizarre lengths that these sentences reached, hundreds of strokes of the lash in the olden days and many years in prison today, have been cut loose from their links to the crimes for which they were legislated. The numbers have developed a life of their own, and have become, in a sense, limitless.

Modern sentencing practice and penal philosophy easily demonstrate how numbers have taken the place of the concrete application of punishment. It has become a common practice of hard-nosed judges in cases of very serious crimes to "stack" a series of sentences on top of each other for a variety of crimes of which the offender has been convicted, with the result that some criminals are sentenced to over one hundred years in prison. Although it may be said that one motivation of the judges in handing down such sentences is to make sure that the offender never sees the light of day again, it is also clear that the numbers have very little to do with the concrete quality of the punishment. That is, it is simply impossible for a criminal to spend over one hundred years in prison.

Here is an even more convincing example. It is the claim of penologists who say they are enlightened that the offender is sent to prison *as* punishment, not *for* punishment, a sophistry that I mentioned in the introduction. This is clearly a symbolic transformation of a concrete punishment into numbers alone. We are told to be satisfied merely with the sentence of so many years, that is, it is the sentence itself that we are supposed to accept as the appropriate punishment, not the pains that go with a punitive sentence. This splitting of the punishment from the sentence opens the door to excess of any punishment, whether incredibly harsh (the pains of imprisonment) or incredibly soft (nothing—that is, a suspended sentence, early parole, "treatment," etc.).

Numbers are, though, essential for modern punishment practice, as we will see in chapters 7 and 8. It is a matter of how they are applied and to what punishment; decisions that may rest not only with judges, but with prosecutors, defense lawyers, and legislators.

Violence

According to enlightened thinkers the essential element of any civilization is its ability to cast off the violence of human (or animal) nature from which it was born. The traditional picture is that of the war of all against all, as Hobbes popularized it, contrasted with an ordered, nonviolent society. It is the latter, of course, that is claimed to be "civilized." Many books have been written about this controversy, some flatly denying that there was ever anything faintly resembling the "primal horde" in our tribal history, others claiming that the dormant (and often festering) feature of today's society is in fact violence.[17]

We can almost avoid this controversy by approaching the question from another direction. Great writers of different disciplines have concluded that what sets a civilized society apart from a barbaric one is the capacity to symbolize, to solve problems abstractly.[18] By this argument, we may say that the attempt to transform concrete punishments, such as mutilating or violent punishments, into abstract punishments, such as numbers of years in prison, was a civilizing process. If this is the case, we should be prepared to defend prison and other numerically based punishments as civilized rather than barbaric.

This argument works pretty well, except for a couple of embarrassing details. First, it does work if we confine the argument to an observation of Western civilization and ignore all the other civilizations that use violent punishments, such as most of the countries of North Africa[19] and other Islamic countries where Shari'a law still pertains. But is it acceptable to label Islamic Shari'a law punishments that mutilate the body as "barbaric"?

The second difficulty rests with the word "civilized." The earliest use of the word, certainly the most common use of it, was by the Romans, who coined the word to define themselves. Theirs was a civilized society that fought the barbarian hordes (so labelled by the Romans), such as the Gauls and others. In many respects, their deliberative politics, social organization, art, markets, and infrastructures formed the basis of what today we think of as essential to our Western civilized society. But the Roman civilization was poised on an incredibly violent society, even during times of peace. During the famous Pax Romana of Augustus, a couple of wars were still fought (and those battles, typical of the time, produced many thousands killed, all in hand-to-hand combat). And, of course, that same civilized society pretty much invented crucifixion as a mass punishment.[20]

The great contradiction in which we find ourselves when we defend the abstracted punishments that have replaced the violent mutilations of the body is that, by the very nature of their abstraction, they are less able to satisfy the essential demands of retribution, which it might even be admitted are "primitive" in the sense that they are many thousands of years old, perhaps embedded in our DNA.[21] As a result, there is today a constant pressure for more and more punishment and more and more violence. Perhaps this dilemma of Western civilization is no better depicted than by the popularity of the hit TV series *Game of Thrones*, a soap opera driven by vengeance, retribution, and as much gory mutilation as possible (not to mention sex), set in an imaginary civilization that is a mixture of ancient, modern, and futuristic cultures.

Is there a way out of this dilemma?

The extended punishment of prison, quantified by time, offers what appears to be the only substitute for those violent punishments that we think violent criminals deserve. The transformation of violent punishments into prison is something more than an abstraction, though. We may argue that prison, used with a clearly retributive purpose—that is, with the intention of inflicting pain on the offender—may reflect certain elements of the criminal's offense. For example, it seems appropriate that if a mugger has inflicted lasting injury on a victim, prison should inflict lasting pain on the mugger. There are additional ways in which prison may be made to match the crime or criminal, such as, for example, hard labor, solitary confinement of various kinds, diet restriction, and so on.

However, in drawing these conclusions in favor of abstract punishments, we must be aware of the clear danger of using such punishments. They separate us from the concrete fact of retribution, the concrete fact being that we must *feel* that punishment has been done. When corporal punishment is used, there is no doubt about our feeling that punishment has been done, because everyone has at some time in their lives experienced pain (whether at the dentist or at the hands of a parent).[22] In contrast, very few have experienced the chronic pain of prison, so we are insulated from such a punishment,[23] unable to identify with the pains that it inflicts. Is this a serious defect of prison as a punishment? Yes it is, and the reason lies in an element of retribution that we have not yet considered in sufficient detail.

Punishment Must Be Done (aka the Rule of Law)

We must feel that punishment is done. A punishment must not only fit the quality of the crime but also the quality of the feeling or sentiment that law-abiding people have about the crime of which they personally have not been convicted (though they may be guilty of it). Thus, the stoning to death of an adulterer in early biblical law was an entirely appropriate punishment, the deep psychology of which was so clearly unearthed much later by Christ's challenge noted earlier: "Let he who is without sin cast the first stone." Each stone was a missile of guilt transferred from the punisher to the punished, from the "innocent" to the "guilty." The offender becomes the repository of society's guilt. The Christian religion is based on this very fact: Christ died for the sins of all. This close link between the punisher and the punished is why in most, if not all, civilized societies minute attention is paid to the process of finding of guilt of the accused, to ensure that the punished truly is guilty, the degree of certainty matching directly the feeling of justice on the part of the punisher (you and me, that is).

This is a crucial point to understand about the civilized psychology of retribution. It is not simply a statement of the crime-punishment connection, the expression of an inherent logic so popularized by Kant. It is the expression of an irrational force: the inherent power of the logic derives from the mass sentiment that underlies much of what we do to criminals, that produces the elaborate rituals of the courtroom designed to reflect the solid unquestionable base of the rule of law.[24] *They* are the criminals, *we* are the law abiding.

Civilizing Punishment by Hiding It

The elaborate rituals of the courtroom have taken the place of punishment itself, a fact that we will consider in more detail in chapter 4. Earlier generations were well aware, in the deepest personal terms, of what punishment was all about when they witnessed a hanging or public whipping; the more the criminal suffered, the more law abiding felt the spectators. Unfortunately, modern criminal punishment no longer openly serves this need. Instead, the state punishes in the complete secrecy of prison.

What could we do to make prisons and other abstract punishments fulfill this basic need? The obvious answer is to make sure that the punishment is public, that people are made well aware of the pains that are inflicted in prison. This would mean opening up the prisons to the public, as they were in the early days of prisons in eighteenth-century England. For security reasons, it is very unlikely that prisons could be made public today. Besides, the additional pain inflicted on the inmates of prisons could not bear such scrutiny. And if corporal punishment were introduced as a substitute for prison, it would have to be public. This is one aspect of punishment that Shari'a law got right, as we will see in chapter 9.

There is another very important advantage to making punishments public, especially in relation to prison: it may help to mitigate their credibility. The media commonly reports examples of prison as "soft" punishment, which conveys to the public the mistaken idea that prisons are not painful enough. For example:

> Convict Thomas White of Arapahoe has served eight months of a 1 to 10 year term in a Wyoming State prison farm for breaking and entering, and for parole violations. He has been allowed on a number of "supervised excursions," and this time it was to a drive-in movie with a prison guard and three other inmates. The movie was appropriately titled, Escape from New

York, in which the whole of Manhattan is depicted as a max-imum security prison. White went to the bathroom . . . and never came back.[25]

However, not only does the media obfuscate what the true pains of prison are, the prison bureaucratic complex indulges in considerable deception. For example, take the official statement of the mission of the Crittendon County Detention Center, Marion, Kentucky:

> . . . to set the standards utilizing progressive and proactive pro-grams, custody, and services which make the most effective use of available resources to protect the public, preserve the integrity of the law, promote community involvement, and return the offender to society with professional and ethical behavior.[26]

Yet, in the 2016 case of *Madden v. Parnell*,[27] Madden was held in that jail in a condition of acute overcrowding. According to Madden, "the cell holds 20 inmates. At all times there was between 6–20 people sleeping on the floor . . . one shower and two toilets . . . no room to hardly walk around the cell."[28]

Madden's suit was overturned, citing the landmark Supreme Court case of *Rhodes v. Chapman*, in which prison overcrowding was found not to be a violation of the Eighth Amendment of the Constitution against cruel and unusual punishment.

The alert reader will realize that public punishment could only go part of the way to preventing punishment excess. Since whipping was used to excess in the past and its use was essentially public, the problem of excessive punishment cannot lie entirely with prison or lack of public awareness of its pain. There are other steps we may take to place limits on numerically based punishments, but a discussion of these must wait until we consider the sentencing process itself in chapters 4 and 5. This is because choosing punishments, in actual practice, is a highly abstract undertaking today and there is much research on how these decisions are made and who should make them. Comparing the effectiveness of punishments is also a very challenging exercise, as we will see in chapter 7.

However, what should now be clear is that if we stand back and look objectively at all past punishment practices described so far that are intended to hurt the offender (that is, real punishments), corporal punishments are demonstrably no worse than prison, and, as I will argue later, they offer a much better prospect to place limits on punishment, to ensure that any punishment administered, including corporal punishment, is moderate and not excessive.

If you are not yet convinced, perhaps the next chapter will do it.

Chapter Three

Rethinking Corporal Punishment

Corporal Punishment Is Not Torture, nor Is It Barbaric

What Corporal Punishment Is and Is Not

The difficulty with many definitions of corporal punishment found in the literature is that they fail to distinguish the mechanical process from the justification for applying the punishment. They almost always sneak into the definition a value judgment as to its negative or barbaric characteristics. Here are some examples:

> Corporal punishment may be taken to mean the infliction of ritualized physical pain or ordeal, the primary object of which is to bind the recipient or observer to the rules, norms, or customs of a larger social institution.[1]

> Corporal punishment is a form of physical punishment that involves the deliberate infliction of pain in order to punish a person convicted of a crime or as retribution for a perceived offense, including physical chastisement such as spanking, paddling, or caning of minors by parents, guardians, or school or other officials.[2]

Both of the above definitions try to do too much. The first suggests that it is ritualistic and therefore lacking in substance. Yet its purpose is to bind the individual to society, perhaps a positive outcome. The second example goes further and is much more complicated. It must be for an infraction, yet that is required for all punishment. No matter what its type, punishment must be for an offense against a rule; otherwise, it is not punishment but violence (or abuse). As for retribution, it is not intrinsic to corporal punishment. It is a feature of all punishment.

Another problem in defining corporal punishment is that those who define torture often equate this with corporal punishment,[3] or, if they do not, they invariably include corporal punishment within a discussion of torture.[4] For example, the United Nations General Assembly definition of torture, announced in 1984, was ". . . the intentional infliction by agents of the state of severe physical or mental suffering . . .";[5] and the World Medical Association, in 1975, defined torture[6] as ". . . the deliberate, systematic, or wanton infliction of physical or mental suffering by one or more persons, acting alone or on orders of any authority to force another person to yield information, to make a confession, or *for any other reason*."[7] This definition obviously also includes corporal punishment, even if it were legally prescribed for an offense, that is, "judicial corporal punishment."

Other definitions expand the boundary of corporal punishment, as does the *Merriam-Webster Unabridged* online:

> Punishment applied to the body of an offender including the death penalty, whipping, and imprisonment.

There is a big problem with this definition. While it is a reasonable extension to include the death penalty as a corporal punishment, probably its most extreme form, is it reasonable to include prison? The death penalty and whipping are clear and direct attacks on the body. Prison, while it may certainly affect the prisoner's body in many ways, does so in mostly indirect ways such as through diet, confinement in a small space, exposure to violence of other inmates, and so on. The Merriam-Webster dictionary continues with its second definition of corporal punishment:

> Punishment administered by an adult (as a parent or a teacher) to the body of a child ranging in severity from a slap to a spanking.

Take note that this definition uses explicit examples of corporal punishment to bolster its definition and makes clear that corporal punishment ranges in severity, as do all types of punishments, some controllable, some not, as we will see in chapter 7.

The Cambridge online dictionary offers two slightly different definitions, one a little more explicit:

> The physical punishment of people, especially of children, by hitting them.

And:

> Physical punishment, esp. by hitting with the hand or with a stick.

Most likely, these definitions reflect the long British tradition of the caning of school children (itself an ancient Roman tradition), a practice exported to most of Britain's colonies during the roughly two centuries of its imperialism.

The following, from the online *Free Dictionary* (source: Collins 12th ed.), offers a simpler definition, embellished by examples of what it is not:

> Physical punishment, as distinguished from pecuniary punishment or a fine; any kind of punishment inflicted on the body.

The *Oxford Dictionaries Online* offers a simpler definition (though it follows it with many variations in its usage):

> Physical punishment, such as caning or flogging.

This simple definition is the one I assume throughout this book, except that I add to it "electronic flogging," for important reasons that I will expand upon later. And, when it suits my argument, I also include prison as a physical punishment. After all, the inclusion of prison in the American Merriam-Webster dictionary definition of corporal punishment cited above destroys the argument of those who claim that prison is the civilized substitute for corporal punishment. Obviously, if prison is also a corporal punishment, one is substituting one corporal punishment for another. Is there a solution to his puzzle? There is. And we shall discover it soon. For the moment, though, we must further understand the distinction between corporal punishment and torture, with which it is often confused. In order to make this distinction, we must further understand the role that pain plays in both torture and in corporal punishment.

Corporal Punishment Is Not, in Itself, Torture

Torture sessions are common in many parts of the world today. Electric shock has become a favorite instrument of torture, although many other traditional methods, such as pulling off fingernails and denial of sleep, are still popular.[8] Jacobo Timerman, in his moving 1981 book *Prisoner without a Name, Cell without a Number*, described his treatment at the hands of the military junta of Argentina. It included electric shock, demands for names of accomplices, manipulation of time, disorientation, all the classic methods. But while one may decry all that happened to Timmerman and thousands like him in many other countries, we must make one very important clarification about the torture he went through: it was a process, one that was psychological as well as physical in nature. Corporal punishment (that is, the intentional infliction of pain) was used only as part of the torture process. It was not corporal punishment per se that was the torture.

It is widely believed that torture is solely concerned with the application of physical pain to the body. When tortures are reported in the media, they are usually reported in the context of stories concerning political turmoil, whether in Latin America, Africa, the former Yugoslavia, or the various terrorist groups, especially ISIS.[9] It is thought that physical punishment only serves fascist political purposes, in that it signifies the absolute domination of the state or other unconstrained authority over the individual.

Using a variety of techniques, the specific function of torture goes well beyond just the direct infliction of pain on the body by use of flogging (electronic or manual), beating, cutting, and so on. In 1990, Peter Suedfeld listed four *psychological* states that the captor attempts to establish in the prisoner through torture:[10]

1. Debility—generally induce physical and mental weakness.

2. Dependency—make the prisoner feel completely in the hands of the captor.

3. Dread—keep the prisoner in a constant state of fear.

4. Disorientation—destroy coping techniques through denial of sleep, sensory overload, prolonged blindfolding, and many other methods.

Moderate corporal punishment, as defined in this book, when used carefully and properly, has no such aims. Its sole purpose is to inflict pain efficiently, quickly, and temporarily. There is no process, there is no aim to engender any kind of psychological state—in fact, the opposite. The aim should be to leave the individual's sovereignty intact. There should be no intention to change the offender in any way. Any attempt to change the offender through corporal punishment is grounds for the charge of incipient torture and, indeed, may easily lead to the transformation of corporal punishment into torture. The types of bodily punishments that are typically presented to the public—indeed, have only ever been considered by criminologists—have been those that were in the service of the torture process: that is, behavior modification, as represented in the novel *A Clockwork Orange*, by Anthony Burgess, which depicted the application of bodily pain (acute nausea) to cause the offender to completely change his ways. This view of corporal punishment makes it appear as torture, leading to the erroneous conclusion that therefore all corporal punishments should never be considered.

Furthermore, because imprisonment unavoidably takes over the prisoner's very mind as well as his body, it resembles the torture process described above. I will argue later that to punish the body using swift application of pain (getting it over and done with) preserves an individual's freedom much more than a punishment that seeks to squeeze the offender's soul, as does the penal harm of prison.

There is a good historical reason why physical punishment is popularly equated with torture. During the height of the Roman Catholic inquisitions, when torture became high art, there were no clear distinctions between the investigatory process, the punishment, and the judgment. The offender was "put to the question," interrogated, tried, and punished all in one:

> We, by the Grace of God . . . , having carefully considered the proceedings against you, and seeing that you vacillate in your replies and that there is nevertheless much evidence against you, sufficient to expose you to torture and torment in order that the truth may be had from your mouth and that you should cease to offend the ears of the judges declare, judge and sentence you by an interlocutory order at such-and-such a time and day, to undergo torment and torture.[11]

The inquisitors applied a carefully planned routine. They began by asking the accused simple questions to which they expected no difficulty in obtaining an answer (similar to modern lie detector sessions), and then proceed to questions that would ask for confession of the less serious offenses. They would then show the accused the various contraptions of torture, and warn her to tell the whole truth. Historians of the Inquisition report that the large majority broke down quite easily, and that the application of machines of torture was unnecessary in many cases. However, there were many for whom this was not the case, and many whose confessions were not believed anyway; and this is the strange paradox of torture, as we shall see.[12]

It is a challenge, then, to extricate corporal punishment from its historical association with the process of torture. In fact, many seem to use the terms "corporal punishment" and "torture" interchangeably, as noted earlier in the UN definition.

In order to rescue corporal punishment from this undeserved bad name, we must see clearly what torture really is.

Torture and Confession

Throughout history, the stated purposes of torture have been to obtain confessions, to purge the lies of the accused, and supposedly get at the truth. This is why, in ancient Rome, testimony by slaves as witnesses (not as accused) was inadmissible unless obtained under torture, since it was thought that there was no way they could be believed, given their low position in society. The information had to be extracted by the purging process of torture.[13]

This difficulty was clearly recognized by the Roman Catholic inquisitors of the Middle Ages, who wrote handbooks on how to distinguish between genuine and false confessions. People under torture were likely to say anything to spare themselves from further pain, which means that they could not be assumed to be telling the truth. This is why burning at the stake, the main death penalty applied by the inquisitors (actually by the secular authorities on their behalf), was reserved for those who, having confessed to a particular crime under torture, later recanted their confession.

Yet, by saying what the torturer wants you to say, it may be false to you, but not necessarily to the torturer. Here lies the dark contradiction, the terrible conflict of the torturer: he forces the accused to confess to crimes and conspiracies that he, the torturer, wants to punish. Yet he knows that, if he had to resort to such extreme measures, the evidence he extracts may be lies. In other words, the torturer has merely created the crimes for which he now convicts and punishes at the same time. For him, your lies must be true, and in the context of your trial by torture, they are true. The torturer has already assumed your guilt, so he "punishes" before he has any knowledge of the crime. By torturing the accused the torturer creates the accused's crime and guilt:

> If you are not a Vietcong, we will beat you until you admit that you are; and if you admit you are, we will beat you until you no longer dare to be one.[14]

The use of torture displays the lie underlying the torturer's claim of justice. He must treat the confessor's lies as truth. It is as if there is a strange pact between the torturer and the tortured that this lie must be maintained. Indeed, in the cases reported where the accused would not break down under torture, it would appear that the torturer can suffer severe mental breakdown, because he has such a desperate need to have the justice of his own position as torturer underwritten by the tortured.[15]

This process has been documented for the ancient Romans and Greeks (not to mention the modern Greeks during the 1960s right-wing coup), the Holy Inquisition, the purges of Stalin and his show trials (perhaps the most sophisticated example of the extraction of justificatory confessions); for various regimes in Africa and in Latin America; and, more recently, for the mild (by comparison) use of waterboarding by the United States against terror suspects. There are abundant examples provided by Amnesty International's regular reports on torture.[16] There is, however, a deeper purpose of torture.[17]

The tortured becomes the object of an obsession, the soul and the body must be completely subjected to the purpose of justifying the torture. On the surface, that purpose appears as the usual utilitarian justification for punishment: the extraction of information so that the war against crime can be fought on behalf of the state more effectively. This utilitarian philosophy, as we will see in later chapters, requires, above everything else, the conformity of the individual so that order can be preserved. A perfect order demands a perfect subject: one converted into an object of utter and complete subjection. Torture is the perfection of utilitarian philosophy. Paradoxically, the perfect object is also one of desire, because it will accommodate authority's personal bidding. It becomes, therefore, the ideal repository for those two very old and interrelated instincts: sex and violence. The psychosexual violation of bodies as an act of political power has a long and bloody tradition,[18] and it continues today in conflict-torn parts of the world, such as in Nigeria where young girls are kidnapped by the Boka Haram Islamic extremists and used as sex slaves before being killed.[19]

It is important to note, though, that any form of punishment can be used for sexual purposes by an individual who is out of control, or by an official who represents an organization that is out of control. Even fines can be used for sexual purposes, that is, their remission traded for favors. So while here we are discussing the dreadful forms of torture, especially the excesses of pain it administers in order for the torturer to get what he wants, we must remember that it is not just violent punishments that are used for torture, but also simple ones. Any punishment can be abused if there are no procedures in place to monitor them, as Milgram and Zimbardo famously demonstrated in their experiments where students administered electric shocks to fellow students.[20]

Time as Torture

Dr. Willard Gaylin, in his groundbreaking book *Partial Justice*, noted that the emotional and suspenseful part of the processing of an offender is not at the trial stage, the finding of "guilty" by the court, as so dramatically depicted on fictional television.[21] This has mostly been decided in a mundane and bureaucratic manner by haggling among the police, prosecutors, and defense. Rather, the big cliff hanger is the sentencing, for often the offender literally does not know whether he will walk out of the court on probation or be carried off to prison for whatever period.

In most jurisdictions in America, separate sentencing hearings are held, often weeks and months after the finding of guilt. We see at work here the torturous use of time in administration of the punishment—although it is at least separated from the solicitation of confessions these days. (Strictly speaking, this may not be so, since lawyers will often advise their clients to display much contrition, to appear subdued and enlightened as to the wrongs of their past in the hopes of obtaining a more lenient sentence. In this sense, therefore, it may well be that confession when seen as an act of contrition is very closely tied to the degree of punishment.)

The capriciousness of sentencing is similar to the process of torture, where it is the "judicious" use of time that is the essential ingredient of the pain to be administered. The convicted offender may be released on probation or fined. But on the other hand, he may find himself sentenced to torture by time: a "stretch" in prison (an expression that clearly reflects the old torture of stretching on the rack).

Another important element in the use of time as torture is to allow the accused to see the instruments of torture, so that he will quake in fear in the anticipation of pain. This is, of course, a way of producing mental anguish, but it also amounts to something else: it is the expert use of time as a way of aggravating the physical application of pain. For example, Timerman's torture was spread out over several months, during which he was given short doses of pain, then removed back to his cell to ponder over what might happen next.

The necessity to control time makes it abundantly clear that the expert use of torture requires as its base a prison system, or at least a prison-like setting. Prison not only provides the possibility of manipulating time, but also the necessary secrecy for the administration of torture. This means that the situations in the criminal justice system that are "at risk" of dissolving into torture are prisons and jails, and in particular police precincts that run their own jails. The danger here is that interrogation, a necessary part of police work, especially in obtaining confessions, provides a highly coercive situation that will constantly tempt eager investigators and prosecutors to go further than they should. It is true that in Western civilization there are strict laws that protect the rights of the accused in these situations. But we must remember that torture is not *really* interested in getting the truth. It is, rather, interested in subjugating the accused and justifying the accuser. This means that corporal punishments should never be used inside or in conjunction with prisons, because it is their special combination with prison that makes real torture possible, indeed, likely.[22]

In sum, corporal punishment is mistakenly associated with torture, but it is clearly distinguishable from it. When physical pain is applied in the process of torture it is done in order to use the accused as a means to an end. It is a ruthless utilitarian process. Used in this way, it is not corporal punishment. In fact, any punishment, including prison, can be used in the service of torture.

Excess and Torture

The outstanding feature of pain as torture, in contrast to pain as corporal punishment, is the excess to which the pain is used. Because the torturer (and the state that usually stands behind him) must prove his "omnipotence," he and the torture system within which he works are prone to excess. In fact, Graziano suggests that it is the excessive use of violence that is the central feature of torture:

> Excess is never incidental, accidental. . . . It is always central to the regimes that employ it. . . . The gruesome catalog of atrocities is . . . a . . . normalization . . . of excess.[23]

The excessive use of prison, as it is used today, fits this quote exactly.[24]

In order for a corporal punishment not to be torture, it must be for an offense against a rule and nothing else, the pain applied must be instantaneous and temporary, and its severity must match and never exceed the severity of the offense committed. In the following chapters, we will see that the retributive justification for punishment fits very closely this prescription and that the idea of deterrence, by far the most common justification for the punitive basis of any criminal justice system, lurches rather close to justifying torture. But first, we must start with the basics. What role does the intentional infliction of pain play in punishment? Is there any such thing as painless punishment? What is pain anyway?

Understanding the Pain of Punishment

A true punishment is one that has its intended effect. We must be sure that pain is actually felt by those, and only those, who receive it. Is pain uncontrollable? Critics argue that, since pain is a subjective phenomenon, we never know whether a person really "feels" it or not, whether he or she in fact "perceives" it as pain or not, or whether all people experience pain in the same way. Does the scientific research back up such a claim?[25]

"Pain" is certainly a subjective phenomenon. It's inside you, not directly observable to others. But the same may be said about much that goes on inside the body, such as thought processes (for example, doing an addition sum) or seeing things, not to mention the unconscious actions of the autonomic nervous system. All such "inner behaviors" can and have been measured, even though they have not been observed directly. It's what the modern science of psychology is all about. Certainly we must guess at much of what is actually going on inside the person's head (the "dynamics"), but these guesses are well-informed guesses, because the external behavior in reaction to pain that we observe is quite similar across many individuals.

Perhaps the more important point is that some kinds of pain are more easily measurable than others. Mental pain (or anguish, as it is sometimes called, anxiety and depression, in clinical terms) is difficult to measure, as are all other kinds of mental states. A glance at any psychiatry textbook, or a look at the many ways in which the American Psychiatric Association's *Diagnostic and Statistical Manual of Mental Disorders* has changed over the past fifty years or so, is sufficient to convince one of this difficulty.

In contrast, physical pain is much easier to measure. Psychologists describe "pain behavior" in quite detailed terms. These include such behaviors as calling out, wincing, calling a halt to a presumed painful stimulus, crying, gritting one's teeth, and sweating. The link between these behaviors and the inferred internal state of "pain" is self-evident. If you don't believe me, just have a look at the many videos on YouTube of individuals shocking themselves with an electronic dog collar. In comparison, those behaviors from which we must infer the vague state of mental anguish or anxiety are more difficult to identify. They could range all the way from restless sleeping to excessive smoking, or even eating too much or too little.[26]

In sum, there are many ways to measure pain. The claim that corporal punishment is perceived so subjectively that it cannot be measured does not hold water. The fact is that we can measure it precisely (more on this in chapters 7 and 8), and if we can measure it, we can control it.

Varieties of Pain

The varieties of pain that may result from punishment are physical, mental, social, and economic. We must recognize at the outset, though, that this classification is not altogether helpful. Thomas Szasz, the renowned critic of the mental illness approach to crime, has noted in his book *Pleasure and Pain* that it is not possible to distinguish between physical and mental pain. In fact, he argues that all pain is reducible to mental pain, meaning, essentially, that all sense data must be processed by the brain, and in that sense are "mental." However, we can see that the opposite conclusion could be drawn: because all sense data are processed by the brain, this is in fact a *physical* process (the firing of neurons in response to pain receptors, neurochemical activity of the brain, etc.), so that all pain may in this way be reduced to physical pain. One might add that the automatic response of the body in response to painful stimuli—for example, heat—is governed first and foremost by the autonomic nervous system before the sensation reaches the brain. The galvanic skin response is probably one of those measures.[27]

The sensible solution to this semantic difficulty is to rely on actual observable behaviors in response to clear and explicit stimuli. If a child is smacked on the wrist and she cries, it is reasonable to conclude that she felt pain. It doesn't really matter what kind of pain. As well as "physical" pain, the child might also feel humiliation, embarrassment, defiance, resentment, or even hatred, all of which might be summed up as "social pain." What matters is that the child exhibited an observable response to an act that is traditionally known to cause pain. However, it does matter what kind of pain is produced by the punishment, and we shall see why shortly.

Physical punishment may inflict social pain as an intended or unintended by-product of physical pain. For example, the branding of "R" on the forehead of a robber in early colonial days was both a physical infliction of pain and an infliction of stigma.[28] In the twenty-first century, this type of pain has moved to another level via social media, where the public humiliation of the stigmatization is amplified considerably. This might reasonably be called "cyber punishment" if used as a formal sanction by a judge or court. To date, I am not aware of any cyber sentence handed down, though there are some examples of public shaming prescribed by judges.[29] Stretching the meaning of the word punishment, though, one might argue that the mandatory registration of sex offenders made public online is an extension of the initial punishment, which is usually some form of incarceration.

The use of economic punishments, such as fines, is not easily distinguishable from social pain, or even mental pain—depending on how important money is to the person punished, and perhaps whether rich or poor. While a heavy fine might be conceived as "painful," it is nevertheless difficult to imagine the actual pain felt. It is a loss, no doubt. But painful? The word "pain," no matter what the psychiatrists tell us of its essential mental element, refuses to shake off its physical connotations.

The punishment of prison clearly combines all types of pain to degrees that it is difficult to specify. Much has been written about the "pains of imprisonment"—the mental anguish, the physical suffering through poor diet, prison violence, the social stigma of being an ex-con, and the economic deprivation of being imprisoned and unable to earn money through a real job.

In sum, it is important to recognize that *the most useful way to assess the pain of a punishment is to examine its outcomes.*

A way of classifying pain that directs us to the question of outcomes may be derived from medical conceptions of pain. In medicine there is a well-established distinction between acute pain and chronic pain.[30] Acute pain is the kind that one feels when one cuts a finger, bangs one's head. Chronic pain is the type that continues for longer periods, such as toothache, and sometimes a lifetime, such as arthritis.[31] We can equate chronic pain with prison, since prison is a punishment that is drawn out over a long period of time and requires that the offender lead a painful life. The actual pains of imprisonment are, however, the subject of much controversy because of the "perks" inmates now lay claim to: cable TV, libraries, gym equipment, and so on (more on this later). Acute pain may be equated with some, but not all, forms of corporal punishment. Some types of corporal punishment, such as mutilations, have long lasting painful effects.

Which is the more severe, acute pain or chronic pain? Chronic pain is potentially more severe, since it could include the prolonged application of pain. That we go to the dentist for a toothache indicates that we are prepared to undergo some intense acute pain in order to get rid of the chronic pain of toothache. We can further explore this question by comparing types of punishment and their consequences. For example, the infliction of twenty lashes might be much less severe than six months in prison. But what do we mean by "severe"? We mean that whipping produces less painful consequences of a social and economic type, even though it may produce more intense physical pain and take a month for the wounds to heal.[32]

Chronic and Acute Punishments

Prison is a chronic punishment. Even a small amount of prison, such as one day, when compared to the few minutes it takes to administer a couple of strokes of the lash, is clearly a punishment of chronic pain. Viewed in this light, this specific corporal punishment may be reasonably termed moderate compared to any amount of prison.

We should also note that much has been made of the physical suffering in prison as a result of prison violence and rape,[33] and the most often cited pain of prison is that of mental anguish.[34] And it is apparent that mental suffering will occur regardless of the material conditions of prison. Mental anguish is a pain that is most likely of long duration, a chronic pain. Most important, it can last after prison, as attested to by many recidivists who have been unable to "go straight" after release. Their mental suffering continued after the actual period of punishment was supposed to have terminated.[35] This element of prison is a serious defect, because it cannot be controlled.

And it is important, if we are to get on top of the problem of criminal punishment, that we inflict the kinds of pain that we can control most easily.

No doubt mental pain may be experienced as a side effect of all punishments. But it is likely that it occurs more as a result of prison than of any other type of punishment, including some corporal punishments, simply because the mental pain of prison is inflicted over a much longer period of time. Yet the defenders of prison argue that the mental pain prison inflicts ("loss of liberty," though it goes far beyond that) is more benign compared to any physical pain of prison, which they view as an unintended (and therefore excusable) side effect of the punishment.

Corporal punishments are the most obvious acute punishments, but there are many different kinds of corporal punishments, and not all have the same physical and mental effects. There is the lash, usually applied to the bare back, and the paddle and other variations of this wooden hand piece, most often applied to the buttocks. Their most obvious advantage is that they get the punishment over and done within a short period of time.

Some corporal punishments are chronic, such as those that produce permanent mutilation or injury or observable scars. Other corporal punishments, while not chronic, do not easily fit into the category of delivering acute pain, since they take too long to administer, and very often require that they be administered under prison conditions. And they assume total control over the person's body for a relatively long period of time. Examples of these punishments are denial of sleep, hard labor, solitary confinement, and harsh diet. While acute corporal punishments are probably illegal in prisons (according to the US Supreme Court, see chapter 9), other pains, such as denial of sleep, solitary confinement, hard labor, are, generally speaking, legal. However, solitary confinement is currently under attack and may be abolished—if such a thing is possible inside the secrecy of prisons—as a result of various class action suits.[36]

Is Pain Evil?

It is inescapable that even moderate corporal punishment requires the intentional infliction of pain (primarily physical, but possibly mental) on an offender. It is also clear that prison intentionally inflicts both mental and physical pain on an offender, though the defenders of prison claim that the physical pain caused the offender is an unintentional by-product of prison.

Is it morally defensible to intentionally hurt someone, even if one has the authority to do it? Perhaps it is more defensible to hurt an offender intentionally rather than negligently (as often happens in prison)? Where is the evil, and where is the good? It is a strange irony that the atheistic utilitarians, such as Jeremy Bentham, advanced the belief in the absolute evil of pain, whereas the religious philosophers (whom the utilitarians like to label as absolutists) saw the two sides of pain. Christian philosophers are spurred on in their efforts to examine the role of pain in society by the prickly problems raised by young minds, like Tracey in the 1977 movie *Oh God!*, who asked, "Why do you let bad things happen?"[37] And God answered, "You can't have good without bad . . . life without death . . . pleasure without pain." How is it that, in a world reigned by a perfect and all good God, there can be pain and suffering?

The classic answer to this question was provided by the eminent Christian philosopher C. S. Lewis in his *The Problem of Pain*. Lewis's argument is that one cannot presume in advance the evil nature of pain. In fact, it is invariably two-edged. The best example of this fascinating question is the Christian view of poverty, very often characterized as a life of pain:

> Those who would most scornfully repudiate Christianity as the mere "opiate of the people" have a contempt for the rich, that is, for all mankind except the poor. They regard the poor as the only people worth preserving from "liquidation," and place in them the only hope of the human race. But this is not compatible with the belief that the effects of poverty on those who suffer it are wholly evil. It even implies that they are good. The Marxist thus finds himself in real agreement with the Christian in those two beliefs which Christianity paradoxically demands—that poverty is twice blessed yet ought to be removed.[38]

If we wish to avoid the religious arguments in favor of the positive side of pain, we have only to look at any medical textbook to find that pain is given pride of place as an important indicator to the doctor and the individual that there is something amiss. It is a way for one's body to cry out, to communicate its condition. Pain therefore performs a double function: it hurts and is sometimes unbearable, and, in that sense, is bad. But, without it, we would often not know there was something wrong with our bodies. Dr. Thomas Szasz, in his classic *Pleasure and Pain*, insists that it is one of man's vital means of communication.

Lewis characterized pain as sterilized or disinfected evil, by which he meant that pain "has no tendency in its own right to proliferate." This is in contrast to the classic Christian view of sin or evil, which is that one sin generates more sins only because it is the product of human error. For example, it is commonly believed that one lie should not be told because it will inevitably lead to many more. Pain, however, will not proliferate by itself—it requires human folly to accomplish that. In other words, pain is "natural" and, in that sense, "disinfected." It is the *expression* of sin rather than sin itself.[39]

With this argument, Lewis makes sure that, in the situations where pain does proliferate, he lays the blame for this squarely on humankind, not on God. For, while he argues that the existence of pain makes for good as well as bad, he claims that the "bad" pain is largely of men's doing, not of God's, and that this probably comprises four-fifths of the pain in the world. As he says:

> It is men, not gods, who have produced racks, whips, prisons, slavery, guns, bayonets, and bombs. It is by human avarice or human stupidity not by the churlishness of nature, that we have poverty and overwork.[40]

The idea that pain is not inherently evil is contained in other major religions. In the West, it is really derived from the early Greek and Roman philosophers. Pythagoras, for example, developed an entire system of philosophy based on the notion of the beneficial effects of pain in heightening awareness and sensitivity. This belief was probably taken over by the Christian religion when it incorporated much of the early Greek and Roman philosophy, especially through the works of St. Augustine and Thomas Aquinas.[41]

We need go no further. The point is well made that pain is of crucial significance to humans in the moral, religious, and physical senses. It is something that everyone experiences almost daily, and in that sense it binds people together. But it also means that, if it is felt so keenly, feared so much, yet essential to identify illness and trouble of a general kind, then it is literally a force on a par with fire. Under our control, it can do great things for humankind, but like all powerful resources, if it is used too much, it can create havoc and reap terrible destruction.

This brings us back to the notion of pain as punishment, because this is where pain should be under our control. We must heed Lewis's warning: that the weakness of humankind will allow the use of pain as punishment to proliferate, the modern example of which is mass incarceration.

Chapter Four

The Retribution of Mass Incarceration

How the Ideology of Retribution Caused a Committee to Fuel Mass Incarceration

In this chapter, we will see that the justifications of retribution described in the introduction contain particular theoretical flaws, causing the powerful twentieth-century American Committee on Incarceration, faced with sentencing chaos, to adopt it as its guiding ideology, thus fueling the rise of mass incarceration. This analysis leads us to reformulate the philosophy of retribution, freeing it from the rigid use of prison and opening the way for the moderate application of corporal punishment for moderate offending.

Sentencing Chaos

If there is any doubt that there is a crisis of criminal punishment in Western society, the following examples, summarized from my 1983 book *Just and Painful*, easily illustrate the point:

> Sixteen-year-old Clifford Smith with a .38 caliber handgun shot to death nineteen-year-old Robert Loftman because he would not turn his radio down in the park. He was sentenced to five years' probation. Loftman's mother, on hearing the sentence, cried: "There's no justice! He snuffed out my son's life for no reason. Why shouldn't he be made to suffer?"[1]

William James Rummel was convicted of theft for a third time, and was prosecuted under the Texas recidivist statute which mandates life imprisonment for anyone upon his third conviction of a felony. The total amount of goods and services Rummel stole came to $229.11. He appealed the conviction all the way to the United States Supreme Court on the grounds that the sentence amounted to cruel and unusual punishment. The court refused to rule that this punishment was grossly disproportionate to the offense. So, Mr. Rummel continues to serve his life sentence.[2]

Nothing has changed. In a recent investigation published in the *Dallas Morning News*, researchers found that 120 defendants convicted of murder in Texas between 2000 and 2006 received only a sentence of probation. In Dallas County, twice as many convicted murderers were sentenced to probation as were sent to death row.[3]

One can see that the sentences of probation for the murderer and life imprisonment for three minor thefts are, to put it mildly, unjust. Judges are supposed to be among our wise and well informed people. How can they—especially in the highest court of the land—affirm punishments of such bizarre proportions?[4] As the Vera Institute of Justice observed in 2010, "Those of us who work in the policy field know there are virtually no political constraints on disproportionate sentences."[5] One might have thought that the Fair Sentencing Act[6] signed into law in 2010 would have corrected that, but unfortunately it was directed only towards correcting the excessively long prison terms dished out for a small number of particular drug offenses. The wild disparities occur for all kinds of crimes, not just drug related.

The answer is that our legislators, our judges, our prosecutors have been thoroughly confused by the twentieth century penologists, who have advocated one reform after another, each reform successively recognized as a failure. And this series of failures has continued into the twenty-first century. The mass incarceration problem in America is downplayed by those on the right arguing that it is the reason crime has dropped so dramatically over the last decade or more (not true).[7] Those on the left, the "reformers," have advocated alternatives to prison, but these turned out to be, for the most part, nonalternatives. They have watered down criminal punishment into nonpunitive alternatives such as probation, halfway houses, or conjugal visits in prison. Or they have insisted that prison should be a "treatment" rather than a punishment. Indeed, the more vocal of them, such as Dr.

Karl Menninger, in his book *The Crime of Punishment*, more than half a century ago argued that criminals are "sick," not bad, an argument that still has traction, though framed within the recent findings of genetics and neuroscience.[8] There continues to be a consensus that these "reforms" have been absolute failures.[9] Prisons have failed to rehabilitate. Offenders have often been worse off "treated" than "punished."[10]

Parallel to these reformers, the 1970s prestigious Committee on Incarceration chaired by Senator Charles Goodell, led a new wave of "reform." This was to be a return to retribution and a strict reorientation of criminal punishment away from treatment and back to punishment. But these reformers drowned in their own solution. Longer and more prison terms were the logical result of their reforms that created a veritable archipelago of prisons overflowing with inmates. It continues today, combined as it is with the powerful and insatiable demands of incarcerating individuals on the grounds not only that they deserve it, but that it will deter those offenders, and citizens like them, from committing further crimes. This latter belief also has been shown to be false,[11] as we will see further in the next chapter.

In 1990, in clear recognition of the confusion created by the treatment alternatives (that is, probation, community service, fines) pushed by reformers of all stripes, Norval Morris of the Chicago Law School attempted to "repunitize" them by calling them "intermediate punishments."[12] The practice of intensive probation and parole arose from that work, but recent studies have shown that such "treatment" does not reduce recidivism.[13]

The increasingly popular ankle bracelet, often used as part of intensive probation (a form of incapacitation, see chapter 6) that allows for electronic supervision, does make this option appear more punitive. However, a lot of work is needed to make this punishment truly a credible punishment, and any appearance of it as a "treatment" will bring it down to the level of disrepute to which regular probation has fallen.[14]

When one reads of the many cases like that of Mrs. Loftman's son, it is undoubtedly clear that a credible punishment must be found that is both just and fiscally sound. The solution lies in the rediscovery of punishment. We must take seriously what the advocates of retribution have been saying for a long time, but not truly understanding: punishment must, above all else, be painful.

The Committee on Incarceration, in the tank for prison, lost sight of the role of pain in punishment. Pain is surely part of the definition of punishment, though the word did not occur in any of the definitions we reviewed in chapter 3. The origin of the word pain is the Latin *poena*, which meant, in Roman times, punishment or penalty. Its meaning as a localized and acute sense experience is of relatively recent origin, probably in seventeenth-century England.[15] In those days, as we have seen, punishment was there for all to see. It was publicly intimate and largely physical. These were clearly painful punishments; there could be no doubt. This is not the case today. We are simply told that so-and-so received "five years," another "two years." What do these punishments mean? What is the concretely felt difference in pain between two years' and five years' punishment of prison? These sentences have no real meaning either to the public or to the criminal who is punished,[16] not to mention the judge who delivers the sentence.[17] The fundamental reason for the mess is that there is no clear purpose to our use of punishment.[18] We must see that pain is not only the prime ingredient of punishment but is also a necessary condition of its justice. For without it there can be no punishment. And there can be no justice without punishment, which was the source of Mrs. Loftman's complaint concerning the murder of her son, described above.

It is also true that too much pain may make a particular punishment unjust. The cases in which too much of it is used result from our failure to comprehend pain in a concrete way, a result, paradoxically, of our having "civilized" our punishments. Today these unjust punishments occur mostly in our irresponsible use of prison, without any clear idea of what kind of pain we wish to administer. The Supreme Court case concerning Mr. Rummel, described above, is a prime example.

This confusion about the use of pain in criminal punishment is well demonstrated by the following quotation from the 1976 report of the Committee on Incarceration, *Doing Justice*. This report set the direction of penology that continues to dominate today. It was a federally funded committee comprised of a prestigious body of clerics, laymen, social scientists, and lawyers charged with reforming the criminal punishment system. The committee, perhaps unknowingly, provided the justification for the excessive use of prison that ensued for some six decades, setting the stage for what we call today, mass incarceration:

> One reason for preferring incarceration is simply that we have not found another satisfactory severe punishment. Historically, the alternative was corporal punishment, but that is worse. Incarceration at least can be divided into weeks, months, and years—and its duration prescribed by standards. Given the numerous possibilities that modern technology affords for inflicting pain and the difficulty of measuring degrees of subjective

distress, effectively controlling the use of corporal punishment is virtually an impossible task.

> Beyond the question of effective control, corporal punishment poses disturbing ethical problems. Besides any physical pain involved, intentional corporal maltreatment evokes in its victim intense feelings of humiliation and terror. . . . Ought a civilized state ever to visit such mortifications? Might there not exist a right to the integrity of one's own body, that not even the state's interests in punishing may override?[19]

The confusion is clear. The committee called corporal punishment "maltreatment," but it did not call prison "maltreatment." It claimed that corporal punishment caused humiliation and terror, yet, to this day, no research substantiates this claim. Prison rests on a platform of humiliation and terror. Some criminals may deserve such punishment, but the humiliation and terror in prisons occur by default (supposedly), not by design, and therefore subject all inmates indiscriminately to such punishments regardless of their crimes.

Not one of the committee's factual claims was—or is—true. Corporal punishment can be controlled, because it can be technologically and scientifically administered, as we will see in chapter 7. It is prison that is out of control, not corporal punishment.

As for the committee's claim that a criminal has the right of integrity over his own body, such a right is worthless if that body is enclosed in a prison cell, especially if that cell contains other violent inmates who may attack each other at will. We will see in chapters 6 and 7 that moderate corporal punishment is designed to preserve the integrity of the offender's body. Obviously, prison does not do that; it does the opposite.

During the committee's deliberations, it was prison that was out of control. And four decades later it is far worse. If you doubt that, consider this. America incarcerates more persons per head of population than any other country in the world, including, horror of horrors, China and Russia.[20] The rate of prisoners per 100,000 population in the United States is almost seven times higher than the rate in Shari'a law countries.[21] Five percent of the world's women reside in the United States, but its prisons confine 30 percent of the world's incarcerated women.[22]

According to the World Prison Brief, the incarceration rates for the United States as of 2013 were 1,485,800 in state or federal prisons, plus 731,200 in local jails, making a total of 2,217,000.[23] The overall numbers in America's prisons have leveled out or even decreased since 2014, possibly due to the policy of the Obama administration to free certain inmates, largely by fiat. While one is tempted to applaud this change, it is likely that this will be a momentary dip in the prison population, sure to result eventually in demands for more prison. Furthermore, the decreases are tiny, relatively speaking, with 13,553 fewer inmates counted in the fiscal year of 2016, a mere drop in the bucket, as is the anticipated release of 3,100 inmates resulting from the First Step Act of 2019.[24]

Not only is mass incarceration a human crisis; it is a fiscal crisis. Since the first large-scale prison, Eastern Penitentiary, was opened in 1829, at great expense, it is striking that, even despite one fiscal crisis after another, the rise of prisons has continued. In the 1980s, a number of states tried to address the penal fiscal problem by floating prison bond issues. In the November 1981 election in New York State, a $500 million prison bond issue was narrowly defeated. Other states have successfully built new prisons, only to find that they did not have the money to staff them.[25] So the fiscal crisis of prisons continues. The Vera Institute of Justice, in a careful study of the costs of prison, recently concluded that, for the 40 states it surveyed, the average cost per inmate was $31,286 in 2010. The study estimated that the total annual costs to taxpayers was in the realm of $39 billion.[26]

Retribution by Committee

The Committee on Incarceration, driven by the retributive ethic, failed miserably to solve the punishment crisis. The philosophy of retribution is supposed to preserve the freedom of the punished and moral righteousness of both the punished and the punisher. What went wrong?[27]

Crime and punishment have been, and will forever be, inextricably bound together. Dostoyevsky popularized this truth with the title of his novel *Crime and Punishment*, a riveting story of a horrible crime and its subsequent punishment, much of it self-inflicted by the murderer (a significant insight, discussed further in chapters 7 and 8 in respect to robotic punishment). Much of the Bible's Old Testament is taken up with the violence of one wrong returned by the violence of another. In all respects, the punishment is the mirror of the crime, and vice versa; which wrong was the crime and which wrong the punishment depended on the context of who was fighting whom, the winner claiming the right of the punisher, the vanquished designated the criminal. Christianity proclaimed both punisher and criminal wrong, though perhaps siding with the criminal, claiming that the punisher should turn the other cheek (forgive).

The ancient Greeks looked on this moral and conceptual puzzle of punishment as a tragedy entwined in a love story, the most famous being Aeschylus's *Oresteian Trilogy*.[28] There, the process of vengeance (that is, getting one's own back), was not able to resolve the riddle (seen as a "curse") of what was the right amount of retaliation for an offense; the constant tendency for it to spiral out of control, often reverberating back on the punisher or retaliator. Modern myths view vengeance in a similar way.[29] From Superman to the Avengers, *Death Wish* to *Dirty Harry*, the story is repeated daily in movies and TV series all over the world.

Revenge is the "psychological reality" of punishment, as Sigmund Freud called it, and it is as old as humanity itself. Philosophers and legal theorists call it "retribution" or "just deserts." Historically, punishment has always been linked to the crime: it must be made to fit the crime.[30] Psychologically, we *feel* that the link between the crime and its punishment is right.[31] We recognize that to reward crimes would make us feel very frustrated; unfulfilled even. At the very least, to sit by and do nothing about criminal behavior makes us jittery, even though most of us personally would rather not be those who actually meted out the punishment. Nevertheless, we insist that something be done to criminals who have committed offenses.

As we have seen, in 1976 the Committee on Incarceration, with Andrew von Hirsch as its director, argued for a return to a just deserts model of punishment, claiming, among other things, that it would limit the overall length of time offenders spent in prison. It would replace the "treatment model" of criminal punishment, which was blamed for the excesses of the "indeterminate sentence" (that is, the offender was incarcerated until such time that he was "cured").[32] The committee argued that punishment according to just deserts would ensure that there were fixed limits to the punishment that could be applied to a particular crime, because the theory of just deserts requires that a person can only be punished "by a punishment that fits the crime."

There is little doubt that this task represents the most serious challenge to advocates of this application of retribution to criminal punishment. Their solution has usually been to give compulsive attention to the fine gradations in the seriousness of offenses, the number committed, and the fine gradations of punishment, essentially gradations of prison. This approach was well illustrated by Alan Dershowitz of Harvard University Law School in his report for the Twentieth Century Fund, *Fair and Certain Punishment*. But he, along with all the other "modern retributivists," failed to break out of the old mold. He took the forms of punishment for granted, unable to overcome the paucity of sentencing alternatives.[33]

Stuck with fines and prison, the Committee on Incarceration, what I would now call, "the retribution committee" could only recommend variations in the amount of punishment as the way to solve the problem of making the punishment fit the crime. The only variations in quality of punishment they considered were those such as probation, which are not convincing punishments, because they are not painful, as we have seen earlier in this chapter. We must therefore look more closely at the question of the quality of punishments, how to solve the retributive riddle of punishment that the committee failed to achieve. How does a retributivist match a punishment to its crime?

Reflecting the Crime in the Punishment

The oldest idea of making the punishment fit the crime was to reflect both the quality and gravity of the crime in the punishment.[34] Thus, the hand of the thief was (as in Shari'a law) cut off—the old principle of an eye for an eye, often associated with the law of Moses, but the principle can be found to underlie the punishment systems of most cultures. There are many other variations of this theme.[35] The great Italian poet Dante Alighieri was a master at concocting reflecting punishments. In Dante's *Hell* (of his trilogy *The Divine Comedy*), suicides, because they did not respect their own bodies, were turned into trees, which were periodically snapped at and chewed by dogs. Thieves who had not respected the distinction between "mine" and "thine" were turned into reptiles, then transformed again into each other, destined never to retain their own true form.[36] How apt, we say. There seems to be something inherently right about the choice of punishment. By "inherently" we mean that we have a "gut feeling" that it is right.

Should we go back to reflecting punishment? There is much to be said for it, although, on first consideration, such punishments do appear terrifying. But we must have the courage to give our criminals the punishment they deserve. We must not shirk our responsibility. How may this be done in a civilized way?

Beginning on a simple level, we may divide crimes according to their type. The simplest and most common division is between those of violence (sometimes referred to as crimes against the person) and those of property (usually various forms of theft, larceny, or fraud). A difficulty with this classification is that some crimes, such as robbery, fit both categories. And some supposedly nonviolent crimes, such as taking drugs, drunk driving, or selling illegal drugs, may have violent outcomes: a drunk driver may run someone down; drug users may die as a result of those drugs. In any event, the simple solution is that, for crimes of violence, the offenders should suffer punishments of violence:

- A man who beats up a little old lady surely deserves a thorough beating himself.

- Those who rape surely deserve to be raped themselves.

- Those who inflict permanent damage or injury on other persons as a result of these crimes surely deserve to suffer permanent injury themselves.

- Those who risk the lives of others deserve to have their own lives put at risk.

- Those who murder should be killed.

Could we face up to inflicting such punishments? The truth is that, for some time now, we have not had the courage to inflict violent punishments directly on violent offenders except for certain acts of murder. But let's not forget. We already *do* allow violence as part of the punishment to be inflicted on offenders, but it is entirely indiscriminate. This is the violence that occurs in prison. It may not be part of the sentence, but it is certainly a known probability as part of prison life. In other words, we do not take direct responsibility for the infliction of violence as part of the punishment. Rather, we view it as an unavoidable part of prison. It is as if it is the fault of prison that violence occurs, rather than our fault. This is the same thinking as that of the Middle Ages when a form of the death penalty was to set the person adrift in a frail boat. If the boat were brought in on the tide, it was lucky for the offender: Nature had passed her judgment. But if the boat were carried out to sea, and the offender subsequently drowned or starved, again, this was Nature's judgment, and those doing the punishing were relieved of the responsibility for the death.

So we must recognize that there are strong historical, cultural, and psychological reasons why it is unlikely that we will take direct responsibility for the infliction of violence to any great degree on offenders, even though it is clear that, for some crimes, they deserve it. It is clear also that retribution has severe limits as a guide to sentencing. But perhaps in nonviolent crimes it would be easier to apply the retribution ethic to reflecting the crime in its punishment?

On the face of it, matching punishments to property crimes should be easier, compared to matching punishments to violent crimes. We don't have to reflect the violence of a crime in the punishment, unless the property crime, such as a robbery, includes violence. When we begin to search for appropriate nonviolent punishments for property crimes, however, we run into a few difficulties. Should we say that the reflection of a theft of X amount of dollars would be the extraction from the offender of the same amount of money? Unfortunately, this won't work for a number of reasons. First, many, if not most, offenders have very meager financial resources. In a large number of cases, they are simply not able to pay the money.

Next, the amount of pain that results from a particular fine cannot be clearly specified, because it depends on how much money the offender has, and how much it is valued. If the offender has never had any money to speak of, any amount of fine may mean nothing to her. If the offender were very rich, it might take a massive fine to have any effect, although, paradoxically, people who make a lot of money often do not value money to the same extent as those who struggle to make money. So we see that even the pain of fines may be experienced subjectively. And if we have to vary amounts of fine according to each individual, we must administer apparently unequal punishments for the same crime, surely, on the face of it, unfair and maybe unjust as well.[37] It is very difficult to come up with fines that are convincingly and consistently painful, yet they must be painful if they are truly to be punishments and if they are to match the pains caused the victim.[38]

Another solution could be to have the indigent offender work off the amount owed. But this immediately transforms the punishment from one of fines to a variation of community service, or some form of forced labor. So we find that the punishment has become a chronic punishment. It may be that, for some thefts, especially large ones, this might be appropriate. But for thefts of middling amount, forced labor would appear to be too chronic a punishment when considered in comparison to one who could pay the equivalent fine. To make such a punishment equitable, therefore, we must insist that all thefts within a particular range, regardless of the economic status of the offender, must be punished with forced labor.[39] Forced labor, that is to say, slavery, is certainly a more convincing punishment that inflicts chronic pain.[40] However, regardless of its "success" as claimed by its advocates, the yardstick being the manufacture of goods competing in the marketplace, it comes at the expense of noncriminals who are unemployed. Labor unions, if they do not universally condemn the practice, are deeply ambivalent in supporting prison laborers' rights as workers, especially, for example, the demand for a minimum wage.[41]

It is common to hold up the considerably more frequent use of fines that are linked to an individual's income in Germany and various other countries of northern Europe, such as Finland, as an example that the United States should follow.[42] While in theory this seems like a persuasive argument, it fails to take into account the difference in political cultures between America and Europe. The European system of fines, referred to as "day fines" (a term used to describe various ways of computing fines on a sliding scale according to the income of the individual being fined), are very similar in structure to a progressive income tax. In fact, the system penalizes income, rather than the offense itself. Thus we see that a specific day fine is no longer a precise punishment and is heavily tainted with a political ideology that targets income.

We can see that economic punishments, whether in the form of fines or forced labor, have many defects. Their functions as painful punishments cannot be clearly specified. They are politically suspect, and their fairness is not self-evident. We would do well to disregard them in favor of other punishments, the painfulness of which we are more certain and the equity of which is more clearly demonstrable.

What would these punishments be? They would need to be punishments that were clearly painful, but moderately so, and adjustable according to the range of seriousness of most crimes. The punishments that clearly meet this requirement are corporal punishments that are acute: that is, punishments that inflict an immediate but temporary pain upon the offender, constituting moderate corporal punishment (MCP). Just how these punishments would be calculated and how they would be administered, we will see in chapter 7. For the moment, it is enough to say that probably the most controllable, least harmful, and least violent of corporal punishments would be electronic flogging: controlled application of a moderate electric shock to a selected part of the body. I know, it sounds barbaric and conjures up images of the electric chair. But understand that your outrage is selective. By now, you know that what is truly barbaric is mass incarceration. Where is your outrage at that? And besides, administering electric shock in a moderate amount is a nonviolent punishment. It requires only the push of a button. More on this in chapters 7 and 8.

Reformers who have had the courage to read this far no doubt are saying to themselves, "This is ridiculous! We no longer do this sort of thing! To punish crimes with violent punishments like electric shock would be to turn back the clock of progress!" But does mass incarceration, the end product of past reformers' unquestioning embrace of prison, represent progress? Indeed, the literature on prisons reflects the opposite: they are a dreadful blight on society, especially American society, which has led the way as the penal state of the twenty-first century with the highest incarceration rate of the entire world.[43]

The reformers, as a matter of fact, are half right. Raping a rapist would be going too far. A thousand lashes for even a very serious robbery would be too much. But so is a life sentence of prison for a $229.11 theft.

How did we reach a point in our criminal justice system that "solves" the problem of punishment by mass incarceration? Retribution is supposed to place limits on punishment, the punishment must match the crime, with no more and no less pain than that caused by the crime. Clearly, it has failed to do so, certainly when prison is the only available serious punishment. Why is this? Part of the reason may be human weakness and error. But the other part of the problem is that the most common justification for punishing criminals is deterrence, not retribution. And deterrence puts us on the slippery slope to torture.

Chapter Five

The Successful Failure of Deterrence

How the Fake Science of
Deterrence Justified Mass Incarceration

If retribution has failed as a policy to limit the severity of the punishment to the severity of the crime (that is, match the punishment to the crime), perhaps deterrence offers a better way? If a punishment deters crime, this is a very powerful moral argument in its favor, because it presumably keeps us safe; exactly what the social contract touted by the Enlightenment thinkers argued for. We give up a little portion of our liberty to the society that in return provides protection. For, they argued persuasively, without security liberty has no value.

In practice, no punishment is ever used purely in the service of one particular philosophy. Each time a criminal punishment is applied, it is serving many, sometimes competing, purposes, and judges invariably invoke several justifications. The most popular, though, is that of deterrence, even though it is pretty much settled science in criminal justice that deterrence does not work; that is, it does not reduce crime rates[1] (general deterrence) or reduce recidivism (stop the punished offender from offending again—individual deterrence), though there are some exceptions. In some very well-defined situations and particular types of behaviors, such as drunk driving, focused deterrence has been found to work.[2] One of the difficulties in testing the effectiveness of criminal punishment as a deterrent, as it is practiced in the criminal justice system, is that its requirements of celerity, certainty, and other parameters established in psychology laboratories cannot be controlled for in the highly complex and drawn-out processes of the criminal justice system.[3] The resultant methodological challenges that confront researchers are immense.[4]

However, from a retributive point of view, if punishment *is* an effective deterrent, therein lies its greatest danger, always lurking, that punishment may slide to excess, demanding more and more punishment to achieve the unreachable goal of crime eradication through punishment. This absolutist utilitarian justification for deterrence is that the end justifies the means. Any amount or type of punishment is justifiable if the end (reduction or prevention of crime) is an absolute good, or even something less than that. In contrast to retribution, its moral value rests on facts: whether or not it works. Retribution is an imperative: a moral assertion that does not rest on fact.

Let us look at the scientific research on corporal punishment as a deterrent. And, by the way, the research on punishment as a deterrent in the laboratory has almost always been on corporal punishment, usually on rats. It has rarely been shown to be an effective deterrent on humans. Be warned, though, that those reviewing (and even conducting) the research specifically on corporal punishment distort the findings in order to reach the conclusion that it does not work as a deterrent, so that they could therefore advocate a policy against corporal punishment. There is a deep bias in the academy and in the therapeutic and educational communities *against* corporal punishment and *for* deterrence. In contrast, when it comes to prison as a punishment, there is no such bias, which makes the findings that prison does not deter so much more powerful.

Does Corporal Punishment Deter?

Many classic experiments on the effects of corporal punishment on dogs, monkeys, pigeons, and humans have been conducted in psychology laboratories. A typical experiment is to place a rat on an electrified grid, put down a piece of food, then shock the rat as soon as it goes for the food. This "trial" as it is called, is repeated around five times, until the rat no longer goes for the food. Its specific behavior has been "extinguished." In a number of similar experiments, corporal punishment has been so successful that some animals have starved themselves to death rather than eat the forbidden food.

Most studies conducted by psychologists in their laboratories use electric shock when they administer acute pain to their animal subjects. The electronic collars used to stop dogs from barking or to suppress any other undesirable behavior are based on this science. It is also of interest that the few laboratory studies of the deterrent effects of isolation (that is, the laboratory analogue of solitary confinement) have produced much more inconclusive results than have those using corporal punishment (defined as a short, sharp shock). There is little doubt that, in the experimental conditions of the laboratory, acute pain is a very efficient and lasting suppressor of unwanted behavior of rats and chickens, but its effectiveness on humans is not well established.[5]

The predominant scientific opinion as to whether it is possible to rehabilitate offenders (that is, do something to them to stop them from committing again) is that nothing works.[6] Yet deterrence is the major justification for the punishment of offenders that judges adopt in pronouncing sentences. And at the same time corporal punishment is singled out as the punishment that should not be used because it supposedly does not deter.

Why is this? It is because those who have reviewed the research on corporal punishment as a deterrent have been biased in favor of deterrence but against corporal punishment. There are three biases evident in past research:

1. Researchers have used a different set of standards for evaluating corporal punishment as against prison.

2. Criminologists have conveniently overlooked all the research on corporal punishment conducted in the psychology laboratory, and, while this research does not have direct application to humans, it nevertheless is an important guide, just as research on the effects of drugs on animals is considered an important guide.

3. When researchers have recognized the laboratory research on the effectiveness of punishment, they have ignored the fact that much of this research has used corporal punishment.[7]

Corporal Punishment in Criminal Justice

There have only been two substantial studies on corporal punishment in criminal justice. They were conducted in the United States, specifically Delaware, and in England roughly seventy years ago.

The Delaware study was conducted by Robert Caldwell in 1947 and published in his interesting book *Red Hannah: Delaware's Whipping Post.*[8]

Delaware was the last state in the United States to abolish whipping as a criminal punishment. Abolition did not occur until 1972, although its use had been rare for some two decades previous.

Caldwell compared the rate of recommittal of those criminals who were not whipped with those criminals who were whipped. However, the law required that whipping should always be coupled with a prison term, so it is clear from the outset that the combined effects of prison and whipping might produce consequences quite different from each punishment when applied separately. But the most important criticism is that, when we look closely at the data of the Caldwell study, it turns out that the whipped group was comprised of those who were the more hardened criminals. This would bias the groups in such a way that we would expect a higher recommittal rate for the whipped group than for the not whipped group. Yet on the basis of his findings, Caldwell concluded that whipping should be abolished.

The British research into whipping displayed a similar bias. The Home Office examined the records of 440 offenders who were convicted of robbery with violence, an offense that was punishable by whipping at the time (1921–1930), and compared those who were flogged with those who were not flogged.[9] However, whipping was always administered in conjunction with a prison term, so the effects of the two punishments cannot be separated.[10] The Home Office concluded that the whipped group displayed a higher recommittal rate than the group not whipped. Buried in the appendix of the report is the statement that the majority of the not whipped group was composed of first offenders, and that the whipped group was made up largely of those who had previous offenses of robbery or who had previously served long prison terms. Clearly, the groups were heavily biased from the beginning and therefore no conclusion can be made as to whether flogging worked or not. We may conclude that the abolition of whipping was not justified on the basis of that deterrence research.

The report of the Committee on Corporal Punishment was published by the Home Office in March 1938. Its conclusion:

> We are not satisfied that corporal punishment has that exceptionally effective influence as a deterrent which is usually claimed for it by those who advocate its use as a penalty.[11]

As laudable, thorough, and apparently unbiased as the report of that committee appears on first reading, it did in fact begin with a conclusion: that corporal punishment should be abolished. And it proceeded to collect as much evidence as possible to support this conclusion. The report began by flatly rejecting any defense of corporal punishment on the grounds of retribution, a philosophy, it said, that "did not fit in with the enlightened treatment philosophy." Today, we know that a "treatment philosophy" (that is, rehabilitation) has not produced the results its advocates expected. As an aside, we should also understand that there are many kinds of "treatment" or "rehabilitation," some of which can and do include the infliction of pain and suffering (prison, for example).[12]

The committee made no effort whatsoever to investigate the comparative effects of long prison terms on crime rates, yet made the following forthright conclusion:

> We have found no evidence that . . . long sentences of imprisonment or penal servitude are so ineffective as deterrents that it is essential to add some further penalty for the protection of society.[13]

That further penalty was, of course, corporal punishment.[14]

The committee then went on to outline a number of other crimes that the judiciary had suggested might be appropriately punished by corporal punishment, and also a range of crimes that various witnesses had suggested. It complained, however, that there was "no principle" underlying the range of crimes that were suggested as fit for corporal punishment, yet at the same time observed, quite astutely, that the crimes suggested were those that "excited the imagination." We can see at work here the quest for punishments that can meet the quality of the crimes. But because of the committee's one-sided view of the purpose of criminal punishment—deterrence to the exclusion of all else—it failed to recognize the principle embedded in "special indignation," the committee's words for retribution.

Conclusions: From Corporal Punishment to Mass Incarceration

Research on corporal punishment in criminal justice has been biased in favor of prison as a punishment. Social scientists' conclusions were invariably that corporal punishment should be abolished because it could not be demonstrated to have a deterrent effect. Yet when similar results are reviewed for the effects of prison as a deterrent, the conclusion that prison should be abolished is never drawn. Furthermore, recent criticisms against prison, complaining of "mass incarceration," are not against prison as a punishment itself, but against its excessive use, especially disproportionately incarcerating certain ethnic minorities.[15] There is no denying it, though, that the excessive use of prison is a direct result of the unwavering belief in the effectiveness of its use as a deterrent (made worse, of course, by the abolition of corporal punishment, so that there is no other alternative). This is utilitarianism at its worst, because the end that it promises, a rehabilitated offender, never eventuates. In this case, it is a false end that justifies an evil means; a morally indefensible position.[16]

The lesson is that deterrence, the practical application of the classic utilitarian philosophy made popular by the Enlightenment thinkers of the eighteenth century, has brought us to the brink not of enlightened punishment but of blind imposition of a cruel punishment, incarceration, upon large sections of our population. It is punishment in excess, hardly civilized and essentially barbaric.

But surely there are some, the worst of the worst criminals, who must be locked up simply for our protection. They ought to be punished for their crimes, but the protection of society overrides all else. Is this not an iron clad utilitarian defense of prison?

The alert reader may have noticed that the third moral justification for punishment that I outlined in the introduction, redemption, was not mentioned in this or the previous chapter. The reason is that it is part of an important solution to mass incarceration, one that requires incapacitation. And I mean incapacitation, not prison!

How can this be?

Chapter Six

The Promise of Incapacitation

Redemption and Control of the Body in an Open Society

Incapacitation without Walls

L et us review the misconception that prison is the only guaranteed way of preventing the very worst criminals from preying on us innocents. This twentieth-century misconception was invented by liberal reformers who fell for the lie of the Enlightenment: it was the mind that incarceration punished, not the body. This supposedly great insight was dramatized by the famous unchaining of the insane in mental asylums by Philippe Pinel in 1797. Indeed, the twentieth-century postmodernists, such as Foucault, made much of this: the insane were liberated, their souls set free.[1] And their coconspirators, the criminals locked up, unchained from the brutality of corporal punishments, their bodies no longer torn asunder.[2] The nineteenth-century prison would deprive criminals only of their liberty, their bodies left alone. And the twentieth-century prisons would punish only the minds of the prisoners, not their bodies.

Such good intentions, enlightened rehabilitation, the prisoners unchained and simply confined! Unfortunately, as is often the case, good intentions are not enough and sometimes downright damaging. Prisons grew and grew.[3] They became monstrous fortresses, visiting all kinds of horrors on their forgotten inhabitants; the guards, themselves instruments of torture, the inmates torturing themselves and each other. For no matter how well or pristine any prison is built or even administered, its very structure dictates that its inmates will be ruled with an iron fist, the humans within transformed into monsters, captured by its rigid structure. The repeated scandals of violence and riots in prisons, now for some two centuries, ought to be enough to tell us that they must be abolished. Instead, they grow, like a dreadful cancer inside and out. Frankly, there is no such thing as, or even the possibility of, a good prison. Progressive prisons are a figment of the progressive imagination.[4]

It doesn't matter, you say. Society has a right to protect itself. Indeed it does. But does it have the right to use a punishment that goes beyond what is necessary, punishing not only the worst of the worst, but many others as well? We have seen so far that moderate corporal punishment, administered carefully and rationally, could be applied to the majority of offenders instead of prison, and chapter 7 will detail precisely how to do it. It is only the terrible few who confound us, and we must protect ourselves by confining them in prisons. The trouble is that, once built, prisons are so effective at hiding the mechanics of the punishment, they are guaranteed to grow, always taking in more and more beyond the terrible few. Once built, they also represent massive investments of human and actual capital.

Besides, just who are the worst of the worst? Just how many terrible few are there in the United States? How are they chosen?[5] I can't seriously answer this difficult question. Attempts by psychologists and social scientists to predict dangerousness of individuals are fraught with many difficulties. Basically, it is not possible to do it with an acceptable degree of certainty.[6] Parole boards have been trying to do it for decades, without much success.[7] An easy way out of this problem is to take stock of how many criminals there are held in solitary confinement in maximum security prisons in the United States, including supermax prisons. In 2006, in his excellent survey of the effectiveness of supermax prisons, Daniel Mears reckoned that there were about 25,000 such criminals, whom we may call the worst of the worst.[8] This is not altogether satisfactory, because Mears also noted that the violence of those in solitary confinement in supermax prisons might have been in part brought on by the very conditions of the supermax incarceration itself. If we take the 25,000 of those in solitary confinement, this comes to approximately 1.2 percent of all incarcerated criminals, based on the roughly two million persons currently incarcerated in the United States. Or, looked at more broadly, the number in solitary confinement computes to roughly 7 per 100,000 US population. Maybe that's an overestimate of the worst of the worst. Another measure for comparison may be the number of serial killers convicted or suspected, which comes to roughly 250 in all, over a period spanning the twentieth century up to the present.[9] Statistically it's impossible to compare this figure to the solitary confinement figure, though it probably comes closer to the death penalty figures of the United States, since most of the serial killers were executed. In any case, this is a tiny number by comparison to the regular numbers of persons in prison.

Why not confine the terrible few, incapacitate them in ways that do not require a prison? We must refocus our energies on the body of the criminal and away from the "mind," unchain ourselves from this Enlightenment thinking.

Once we get rid of the idea of prison, we can think of many different ways to incapacitate a criminal of the terrible few, taking into account the amount of threat he is to society (deterrence), and, secondarily, the extent to which any painful punishment matches his crimes (retribution). In this case, his threat to our safety and security trumps any attempt to match a punishment to his crime; it may not be possible anyway, given the awful crimes the terrible few commit, especially at the extreme end where no punishment could be severe enough, including death, to match the horror of the crime.

Types of Incapacitation

Prior to the Enlightenment, punishments that incapacitated were common, as we have already seen. The scold's bridle incapacitated her mouth so that she could not nag her husband, the stocks and pillory constrained the whole body within a fixed apparatus, the hand of the thief was cut off, and, in Shari'a law, a variety of hands and feet continue to be cut off, thus incapacitating particular parts of the body. Finally, in some common law jurisdictions, castration, whether physical or chemical, is applied to serial rapists.

In the twenty-first century, and in the near future, we have many more options, once we envisage incapacitation that does not need a prison. There are basically two types of incapacitation: geographic incapacitation and bodily incapacitation.

Geographic incapacitation is where the offender is confined by instruments that keep him within a defined boundary. "House arrest" is a common method, but for the terrible few, this is of course not enough. Some jurisdictions forbid sex offenders of various kinds from living within a particular distance from schools. How these sentences can be enforced, however, is another matter. Some jurisdictions use mechanical or electronic means, such as an ankle bracelet that can, using GPS technology, track the offender's whereabouts, and soon to come, embedded tracking chips and drone surveillance. In any case, we should think of this type of incapacitation as relatively benign for the terrible few, unless enforced through the use of modern technology, which leads to the second type of incapacitation.

Bodily incapacitation may be achieved by several different means. Cutting off hands or feet limits dexterity and bodily movement. Using this means of incapacitation makes it possible to limit the body to specific movements. Another way of looking at it is that to cut off, say, the foot of a horrible offender is to punish him with a disability. That disability he would have to overcome if he were to manage his life in society, and it would clearly mark him as a horrible offender of some type. The negative side to this incapacitating punishment is that it would, obviously, stigmatize those who, for reasons of birth, accident, or war, have lost a part of their body. Those who are not used to Shari'a law are probably shocked by this suggestion. But it is important to remember that the only modern alternative to such severe punishments in Western culture is the use of prison.

If the shedding of blood to amputate a part of a terrible criminal's body is culturally unacceptable, then why not use a disabling mechanism that can be applied to the body? The forerunner of these mechanical devices was the ball and chain that the offender had to carry around with him everywhere he went, a very effective way of limiting movement. It is also a very visible incapacitating punishment. A little imagination would produce no doubt a variety of many different kinds of restraining devices that would restrict specific bodily movements, and also confine movement to particular areas and locations. These instruments could be designed also to administer certain amounts of pain, should the terrible criminal deserve it, and to be either more or less visible. These restraining devices also have long term effects, causing musculo-skeletal damage, for example, as was the case with the 28 lb. Oregon boot used in Oregon State Penitentiary early in the twentieth century.[10]

However, there are many restraining devices already available that physically restrain individuals. It is of interest that all such devices have been invented for use within institutions that are designed to house people against their will, whether hospitals, prisons, boarding schools, or asylums, or nursing homes. Here is an incomplete list:[11]

1. *Low technology:* ankle cuffs, anklets, hand- or leg cuffs, fetters, waist bands, wristlets, plastic cuffs, wraps, belts, shackles, chains, (weighted) leg irons or leg cuffs, gang chains, finger and thumb cuffs, soft/fabric restraints, straightjackets

2. *Heavy duty:* four-, five-, six-point restraints—such as restraint chairs, shackle boards, and restraint or isolation beds

3. *Electronic:* body-worn electric-shock restraint devices—such as stun belts, sleeves or cuffs, embedded devices that shock or otherwise control behavior.

Technology of the twenty-first century makes it possible to go beyond the ancient mechanical devices that confined the body to particular places or restricted bodily movement in particular ways. Those devices are and always have been very visible. We can, in fact, incapacitate the body through ways that are not at all visible, achieving either geographic incapacitation or bodily incapacitation. Keep in mind that the so-called incapacitation of offenders in prison is hidden from public view, by necessity, because to allow the public access to view inmates in prison would raise all kinds of security concerns. The extreme form of incapacitation in prison, by the way, is solitary confinement, which is currently reaching full throttle, though its cruel effects are currently under scrutiny.[12]

Hiding the incapacitation of the terrible few in plain sight is most certainly feasible through two main methods: (1) a tracking chip implanted in the body that is inaccessible to the offender or (2) an implanted mechanism that administers particular kinds of drugs that immobilize the offender in various ways. Note, though, that neither of these methods administers pain, except for the initial insertion, and since this punishment must be both incapacitating and punitive, a variation of this mechanism might also administer an electric shock or other painful stimulus.

What we are talking about here is whether or how we want to incapacitate the offender. It is possible using these implanted mechanisms to shape the offender's behavior in various ways, just as we saw in the last chapter, where the rat received a shock each time it went for the food, or as Alex, in *A Clockwork Orange*, received a vomit-inducing drug when he tried to commit violent acts. In other words, using the available technologies, we can shape the offender's behavior in ways that we want, especially preventing him from repeating his terrible past crimes and at the same time also make the experience painful. These mechanisms can do more than incapacitate, or, more precisely, they incapacitate by shaping the offender's behavior. Finally, the punishment mechanism would also induce painful or very unpleasant consequences should the offender attempt to circumvent it in some way, additionally communicating through a monitoring mechanism that such an attempt was made. Some may be tempted to call this a kind of "rehabilitation," even "deterrence," since we are trying to shape and modify the offender's behavior. In one sense, this is true—rather like we try to do with prison (that is, total control of the body and mind of the offender), except we are doing it outside of prison, in open society.

By far the most difficult issue we face in implementing this design of incapacitation hidden in plain sight is this: Are we able to live with the knowledge that very serious criminals, indeed, the worst of the worst, might live among us, without us knowing who they are?[13] Here we confront the most difficult aspect of criminal punishment. Prison solves this very difficult problem by putting criminals out of sight. Unfortunately, it is now very clear that the moral, social, and economic cost of this punishment is far too great.

There are two viable solutions. The first is to revert to the old tried and true method of stigmatizing the criminal with a visible sign or other means of making his or her crime public; a version of the "scarlet letter." These days, social media take care of this. It is in various locations in the United States and other countries applied to sex offenders who are officially registered as such. Their places of residence, name, and other personal details are often openly published on the Internet, depending on local laws. Why can't this be applied to all very serious offenders, even the worst of the worst? It might be, but it would not solve the problem and would bring additional problems with it. The constitutionality of sex offender registries has been challenged for some time now, particularly according to the denial of due process—the claim that offenders' punishment is continued beyond and above that intended by the original sentence.[14] Of course, we can see that this very same argument can be applied to prison itself.

The second is to incapacitate the worst of the worst in plain sight, but making sure that they can do no harm. What kind of lives would these horrible criminals lead? They would be under constant surveillance, their every movement monitored robotically—total surveillance. Now this is *real* deprivation of liberty, without the colossus of prison that has been the blight of so many communities. And the big advantage of this kind of incapacitation is that it is achieved quietly and without spectacle. The horrible offender, the worst of the worst, cannot make himself a spectacle, cannot make of himself the horror of people's imaginations, such as occurred with Charles Manson. The idea of total surveillance of criminals was first imagined by Jeremy Bentham with his plan of a prison (the panopticon) built so that all inmates would be under surveillance twenty-four hours a day. We no longer need a prison to achieve this end. It can be done in open society, robotically.

It may be argued that this is impractical and dangerous because the worst criminals will, of course, do what they can to escape, break the monitoring system or whatever other incapacitating device might be applied. It is true that traditional home confinement, used in the US federal system since at least the early 1980s, has an "escape rate" of roughly 20 percent, though there are no known definitive studies that have clearly established this.[15] This rate compares unfavorably to the prison escape rate that is estimated to be around 5 percent, and from maximum security prisons, around 2 percent. There is, however, a very effective answer. Keep in mind that the steps we take to achieve security for communities when the terrible few are incapacitated, whether in their homes or elsewhere, may be draconian, but are still far more just and humane than putting these criminals in prisons.[16] Whenever we use prisons, even for the worst of the worst, once they are up and running, their appetite increases and must be fed. Hence, mass incarceration begins again.

The Ultimate Solution: Dependent Incapacitation

In the 1970s, after the enormous success of the movie *One Flew over the Cuckoo's Nest*, the movement to deinstitutionalize insane asylums took hold and many mental institutions were closed or reduced considerably in size. The evils identified in that movie were essentially two: (1) the horrible and inevitably inhumane conditions that arise inside any kind of institution, even one whose purpose is to treat, not to punish, such as a hospital or insane asylum; and (2) the use of drugs to deprive the inmates of their consciousness, to make them docile and easier to handle by the staff, portrayed by the memorable character of Nurse Ratchet.

The inherent, inbuilt dangers of institutions of all kinds came under attack by many social scientists, such as Erving Goffman, in the 1960s and beyond.[17] Yet it was the gradual availability of mind-controlling drugs that made it possible for many to be released from mental institutions, though, unfortunately, the ability to make sure that they took their medications as prescribed was severely curtailed. Today, there are many more powerful drugs available to control a variety of mental problems and difficult behaviors. Why not use these drugs on the terrible few as a means of incapacitation?

Finally, we know that some drugs, heroin and other modern derivatives or reconstituted drugs, are extremely addictive. Why not induce addiction to such drugs so that the only way the terrible criminal can survive is to have his addiction satisfied by the drug that is dispensed to him at his place of residence? A maintenance dose may be administered so that the terrible criminal is even able to work in some limited capacity. There are a number of studies that have shown, for example, that the careful monitoring of heroin can maintain an individual so that he can carry out day-to-day activities.[18] The punishment, then, is not painful unless the horrible offender fails to take his medicine, at which point he suffers terribly the withdrawal symptoms of drug addiction.

But what of those who still scare us, who are so violent, that they will do anything to overcome their robotic implants? In the few cases where the implants can be overcome—these would be the terrible few of the terrible few—ultimate immobilization might be the only solution. Here, the death penalty might be applicable, except that we know that the death penalty cannot be applied in practice without also confining those sentenced to death in prison while their cases slowly make their way through the courts, which on average takes at least ten years.

Maybe this is not really necessary. Perhaps there are ways to immobilize such offenders with paralyzing drugs, even induce a coma. Such an incapacitation would be close to the death penalty, but would not be death—rather, a suspended animation. True, such individuals would have to be constantly monitored and fed to be kept alive. But this avoids the expensive process of locking them up in death row. Instead, they are kept alive in a coma. It is not a death penalty, but it is a deprivation of life. Instead of "life in prison," they receive "life in coma" (for whatever number of years). Would it be cheaper to keep an offender on life support rather than conscious in a maximum security prison, with all the security and other activities necessary to provide a "humane" existence in a supermax prison?[19] The worst of the terrible worst could be maintained in such a state in a hospital-like setting, or even in a private home monitored by robot, visited by a caregiver. In fact, we already know that it is cheaper to care for a sick (usually aged) person at home rather than in a hospital.[20]

We are pushing the envelope here. From the point of view of punishment, the difficult issue obviously arises with induced coma: where is the pain? The traditional definition of punishment is that it must involve the application of pain or "consequences normally considered unpleasant."[21] In order to call an induced coma punishment, one must expand the definition of punishment to include loss of life that is short of death. It is painless, except perhaps for a fleeting prick of an injection, though even this could likely be avoided by using a nonintrusive method of applying a drug through a patch on the skin.

We must remind ourselves once again that we are talking here about the punishment of the terrible few of the terrible few. It is an extreme case in which incapacitation overrides punishment, though one can argue that the outcome, loss of life without death, is a punishment, even if not painful in the classical sense.

You may well ask, why not just kill the offender and be done with it? My answer is that enforced coma is in lieu of a death penalty. Obviously, the death penalty is the ultimate incapacitation and when used is mostly justified as a means of protecting us from the worst of the worst. We know that the horrible offender cannot repeat his crime on someone else. This utilitarian justification is the only justification for the death penalty that holds water. The retributive justification that the horrible offender deserved to die for his terrible sadistic murders overlooks the impossibility of matching the death penalty (these days, if administered, done so with every effort to make it painless) to the horror of the crimes. The killing of a murderer for one murder fulfills the demands of retribution that the punishment match the crime. But what if the murderer is a serial or mass murderer? It is not possible to kill the murderer more than once to make up for the multiple murders. The only way to attempt such a match would be to apply an aggravated death penalty as occurred two centuries ago, such as drawing and quartering and so on. And who would agree to that? And would it be enough, say, for a Hitler or a Pol Pot? The amount of punishment could never be enough, could it?

Forcing a horrible criminal to become addicted to a drug may appear callous and even inhumane. But we must remember, once again, that this is a last ditch effort, an effort to incapacitate the most terrible of the terrible offenders. But the question is often asked, what if the terrible offender of the terrible few was wrongly convicted and was after all innocent?[22] Clearly, in the cases unearthed in recent years of wrongful conviction, for the death penalty, this punishment cannot be reversed.[23]

In general, no punishment can be reversed, in fact, in life. No deed, painful or pleasant, can be undone, can it? In the case of criminal punishment and the crimes that invoke it, neither can be taken back completely. This is why offenders generally cannot be "rehabilitated," because they cannot undo their crime, even if they wanted to. Past wrongs cannot be undone, unless they are completely forgotten.[24] In fact, as Sigmund Freud so remarkably demonstrated early in the twentieth century, we are unable to forget past deeds, even when we think we have (they stay in the unconscious).

However, some punishments are more reversible than others. Obviously, the death penalty is final and cannot be reversed. The scars of some punishments, such as cutting off a hand or foot, the stripes on a bare back from the lash, are not reversible either, though new technologies do promise to replace parts of the body with transplants or bionic parts. Nor can a life in prison or even less be given back. Those scars are irreversible.

However, so long as a person is alive, there is the opportunity to at least mitigate a mistaken punishment, and if the punishment is not mistaken, to make up for past wrongs by making adjustments. Keep in mind that throughout this chapter we are talking about how to punish the worst of the worst. The kindest punishment of most offenders is moderate corporal punishment. The harshest punishment is prison, which is so evil it should be abolished. Bodily incapacitation, also very severe, should be kept for the terrible few, those who are a clear and present danger.

A Cautionary Note

There are some people—it is often difficult to say who they are or what is wrong with them—with whom family members, relatives, or friends, even, just can't stand to live. I suppose one could say that some people are "uncivilized," "incorrigible," or just so crazy or violent that we can't stand to live with them. We want them "out of sight."

Western civilization, in the darker periods of the eighteenth century, found a solution to this social problem: put them in an asylum and keep them out of sight. Prisons do just that also. In fact asylums and prisons have parallel histories, having arisen at roughly the same time in the eighteenth century in the West.[25] Michel Foucault, in his best book, in my humble opinion, described this history of those who revolt us in his *Madness and Civilization*. The outcasts of society were transported, always on the move, banished from small towns and villages, drifting from one town to the next, likened to the "ship of fools." This lot, constantly on the fringe of society— the sick, blind, deaf, dumb, deformed, leprous, violent, and mentally and physically handicapped—were eventually scooped up and put in asylums, chained to the walls, on display as things of curiosity and disgust. All this happened in the West sometime in the late seventeenth century and into the eighteenth century, until Pinel famously unchained them. Prior to that time, they were either forced out of villages and towns to beg or starve, or were, for those families who could put up with them, hidden away in their home, the classic monster in the closet or attic, a source of shame and embarrassment to the family.

Institutions for the insane or other misfits of society did do a great service for those family members who couldn't stand to live with their incorrigible or monstrously deviant family members. Thus it happened that, in civilized society, institutions arose where families could deposit their obstreperous or shameful family member, and thankfully go back to normal lives, without the disruption or shame of the deviant. The process of removing deviants from society into institutions took hold in every social institution of Western society: families, schools, workplaces.[26]

All of the above is a longwinded acknowledgment that there may be no other solution for some families who cannot stand to live with a particular family member to get rid of that person. Today, this observation probably concerns mostly those families that have a violent family member, especially one who abuses family members, most often in the form of spouse and child abuse. Sometimes, the twisted solution is for the victimized spouse to leave the family behind, rather than for the offender to be moved out.

I do not deny that what to do with such family members is a very serious and intractable problem. Yet, the idea of nonincarcerative incapacitation does resonate at one level. Maybe it gives the family members an opportunity to live with that offender in his incapacitated condition, even if it is an induced coma or controlled drug addiction. There is a sense of poetic justice here, where the family member who is the problem, perhaps the violent problem, who rules the roost in the house, subjects family members to his tyranny, is put into a dependent condition where he depends on that very family for his livelihood, even survival.

We need to give much more thought to this question in regards to a criminal's family members. Much is made of the damage to families, both financial and psychological, when a family member is sent to prison. However, there may be some families where the opposite is the case: they are glad to be rid of that nuisance, even if it means they may suffer in other ways, possibly financially.

In any case there are ways to put incapacitation to good use. This requires us to revisit the old conflict between the two justifications of criminal punishment so far distinguished: retribution and utility.

Redemptive Incapacitation

We have seen that the utilitarian justification of punishment, especially that of deterrence, is an essential justification when it comes to punishing the worst of the worst. Its advantage over retribution is that it can be tested scientifically. If it can be shown to work, then its moral purpose is justified. Retribution is not open to scientific testing, since it is based on a moral assertion rather than a question of fact. It argues that a wrong must be corrected by a punishment that matches that wrong. There is no scientific way to test such a moral assertion, least of all a scientific procedure that validates the matching of a particular punishment to a particular crime. We will see later that there are procedures for matching punishments to crimes, but they are legal procedures, not scientific ones.

In fact, there is a serious semantic difficulty involved, because utilitarians argue that retribution itself is actually part of the definition of punishment; it is what distinguishes punishment from violence. It seeks simply to punish just because a crime has been committed; it is "backward looking," has no interest in looking to the future, hoping to prevent further crimes. So critics commonly charge that retribution is entirely negative, concerned only with inflicting pain or suffering for its own sake, with no positive value, no concern to make things better.[27] Surely there's something positive that could be done, and, if so, wouldn't this be preferable to an entirely negative "injury for injury" approach to the offender? At least, with their concern for order and for the greatest happiness for the greatest number, the utilitarians are trying to do something positive.

The morality of retribution is both theoretically and practically negative. For example, a common complaint by those who criticize the death penalty is to question its wisdom that the evil done by the murderer can be "made up for" or "erased" by killing the murderer. How can the destruction of a second life make up for the loss of the first life? The defenders of retribution must resort to mystical and perhaps religious theories to show how taking the offender's life "replaces" the life of the murderer's victim (Moses said so). The standard defense of this "moral equation" of retribution (a life for a life) is that it is "just" (hence, "just deserts"), that the "balance" of injury or evil is recovered. However, this does not alter the fact that this "balance" is still weighted towards one side (that is, the state inflicts injury on the murderer, leaving the victim or victim's family out of the equation). It is a "negative reciprocity."[28]

Even more unsettling is that intentionally inflicting pain and suffering for its own sake (that is, punishing according to retribution) appears to carry with it the identical elements of the behavior of the one we punish. Did not the criminal intentionally inflict pain or suffering on his victim? This is the conundrum of criminal punishment (and perhaps all punishment):

in order to punish, we must actually indulge in some of the same behavior as the offender. While we indulge in certain sophistries, such as "the state does it legally," which is true, there is still no arguing that the actual behaviors or behavioral intentions are very similar: to intentionally inflict pain and suffering, whether by offender or judge. The Judeo-Christian tradition understood this contradiction of punishment by trying to turn it to its advantage: it used pain and suffering as a method to teach the offender a lesson, to correct him. It is upon this edifice that Judeo-Christian guilt rests. The offender, through punishment, is taught to take upon himself the guilt of his actions, essentially punish himself—which is what guilt is all about, after all. And while guilt remains with us, the idea of self-punishment, real self-punishment, has dropped away in secular society. In any case, it is this close affinity between the punisher and punished that points us towards a positive side to retribution.

Retribution is all about reciprocity. The reciprocal aspect of retribution is hidden by its concern with inflicting pain and suffering equal at least to that inflicted by the offender. However, there are types of retribution that are not wholly wedded to this view, or that at least try to place the pain and suffering into a framework in which the pain is used to "mean something"—that is, for pain to have a positive purpose. And that purpose is when punishment is used as a "cure" (or purgative, an expression no doubt derived from Dante's *Purgatory*). In this model—basically the Christian tradition—offenders are required to indulge in certain acts of suffering, such as penance, physical pain, or solitary confinement (meditation or prayer), to come to an understanding that what they did was wrong. The complete psychological and cultural explanation as to why it is thought personal suffering is necessary to learn the wrong that was done would take us far afield of this book. Suffice it to say that our Western way of life has, as long as we can remember, always linked the absolution of guilt with physical and mental suffering.[29]

Dante's *Hell* and *Purgatory*, provided many examples of punishments that, while they were intended to be painful, nevertheless served to demonstrate that, while pain is a necessary part of eradicating guilt, it is not sufficient in itself. Dante introduces a positive element to the reciprocal relationship between the crime and the punishment: the offender must practice the virtue that is opposite the vice he committed. For example, those consumed with pride or self-love, must practice humility: whereas their heads were held so high on earth, now they are bent double under a big stone, their heads low. The slothful and lazy—they must spend all their time running continuously. Instead of concentrating entirely on the pain and suffering as a match to the suffering caused by the crime, Dante's punishments show that the practice of a virtue (that is, doing good) may in addition help to cancel out the injury of the offense. Yet he manages to translate the practice of a virtue into a horrendous punishment.[30] Keep in mind, now, that we are, in this chapter, talking about how to punish horrendous criminals, the terrible few.

There is one important element left out of this equation: the victim. Dante's punishment and the retribution idea, generally, of the last several hundred years have had little regard for the victim in Western civilization. The balance has been treated as a more abstract balance: that between the individual actor and his own past acts. The punishments of Dante are oriented entirely toward the individual coming to account with himself (and, through this experience, with God).[31] This "keeping of accounts" is clearly an important part of retribution, and it is also crucial to the idea of restitution, of paying a debt.

There is little agreement upon to whom the debt is owed.[32] The argument usually revolves around whether or not society in general can be conceived as a victim of any crime (including "victimless crimes"), either instead of or as well as a victim who is directly damaged by an offender. For example, those who advocate a "pure" restitution, take the position that society has no place getting involved in the essentially private offender-victim relationship. The only victims they will recognize are direct, concrete victims.[33] Shari'a law in its traditional form also affirms this view, where victims may play an important and active part in the application of the punishment (see chapter 9).

However, others argue that a debt is owed by the state to those who have not broken the law, to punish those who have. Otherwise offenders have an unfair advantage. Yet others argue that the offenders also have a right to be punished, and that society, by punishing them, fulfills the debt it owes to the offender.[34] Finally, some who are strongly opposed to punishment of any kind take the position that the actual involvement of the victim and the offender in the process of resolving the conflict themselves is a good thing in the sense that each can learn and grow from the experience (these days called "restorative justice").[35]

In practical terms, there seems little point in quibbling over to whom exactly the debt is owed, since it is always difficult to identify exactly where that damage or injury to persons stops. If an individual is mugged, clearly he or she is the victim. But his or her family are also victims in that they share in this suffering. The injury and damage caused by most crimes can rarely be limited to one victim. Because of the complexity of interpersonal relationships, the effects of a crime will be felt by many.[36] The same goes for the effects of punishment, as we will see in more detail in chapters 6 and 7.

The question, therefore, of whether or not the debt is owed specifically to the direct victim of the crime is, from an historical and even practical point of view, unimportant. Let us simply observe that many writers of varying philosophical and ideological persuasions seem to agree that there is a debt owed by the offender on account of his having committed a crime. For the moment, let us put aside the question of to whom the debt is owed, and turn instead to the ways in which one may pay a debt.

Historically, there have been a number of different solutions to this everyday problem of life. These may be summarized briefly as follows:

- The victim may return injury for injury (vengeance). Here the debt is seen as that familiar imbalance created when one party wrongs another.

- The offender may pay blood money in return for an injury done to another party. In this case, monetary values are attached to particular types and amounts of bodily or property damage. This dates back at least to the Middle Ages.[37]

- Depending upon the religious persuasion of the offender, he may indulge in certain acts of suffering or penance, to pay back to his God the debt he owes from having committed evil acts. The common picture of St. Peter or the "Recording Angel" keeping a ledger of good and bad deeds of each person testifies to the well-established notion of a debt interpretation of punishment in the Christian tradition.[38]

- The offender may make it up to the victim, by offering valued services (such as his labor) or other goods valued by the victim.

- The offender may shift the debt to another person. That is, he may borrow from another, to pay his immediate debt. While this might work with financial arrangements, it is difficult to see how it could be implemented for bodily injuries, unless the victim bypasses the criminal justice system and seeks recourse through institutions that specialize in collecting and disbursing such debts, such as the Mafia.

We can see, from the point of view of punishment as payment of a debt, that both the retributive and restitutive models embrace this philosophy because they view punishment as an exchange—ideally an equal exchange. They seek the reestablishment of the balance between offender and others, they both reinforce the norm of reciprocity.[39] It will be remembered, though, that in chapter 3 we rejected some of the punishments outlined above as not credible punishments, because they were not painful enough. And in this chapter, where we are concerned only with what to do with the terrible few, they may not apply in practice, but they may apply a satisfactory justification for making the terrible few at least attempt, through their incapacitation, to do some good. Could they make restitution?

Advocates of restitution maintain that, instead of the totally negative approach to the offender adopted by both the retribution and deterrence advocates, restitution offers a way to have something positive come out of the punishment process. This is considered to be a more enlightened approach to criminal punishment, the presumption being that a civilized society, if it must inflict pain, should attach some higher meaning to it. That is, there must be an identifiable consequence of the punishment that goes beyond the mere infliction of pain and suffering. There are two identifiable forms of restitution: pure restitution and punitive restitution.

The strongest advocates of pure restitution argue that restitution is inconsistent with punishment and that it should totally replace punishment as a new paradigm in criminal justice.[40] However, it takes little effort to expose this position as indefensible.[41] The purists argue that we serve justice not by punishing individuals, but by requiring offenders to make restitution to their victims: "The armed robber did not rob society; he robbed the victim."[42] We have already seen that it makes no practical or moral sense to draw hard and fast lines between the one individual victim and others who are also affected. But, more importantly, the attempt to focus upon restitution rather than punishment puts restitution in a position of having to excuse itself for being "soft on crime." Punishments must be credible, and, to be credible, their infliction of pain or suffering must be unambiguous.

Furthermore, pure restitution allows for the possibility of other interventions into the offender's life that would otherwise be seriously questioned if they were labelled clearly as painful punishments (such as forced labor for the victim). That is to say, their harmful effects are cleansed by the apparently good intentions of this form of restitution (to provide an alternative to punishment). If an act is labelled as "intentionally painful" or "punitive," it is much more likely to be scrutinized for its ethical and political justification than is an act labelled as "helping" or "doing good." On these grounds, we must reject pure restitution as being incompatible with retribution.

Punitive restitution is the more widely recognized form of restitution,[43] the one closest to that expressed so well by Dante. By insisting that the offender suffers for his crimes (which the retributivist says he deserves) punitive restitution avoids the criticism that it is naive (to think that the public will give up punishment and accept some kind of nonpainful alternative).[44] The problem remains, then, how to make restitutions credibly painful.

In sum, if restitution is to "work" as a retributive punishment,

- it must be credibly painful,

- it must provide a satisfactory balance to the offense (that is, the restitution must match the crime), and

- its effects both on the offender and the victim(s) must be clearly identifiable.

In other words, what is needed is a restitutive punishment that is easily identifiable as a punishment, can be readily matched to the offense, and the positive effects easily identified. There is such a punishment: redemption.

The death penalty, if we must have it, does provide us with an excellent opportunity to turn what many see as an outrageous and wanton destruction of an additional human life, into something that could *save* one or more human lives, and certainly to dramatically improve the quality of life for many others. Why should not the bodies of the executed be used for donor organs for those awaiting transplants? There are such long waiting lists, and the expense of such organs is extremely high.[45] Indeed, one could even argue that, in order for the use of organs not to be appropriated by the rich (as can be the case now, because of their high cost), organs of the executed could be specially allocated to those who are too poor to receive transplant operations.

The death penalty offers a unique opportunity for the murderers to do what many say is impossible for them: while they may not be able to bring back the life of their victim, they can certainly save another life— maybe more than one. This is surely a wonderful opportunity to enhance the retributive aspects of the punishment and truly "cancel out" the injury done by the original murder. Just think of it. According to the Organ Procurement and Transplantation Network,[46] one organ donor can save eight lives. As of June 20, 2017, 117,589 people in the United States needed a lifesaving organ transplant. Of those, 75,851 people were active waiting list candidates. The number of people who die every year awaiting a transplant is, on average, 11,000.[47] Many such lives could be saved by murderers.[48]

Indeed, one could go so far as to say that the individuals' lives that are saved by the donations of the offender are more worthy, as lives, than that of the offender. After all, according to retribution, society is saying that the murderer's life is worthless; but that his death is of great value. The retributivist can only say that the value of the murderer's death is simply in the fact that he took another's life. Both, therefore, are negative values. But, with what we can now call "restitutive retribution," we can see that the value in the death of the offender lies in the extent to which it can save and enhance the lives of others. And we could even choose others who truly deserved to have their lives enhanced: the poor, who, as it happens, do not have the money for the expensive transplant operations, and in some countries, in fact, may end up selling their body parts in order to live.[49]

We should be aware that the argument for using the bodies of executed offenders to save lives is made easier if we leave it to others to decide *on other grounds* whether or not it is justified to inflict the death penalty in the first place. So far, I have simply argued that, given that some US states have decided that the death penalty is an acceptable punishment, then there is no need to address the difficult argument of whether it is justified to violate the physical body of the offender to do good. The decision to execute is already the decision to violate the offender's body.

If we extend the idea that we wish to save lives of innocent people by using the bodies of offenders—alive or dead—then we have much more difficult issues to address, especially from a retribution point of view. In fact, utilitarians have told us for a long time that they only inflict punishment when they can maximize the greatest good for the greatest number. And we are well aware of the defects of the utilitarian justification for punishment, the major one of which is that the individual is used as a means, whereas the retributivist argues that the individual is an end, not a means to anything.[50] If we want to keep true to a retribution position, there is difficulty justifying the use of offenders' bodies while they are alive.

Unless, that is, they are the worst of the worst. In which case it may be better for all concerned that we keep them alive while we harvest their body parts. We would be doing good by the principles of both utility and retribution. We offer the terrible few a chance at redemption.[51]

Redemption softens the harsh utility of using criminals as a means to an end. We have seen that the bodies of the worst of the worst could be incapacitated in a number of ways, without resorting to prison. So far, we have confined the discussion purely to incapacitation, with the sole aim to make sure that criminals could do us no harm while living among us. We used the utilitarian justification of punishment to defend the justice and morality of such a punishment.

Without going into too much detail concerning the defects of the utilitarian position, it is important that we recognize that its claim to serve the "greater good" (we, the people) is a double edged sword. The "greater good" redefines the negative aspects of any punishment as positive. So, by calling imprisonment rehabilitation, utilitarians can justify extended prison terms (the indeterminate sentence) for comparatively minor offenses. This crass justification of punishment has contributed significantly to the excessive and irresponsible use of prison.

In contrast, it is always, without qualms, the intent of retribution that the offender suffer a pain that matches the severity of the crime he has committed. It is "just" and it is the criminal's "deserts." In this chapter we have tried to make room in retribution for "doing good," through redemption, offering up the body of the convict to society. In this case, punishment serves both utility and retribution. More important, it also offers a way to verify scientifically that the punishment has worked by counting the lives saved by "donation" of the offender's body parts.

Can punishment serve two masters? It always has. But a crucial difference remains hidden in the definition of "doing good." The utilitarians' abstract formula of the greatest happiness (who on earth has any idea what this could mean?), in practice define their "good" as conformity, expressed through various policies of deterrence, treatment, and incapacitation via prison. As we have seen, there have been many scientific studies that have attempted to measure the effectiveness of the various utilitarian policies of deterrence and rehabilitation. None has been able to demonstrate definitively that they have "worked." Indeed, if they really did work, would total conformity be a good thing, bring about the greatest happiness?

In contrast, the retributive use of bodily incapacitation in the cause of redemption is highly visible and conclusive. Other specific lives can be saved and enhanced. Furthermore, after they have made their organ donations, offenders who did not receive the death penalty would be free to go about their lives again, depending on the extent of incapacitation required of their crime, that is, the extent to which they remain a threat to society. Remember, we are here talking about only the worst of the worst.

There are, of course, many obvious objections to this idea. For example, some may complain that the government will execute murderers in order to harvest body parts, especially as this has already happened in China.[52]

But America is not China. We have due process and many legal safeguards against tyranny. It should be possible to introduce legislation and structure the "donor" program to prevent its abuse. (The reader will recognize this as the familiar utilitarian propensity for excess.) It would also be a mistake to conclude that the use of the organs of the condemned is either a cause or symptom of the nondemocratic government of China. Dissection and use of the body of the condemned has a long history in the West.[53] It was certainly around long before China's modern government.

There may also be some concern about an individual living with a serial murderer's heart or other body part. Patients receiving such organs would need to be counseled carefully. Whether it should even be known from whom the organs came is a question that would need to be addressed. There is also the risk of HIV and other infections in taking transplants from prisoner donors.

Others might complain of a slippery slope, since some organs, such as kidneys, could be extracted from prisoners without permanently incapacitating them. So long as prisons exist, there will be this danger. Please remember that in this chapter, the prime purpose of bodily dissection is in the service of getting rid of prisons altogether, in an attempt to address the old question of what to do with the terrible few. So long as it is justified to lock up the terrible few, the temptation will be to put more and more people in prison, to define more and more as the worst of the worst. By incapacitating them in plain sight, we at least keep visible our punishments and, more importantly, avoid the many excessive and uncontrollable features of prison as a punishment.

In sum, the retributive way of doing good through bodily incapacitation offers a clear and concrete consequence of the punishment. The pain of the punishment is clear; the good is a concrete good, not an abstract good of the kind offered by utilitarians.

Consider the fantastic service that executed murderers could provide to the saving of hundreds of innocent lives. While their suffering may not make up for the specific suffering and loss of the particular victim, the victim's family, even the offender's family, can at least take comfort in the fact that two terrible deeds—the murder and the execution—have been turned to a truly positive act: the saving of lives and improvement of quality of life of many others. This is real community service, while at the same time preserving the punitive element of the punishment. Here are the actual words of a death row inmate, Christian Longo, who strangled his wife and daughter, and tied his two toddlers inside pillow slips and drowned them in a pond:

Eight years ago I was sentenced to death for the murders of my wife and three children. I am guilty. I once thought that I could fool others into believing this was not true. Failing that, I tried to convince myself that it didn't matter. But gradually, the enormity of what I did seeped in; that was followed by remorse and then a wish to make amends.[54]

Could he make amends? Obviously not, given the enormity of his crimes. But he continued:

There is no way to atone for my crimes, but I believe that a profound benefit to society can come from my circumstances. I have asked to end my remaining appeals, and then donate my organs after my execution to those who need them.[55]

And why couldn't a vicious serial rapist (remember, the worst of the worst) give up a kidney or two for persons who will most likely die, especially if they happen to be poor? A lifetime on dialysis for a serial rapist would seem a just outcome, and, at the same time, it would incapacitate without prison. We can see that the chance to do good is tremendous. Actual lives could be restored and improved. There would be no question about the good that came of such acts. At last, punishment would have a positive aspect, yet retain its credibility as a punishment. And the offender would have made true restitution, undeniable redemption. If we must punish (and it seems we must), what better good could come of punishment than this?

But enough of the terrible few. It is time to return to the punishments that most offenders should receive, moderate corporal punishments. You may be wondering, surely there must be other kinds of punishments that we could use that are not violent and that do not attack the body. *Must* we go to corporal punishment? It's a fair question. Its answer lies in how one can compare punishments—all kinds of punishments—and sensibly, rationally, and morally choose those that will best match the crime and our moral sensibilities. The following chapter does just that.

Chapter Seven

A New Way to Punish

Moderate Corporal Punishment Is the Least Imperfect of all Criminal Punishments

When we look at the range of punishments that might be possible once we free ourselves from the dominant paradigm of prison, the variety of punishments is considerable. And when we include moderate corporal punishments and incapacitation in the mix, a way of comparing them and applying them is needed, especially for comparing them to current practice. However, the choice of what punishment for what crime is a difficult one. In the first section of this chapter, we examine how to compare punishments according to their outcomes—intended or unintended. The major punishments used today in our "modern" criminal justice system, have very severe outcomes that are unintended, and these are often justified, paradoxically, on that very basis.

The second section will examine how to apply them. The solution to comparing and administering punishments—they are deeply linked—is to punish by numbers, that is, to assess the severity of a punishment by its quantity, such as years or months in prison, or months on probation. This abstract way of viewing punishments splits the actual effects or outcomes of the punishment from the sentence that is always pronounced in numbers. This abstraction of punishment, while it has had serious deleterious effects when applied to prison sentences, has an important role to play in criminal punishment, because it helps to separate or "dehumanize" the punishment process. That is, the criminal is punished by "the law" not by a human who may or may not hold malice. This is an important civilizing aspect of criminal punishment that, when applied to moderate corporal punishment (MCP) and open incapacitation (OI), makes it an entirely new and humane way of punishing, while at the same time making it easy to apply in practice. We will shortly see that by far the greatest benefit of MCP and OI is that, if applied carefully, while they dehumanize the punishment process, they respect the humanity of the criminal.

Comparing and Choosing Punishments

Although the famed learning psychologist B. F. Skinner claimed that his experiments showed that punishment "did not work," decades of research in the psychology laboratory have since demonstrated that claim to be wrong.[1] In any case, when we say that a punishment "does not work," what do we mean exactly?

We may begin by noting that there are no perfect punishments. All punishments, even the most effective, bring with them negative side effects.[2] Given that no society is likely to give up punishment, even in the distant future, we ought to compare punishments according to the negative side effects they produce relative to their effectiveness. By "effectiveness," in this chapter, we mean something quite different from Skinner and his followers who were concerned with whether a particular punishment will suppress (temporarily or permanently) an unwanted behavior. That is an important utilitarian justification of punishment, as we have seen. Our interest is broader in this chapter, taking into account retribution and other moral, societal, and political factors relating to the administration of punishment in criminal justice.

As we saw in chapters 4 and 5, in the 1970s, sentencing reformers began to examine the array of possible punishments that could be used in sentencing offenders. However, their focus was not on the outcomes of such punishments, but primarily on trying to devise a formula for the equivalence of different kinds of punishments. For example, they asked, how much probation is thirty days in jail worth?[3] Their failure to examine other aspects of the punishments was conditioned by the fast growing fixation on the quantification of punishment rather than examining its qualitative attributes.

There are a number of criteria on which we can base a comparison of punishments. Table 7.1 shows a schema for a selection of eight punishments arrayed according to eight criteria for evaluating outcomes. How would you fill in the boxes? I have filled in my own assessment, but this, of course, is

Table 7.1. Schema for Comparison of Punishments

Criteria	Bodily incapacitation	Prison	Electronic flogging	Shock incarceration	Fines or restitution	Digital punishment	Community service	Probation
1. Control	High	Low	High	Medium	Low	Low	Low	Low
2. Credibility	Medium to high	False	High	High	Low	High	Low	Low
3. Visibility	Medium to high	Low	High	Low	Low	High	High	Low
4. Calibration	Medium	Low	High	Medium	Medium	Low	Low	Low
5. Side effects	Medium	High	Low	Medium	High	High	High	Low
6. Overflow	Medium	High	Low	Medium	High	High	High	Low
7. Cost	High	High	Low	High	High	Low	High	High
8. Quality					Determined in relation to the crime			

Source: Adapted and extended from Newman, *Just and Painful*, 2nd ed. (1995). Table 1, p. 91.

affected by my own perceptions and understanding of existing research. In the explanation that follows, I will concentrate only on the more obvious aspects of punishments that illustrate the comparison criteria. The criteria are listed in no particular order of importance, although, if I were asked which was the most important, I would say "credibility."

The types of punishment are self-explanatory, with one exception, "digital punishment." This is essentially a punishment of "humiliation," a twenty-first-century, possibly extreme, form of the old punishments of the pillory and stocks, but implemented through the Internet and social media. To date, there is no actual legislative use of this punishment, although these days it is possible that most types of punishment carry with them a dose of humiliation. Social media and traditional media celebrate the exposé of individuals' wrongdoing, or, more accurately, accusation of wrongdoing. The extreme form of this punishment is digital lynching (an expression first coined by Clarence Thomas at his senate hearing for nomination to the US Supreme Court), which by definition takes the law into its own hands and is essentially "unlawful." An example of this type of uncontrolled, unsanctioned punishment was the case of Nobel Laureate Tim Hunt whose chauvinistic comments at a convention in South Korea in June, 2015, were tweeted by a woman in the audience and within days he was forced to resign his prestigious academic position.[4]

It is hard to separate out humiliation from any punishment that is made public. Certainly, one could aggravate any punishment by manipulating the amount of public abuse or derision. To some extent mandatory sex offender registries may achieve this, but these serve the purpose not so much of humiliating but of tracking individuals so that they may be informally ostracized.

Let us examine each of the evaluative criteria and consider generally how they might occur in each different type of punishment.

1. Control. How specific can we make the effects of a particular punishment? Can we apply the pain narrowly for that particular part of the offender's behavior we wish to control? Behaviorist psychologists specialize in this technique, using conditioning schedules. It was the supposed method of the doctors in the movie A Clockwork Orange. In contrast prison is a punishment that is generalized and nonspecific. It is virtually impossible to control experimentally, because it places the offender in a setting that is in itself extremely ill-defined.[5]

While prisons appear from the outside to be highly controlled (the walls, bars, etc.), these only serve to keep the inmates inside the prison and the rest of us out. They do little to ensure that the punishment is directed specifically at the particular aspects of the offender's behavior that have broken the law. Drug offenders, violent offenders, rapists, burglars, all are heaped in together. Prison does not primarily differentiate among such prisoners, in spite of sometimes elaborate classification procedures. All prisoners suffer punishments of diet, liberty restriction, boredom of prison life, and so on. Many prisoners suffer differentially because they are weak or young and can be preyed upon by the strong. The pain of prison is applied differentially to inmates not according to the crimes they may have committed but according to their physical and mental attributes as they appear in the prison setting.

Bodily incapacitation, the substitute for prison in the case of the terrible few, is highly specific in its application, whether through a form of the death penalty or the incapacitation of particular parts of the body by either medical of mechanical means.

Fines may stop the unwanted behavior, but they may also result in the offender not having enough money to put food in his mouth. In fact, all punishments shown in Table 7.1, with the exception of electronic flogging, may have long-term negative effects on the offender's ability to lead a normal life, effects that go far beyond the present offense for which he is punished. If these effects were "positive," in the sense that they made the offender a "better person," this would be a reason in favor of the punishment, so long as, from a retribution point of view, the integrity of the individual was maintained. Redemptive incapacitation fits this requirement quite well. It does, of course, intentionally, have long-term effects on the horrible criminal's life (remember, the worst of the worst).

Critics will argue that moderate corporal punishment (MCP) surely has long-term effects on an individual's life and cite the extensive research of the "cycle of violence" as evidence. There are a number of answers to this criticism.

First, critics make the error of equating moderate corporal punishment with violence (and, by implication and error, torture). While corporal punishment does necessarily use some "force," because the offender has to be restrained in order to carry out the punishment and we must ensure that the offender is not wantonly or accidentally injured, it can be administered with very little violence. MCP simply requires turning on the switch of an electric current, which is hardly a violent behavior. Some physical restraint is necessary in all punishments that aim to control the body of the accused, and this obviously includes prison. Fines, probation, and certain forms of community service would seem to avoid this problem, but because they do so, they lack credibility, as we shall see.

Second, there is no conclusive evidence that the so-called cycle of violence operates on a broad scale. In the individual cases where it has been shown to operate, it has been extreme child abuse that has cycled violence over generations, not corporal punishment as used in the normal discipline of a child.[6]

Third, the research on the long-term effects of moderate corporal punishment has been conducted entirely on the effects of receiving corporal punishment as a child or teenager—as reported by adults, as far as they can remember. The specific (or even general) long-term effects of receiving such punishment have never been demonstrated, in spite of the claims of Straus and his colleagues, the dominant researchers in this field.[7] Since all of these adults were leading fruitful lives (many of those surveyed by Straus turn out to be college students), one can simply conclude that they were not seriously affected by corporal punishment as children; if anything, the fact that they were at college suggests that they had done quite well.

Fourth, specific research on the effects of electric shock used as a punishment has found negligible side effects, and significant positive effects.[8]

Fifth, shock incarceration, while it is a form of prison, is more controllable than "regular" prison because it is focused on one principle: the total subjection by physical abuse and mental humiliation of each inmate. It is also usually limited to a specific short term (from six weeks to six months). However, because this control is administered in a prison setting, and is therefore not open to public scrutiny, there is the danger of the principle of total subjection (not unlike the principle underlying torture) leading to excess.[9]

Sixth, as for digital punishment, it is pretty much by definition out of control. In some cases individuals have been driven to suicide (a form of self-punishment) by revelations of their (usually sexual) behavior on social media. Self-administered punishment is a particularly interesting form of punishment that we will examine more closely later in chapter 10. Of course, the use of digital punishment by terrorists who execute their victims on social media is an example of the use of digital media to enhance the terror of the punishment, a direct illustration of the utilitarian use of punishment. Its specific effects, however, are largely beyond the control of the terrorists—they may excite their supporters, but firm up the resolve of their opponents.[10]

2. Credibility. In order for punishments to fulfill their role as effective punishments, they must be credible as punishments. That is, the public must be able to see that they are punishments, pure and simple, not some kind of treatment. This is why probation has become so unpopular and has given punishment in modern criminal justice such a bad name. Probation is an ambiguous punishment. It mixes handholding and treatment with the administration of the punishment (if it can be determined that the offender suffers as a result of probation). In contrast, the unambiguous application of pain by the acute but moderate corporal punishment of electronic flogging makes it a highly credible punishment even though one might argue that it is actually "less severe" than, say, even ten days in jail. In fact some might even consider it less severe a punishment than a $1 thousand fine. It is the credibility of a punishment that makes it effective as a punishment, seen from a societal point of view. This is no doubt why shock incarceration, a version of boot camp, in which humiliation is traditionally used as a means of discipline along with severely regimented prison life, including extreme physically demanding daily routines, is popular in some quarters of the United States. This punishment has never been shown to deter crime or reform the young offenders for whom it is reserved.[11] But it is popular among many legislatures today. This is because its publicized severity makes it a credible and unambiguous punishment.

Similarly, the humiliation attached to digital punishment is unambiguous, though there is, perhaps, the possibility of some offenders turning the humiliation into notoriety, becoming "digital outlaws." Bodily incapacitation is demonstrably painful if it includes the removal of body parts; but if incapacitation is achieved through the use of drugs, or addiction to a specific drug, then the "painfulness" of this punishment may be in doubt, since some drugs that are addictive are not painful, though the withdrawal from them is.

Prison has a great deal of credibility as a punishment, given the extremes of mass incarceration. One may say here that this credibility is undeserved, since it has so many defects as a punishment, as already outlined in this book. One might term this as "fake" credibility. The pains that prisons cause are widespread and uncontrollable, yet much of the public believes that they are not painful enough, resulting in the illogical response of extending prison terms, thus adding to mass incarceration.

3. Visibility. Before prison, almost all criminal punishments were public, so public that they were a spectacle. The challenge with today's punishments is to keep them before the public eye but avoid making them a spectacle. There are many theories as to why punishments were so public in earlier times, the most popular being that they put the fear of God into the onlookers (general deterrence)—a theory made fun of by the great illustrator Hogarth in the seventeenth century in his illustration of a public execution, with one of the crowd picking someone's pocket, a crime punishable by death at the time. But the most pervasive popular and academic theory remains Freud's idea of catharsis (taken from the Greeks), that humans (especially men) have a violent nature which must be constantly satisfied, and so watching violent gladiators in the Roman colosseum or a violent sport like American or Australian football serves that purpose. Today, we do not need to watch actual violent punishments carried out in public to obtain release or satisfaction of our need for violence. Nor do punishments need to be violent. Modern movies and video games, now in high definition or 3D, along with deep sound, provide experiences of virtual reality that far surpass any actual experience of violence.[12] The actual concrete visibility of violent punishments is no longer necessary for catharsis. However, their visibility is necessary for two different reasons: (1) to hold those who administer it accountable to the public and (2) to make the punishment credible.

To be a credible punishment, a punishment must be seen to be done. Prison is an isolated, secret punishment kept mostly out of the public's eye. The only times in which it becomes a public punishment are through the national media when prison riots erupt, or when the national media occasionally decide to do an exposé of prisons.

The media often present a picture of prison as nonpunitive, emphasizing its provision of TV sets, libraries, and other amenities that many might consider convicts do not deserve. The result is a conflicted public view of prison as a punishment: the most serious of punishments (apart from the death penalty) available for offenders, but at the same time a punishment that is not serious enough.

The visibility of other kinds of punishments is also important. Probation (whether regular or intensive) is a punishment of low visibility, simply because its aim is to blend the offender into the community. Reporting to the probation officer is not a particularly onerous or exceptional task, a bit like going to the bank (certainly not as painful as going to the dentist). It is not surprising that probation is viewed popularly as a nonpunishment. Intensive probation requires more thorough control and supervision of the offender in the community, but it occurs blended in with the community, and so is essentially invisible to the public. Probation continues to suffer from a credibility problem because it is administered largely by social workers, so the public does not believe that it is punitive enough. Other "painless" alternatives such as weekend incarceration, enforced attendance at classes, and community service have been tried around the Western world. Some work (that is, generally reduce recidivism) within a very limited setting and for mild crimes.[13] But they are, by and large, not sufficiently punitive to take the place of prisons,[14] making it likely that they become add-on "punishments" rather than alternatives to prison.

Community service can be a highly visible punishment, depending on how it is administered. Road gangs, a form of community service often ignored by liberal reformers, could certainly advertise the fact that the road workers were convicts by dressing them in distinctive prison uniforms. This would make it a credible punishment, although there are other problems with inmate-enforced labor, as we have seen and will see further below. Other kinds of community service would have to be evaluated according to their special characteristics. It should be possible, though, to emphasize the visibility of most types of community service. Of course, along with visibility comes the possibility of humiliation. The extent to which this type of punishment should be combined with all kinds of punishment needs to be carefully assessed. Digital punishment, as already noted, is totally visible and therefore 100 percent humiliating.

MCP also needs to be public if it is to be credible. And it must appear as sufficiently painful to the public. There may be risks involved in this, as we know from the hysteria that occurred historically at public executions. There are ways to avoid this, as we will see in chapter 10, where robotic surveillance is the means of ensuring public visibility. It goes without saying that mutilations, if used for incapacitation, a form of chronic corporal punishment, are very visible, in all cases, visible for life. However, if bodily incapacitation occurs robotically within the privacy of the terrible criminal's home, there may be a question of visibility. Here again, robotic surveillance may be the answer.

4. Calibration. The extent to which a punishment may be calibrated—that is, applied to the offender according to a specific amount (intensity and duration, described in the following chapter)—is important if a punishment is to be used to match a particular crime. Finely adjusting punishment amounts to match more closely the appropriate level of crime seriousness is not as simple as it seems.

Prisons have been championed on these very grounds: that, because they are measured in terms of years and months, they can be finely calibrated to meet the particular crime. Unfortunately, this is only superficially true. Months and years, or even days, of prison are certainly legislated by politicians and delivered by judges in an appearance of matching the seriousness of the punishment to the seriousness of the crime. But in fact the calibration stops with the pronouncement of the sentence. The offender is then passed on through many hands into the correctional system, subjected to an enormous variety of pains of imprisonment, none of which have been specifically prescribed by the judge or legislator. For example, how many times should a young drug offender be raped in prison? A judge would be offended by this question, yet in prescribing a certain amount of time in prison, she is by default prescribing the possibility of such pain. The calibration of punishment and its specificity are closely related. This problem relates to any punishment that is calibrated in terms of time. In contrast, the application of MCP by electronic flogging can be carefully and specifically calibrated to ensure that both the intensity and duration of the pain are controlled.

Because of the high level of control exercised on inmates in a shock incarceration program, it is possible that conditions inside the camp could be calibrated (that is, the intensity of the punishment varied) in such a way as to visit quite specific forms of punishment on various individuals and groups. However, the "ethic" on which boot camp philosophy seems to operate is that all are treated "equally" (that is, equally horribly), with a few set apart for humiliating examples. Whether these few are those who deserve it (in terms of their crimes, not in terms of their behavior in camp) is a question unanswered. Because the duration of shock incarceration is ostensibly limited to six months or less, calibration of time could also be adopted, and perhaps be made more meaningful, since we are not talking about enormous expanses of time, as with regular prison.

Fines also have the appearance of easy calibration, since we value commodities and services in terms of money every day. However, as we saw in chapter 4, we do not know what the deprivation of money means to individuals. Unlike physical pain, the value of money is perceived in a much more diverse way. There ae many shortcomings of this type of punishment, especially its subjectivity (or, more precisely, its false objectivity).

Digital punishment via social media appears to work as a kind of infectious disease. It runs its course then peters out. However, the problem with the digital world is that tweets and other digital communications never go away completely. There is always the possibility that they will come back. Politicians running for office know this: one's digital history can be easily dredged up and used against one. In this sense, digital punishment, if used as an official sanction, is a chronic punishment more like a cancer than an infectious disease that runs its course.

5. *Side Effects on the Offender.* All punishments have unwanted side effects. The question is, which punishments have the least? The side effects of prison are countless. Plenty of research has shown that it has effects on the offender long after release. While its advocates argue that the punishment of prison is "only" deprivation of liberty, many other deprivations come along with the loss of liberty. There is deprivation of diet, normal sexual activity, family life, a work environment—one could go on and on. To claim that prison only represents deprivation of liberty and nothing else begs the question of what conditions prison advocates would envision. In an attempt to remove all the other pains of imprisonment and make it purely and simply deprivation of liberty, prison apologists have pushed for making prisons as comfortable as is possible, given the circumstances, a "home away from home." One can see that this simply eats away at the credibility of prison as a punishment.

Acute temporary corporal punishment of electronic flogging (MCP) has few if any side effects on the offender. The pain can be applied in very short duration, can be calibrated just enough to have a painful effect without carrying with it additional injury, and can be administered in conditions that are not humiliating, degrading, or violent.

Digital punishment certainly inflicts humiliation, but its intensity and extent are very hard to control. If it were for a sex offense, for example, and the details of the offense were graphically portrayed on a YouTube video, it could lead to all kinds of repercussions for the offender (not to mention the victim). A number of well-publicized sting operations to entrap sex offenders, for example, led to the suicides of the accused.[15]

Community service could be managed to provide an uplifting, as against a humiliating, experience (one presumes that a uniformed chain gang member is humiliated by the visibility of the punishment) if the community service were some form of "doing good." But what "doing good" for a criminal would entail is a question of considerable difficulty. The traditional notion of community service usually means something like assisting in a nursing home. Why such persons (or any objects of charity) should benefit from having criminals take care of them is puzzling. It also demeans the role of true volunteers, which brings us to the next point.

6. Punishment Overflow. The most perplexing and frustrating aspect of punishments is that they all have overflow effects. That is, the effects of the punishment of a single offender overflow into other areas and on to other people in ways that are commonly dismissed as unavoidable. In many cases, the imprisonment of an individual family member causes very severe hardship for the rest of the family members.[16] Not only is the suffering financial, but the children lose a parent and suffer the ignominy of a parent who is in prison. It is often claimed that it is not our responsibility that the punishment has overflowed, that the offender should have thought of his family before he committed his crime. Of course, this is true as far as the offender is concerned. But it is not true as far as a responsible society is concerned. Are we not accountable for the effects on innocent people of punishments that our judges and legislators have prescribed? The family members of a prisoner are surely innocent (in most cases).

One can only guess at the punishment overflow of shock incarceration. Since this punishment is leveled at older juveniles, one can perhaps minimize the overflow effects on family, although, these days, it is certainly possible that many of them are parents.

Punishment overflow also occurs when fines are levied against the offender. This is easily measurable. For example, welfare has to cover for the lost family income of an imprisoned family member. The overflow can reach far and wide.

Punishment overflow is especially severe in the case of digital punishment, since tweets, Facebook, and other Internet outlets for scandal and notoriety make character assassination a tempting proposition for many and ensure that the family and friends of an offender whose crimes are digitally broadcast will also be punished and humiliated. How would a child feel if the crime and punishment of his or her father were broadcast far and wide so that she would be teased and bullied at school, especially if the parent were a sex offender?[17]

The use of moderate corporal punishment (MCP) minimizes (though it does not eradicate) the punishment overflow effect. It is done quickly, by appointment as it were, does not leave lasting effects, can be done without financial cost to the offender, and does not remove the offender from the important role of family member. Possible overflow effects could be the stigma a child suffers from the parent receiving corporal punishment in public (though, as we will see later, it can be minimized, if not avoided), but this is far less by comparison with the overflow effects of the punishment of prison. It may also be counteracted to some extent by the clear and simple message sent to the child with the swift and unambiguous punishment of the father: that when you break the law you get punished, and it hurts.

7. Cost. The cost of a punishment should be the last consideration in choice of punishments. Clearly, a society that is morally accountable for the punitive actions it takes against its members should consider moral considerations ahead of cost. After such considerations have been met, the comparative cost of punishments should be taken into account.

The costs of both the death penalty and prison are exorbitant, as is well known.[18] Which costs more in the long run is a subject for debate, but the costs are so high for both punishments that there seems hardly any point in engaging in the debate.[19] It is often argued that community supervision of some kind, including community service, is cheaper, but this remains to be seen. Certainly community punishments would not have to be all that cheap to be cheaper than prison. It was argued, when probation was put forward as an alternative to prison, that it would be cheaper than prison. However, there has long been a preoccupation with the cost of probation supervision, and the extremely high caseloads of probation officers is well documented. These community-based corrections have become massive bureaucracies answering mainly to themselves, yet suffering constantly from lack of adequate resources, which renders them, even allowing for their confused purpose, relatively useless.[20] Thus, in terms of cost effectiveness, probation probably brings the worst return on investment. At least with prison criminals are locked up and kept away from us, so we do get something for our money. However, as we saw in the previous chapter, criminals can be incapacitated in the community without being locked up.

Perhaps fines offer the most promise for return on investment? Inflict big fines and demand restitution? This could be a punishment system that would pay for itself! Unfortunately, in the United States at least, it doesn't work:

> Federal statistics indicate that the U.S. government collects from criminals about a penny for every dollar they owe in restitution and fines, money that should go to the public treasury and victims.[21]

Not only does this particular punishment not meet any decent standard in terms of cost, it does not meet the standard of punishment itself, since it seems that the majority of offenders don't actually pay their fines. This means that they are not, in effect, punished. They are only sentenced. And, in one case, a judge even required offenders to give a pint of blood in lieu of a fine—a form of redemptive corporal punishment.[22]

Digital punishment, if used officially, probably would be the least costly, since a connection to the Internet provides access to a limitless number of people to whom the crime and the punishment can be broadcast. However, because its overflow effects are considerable, it does not compare to moderate corporal punishment that is acute and temporary, and not broadcast digitally.

If a primitive form of corporal punishment were used, such as paddling or the lash, not a lot of capital equipment would be necessary. However, in order to maintain equity and consistency, individuals who were commissioned to carry out the whipping would have to be trained so that they used the right amount of force equally and to the correct part of the body. Training individuals would be very costly. A better solution, if a corporal punishment requiring impact of an object on the body were preferred, would be the use of a machine, these days certainly feasible, a robot that could be calibrated to administer whipping or paddling with consistency and accuracy. This would obviously cost a lot to set up, but in the long term would be cost-efficient, because there would be no human employees, who are of course always the most costly. A more efficient and consistent corporal punishment would be electronic flogging, as will be described shortly. There would be a minimal set-up cost, and a small amount of training for administrators, but it mostly could be administered without much, if any, human intervention, so, in the long run, would be cost-effective. As a matter of fact, it might even be self-administered, as I will examine in the final chapter.

8. Quality. I have reserved the most difficult and fascinating criterion till last. By "quality" we mean the inherent "matchability" contained within a punishment. There are some punishments that seem perfectly to "fit the crime" regardless of whether their apparent severity matches the seriousness of the particular crime.[23] For example, cutting off the hand of the thief seems to "fit the crime" even though most of us would probably consider its severity out of proportion to the particular crime, regardless of the amount stolen. This difficult-to-describe quality of punishments is perhaps the pivotal factor in choosing punishments. It is the art of punishing that has been lost, or at least buried in our modern obsession with quantification of punishment. One roundabout attempt to get at the qualitative aspects of punishment has been restorative justice, though this has its own problems.

The informed criminal justice reader may wonder why I have not included restorative criminal justice in my list of possible punishments. This is because it is not put forward by its advocates as a punishment but as a replacement of punishment, in fact, not just of punishment, but of the entire criminal justice process. I once witnessed its application to an event in which a male supervisor had harassed his female inferior in the workplace for a period of seven years, making her life a misery. The negotiator (or counsellor, or mediator, there are many different names given to the individuals whose job it is to bring the two sides together) after lengthy give-and-take between the two parties, had them shake hands at the end. And that was it. A handshake supposedly made up for seven years of harassment. This case, while not about criminal offending (at least not yet), displays the extremely difficult problem of how to match the "punishment"—here the counter response, an expression of "love" and "reconciliation"—to the severity of the "crime." It is very difficult in cases where the crimes have been enormous, such as the human rights violations that occurred in South Africa in the days that led up to the eradication of apartheid—where the now popular idea of reconciliation and restorative justice originated. The best one can say about this way of avoiding punishment completely is that it is a brave (romantic) attempt to get victims to forget (that is, forgive) what was done to them.[24] This is a paradox, of course, since the process involves dredging up in face-to-face encounters all the terrible things that the offender has done to the victim, which would seem to run counter to the victim forgetting what was done to her.[25]

Finally, in some respects, the Shari'a law approach to offending also encourages the participation of both offender and victim in the criminal justice process, giving the victim some say in the outcome, should the judge decide that the offender is guilty. The difference, though, is that the purpose of a Shari'a trial presumes punishment as its outcome; the victim gets a chance to mitigate or aggravate the punishment once guilt is established (see chapter 9). That is, the purpose of a Shari'a trial is to bring about a just punishment. The purpose of restorative justice is to replace punishment with love and reconciliation.

So far, we have seen that MCP has distinct advantages over other kinds of punishments, especially, of course, that blunt instrument of punishment, prison. MCP, acute temporary corporal punishment, falls somewhere in between the need to quantify the punishment so that it matches the seriousness of the crime and the need to match qualitatively the pain or moral imbalance caused by the crime (retribution).

The criteria presented here for assessing the effectiveness of criminal punishments go well beyond the criteria used in penology and criminal justice research that seeks to investigate whether particular punishments "work" or not. Such research confines its assessment of what works simply to measuring recidivism (that is, whether offenders recommit after they have been punished, almost always the punishment being prison of one form or other). Rarely, if at all, do any scientific studies attempt to compare the effectiveness of one type of punishment with another. And, finally, no studies have ever assessed the visibility, credibility, calibration, side effects, overflow, or ability to control the application of a criminal punishment.[26] Interestingly, when comparisons have been made between prison and other interventions, these are not with other alternative punishments but with alternative treatments, such as with drug offenders.[27]

Having developed the criteria according to which we may compare the effectiveness of criminal punishments, we turn now to the most difficult challenge, choosing the punishment. That is, matching the punishment to the crime. Much of the book so far has been preparing you for this. We have seen how chaotic the matching of punishment to crimes has become, how difficult it is to identify whether retribution or deterrence are effective guiding principles for choosing and matching punishments to crimes. In the modern age, there is but one solution.

A New Way to Punish

The father of modern criminology was Cesare Beccaria, who, in 1764, wrote a famous treatise called *On Crimes and Punishments*, a coy attempt to liberalize what he and other reformers of the Enlightenment period considered to be the primitive, sadistic, and unfair criminal justice system. He especially pointed an accusing finger at the judges of his day, whose unbridled discretion, he thought, had led to the horrendous punishments of the eighteenth century, though he did not oppose corporal punishment for violent crimes.[28] Two hundred and fifty years later, reformers, citing Beccaria, boast that we no longer use violent punishments and continue to identify the unbridled discretion that pervades the criminal justice system at its evil core. The modern complaint is that there is too much "disparity" in the sentencing of offenders (that is, similar offenders receive different penalties for the same crime) and that it is the judge's discretion that is the cause of this disparity.[29]

The truth is that judges have had very little discretion in respect to serious crimes since the "reforms" of the eighteenth and nineteenth centuries, especially since prison has become the main punishment for serious crimes. The only discretion judges have is limited to a pathetic single alternative: in or out of prison. In contrast, in the days before prison, there were many different punishments available to the judge, who therefore had more discretion as to the choice of penalty. In this century, discretion has been limited largely to assessments of the offender's background and the "seriousness" of the crime, because there is so little choice as to the possible sentence. In this respect, one might argue that the widely disparaged (in the West) punishments meted out in Shari'a law, as described in chapter 9, do at least offer a variety of punishments for serious crimes, much more than just prison that is available in Western criminal law.[30]

There also exists a strong feeling among judges that "each case is unique."[31] But sentencing researchers have found that even when judges have a lot of information about the criminal available, they apparently use only two pieces of it: the seriousness of the offender's offense and the prior criminal record.[32] Clearly, when there is such a paucity of sentencing alternatives, there is only so much information that one can use in making such a decision, since there is only one choice of any import: in or out of prison. Enter, sentencing guidelines.

Sentencing guidelines, introduced in the 1970s into the federal system and later adopted in many states, made a small step towards a solution to judicial discretion. They offered a way to set limits on the punishment lengths to which a judge may go in sentencing, establishing generally mandatory minima and maxima.[33] The extent to which a judge can adjust the mandatory minima or maxima has been subject to some Supreme Court decisions in recent years, generally favoring the discretion to be shifted to juries rather than judges.[34] More importantly, they structure the sentencing process, focusing on the amount of punishment to be delivered, and systematize it. This focus has important implications for both the function and delivery of moderate corporal punishment, as we will shortly see.

There are many different kinds of sentencing guidelines,[35] but it is possible to describe a general model.[36] The way these guidelines work is that social scientists tabulate the sentencing decisions of judges, and the criteria that they either say they use or can be shown to have used in their decisions. Such variables include criminal's prior record (the severity and number of prior offenses), seriousness of the current offense, age, sex, race, income level, and many more (some not necessarily legally valid criteria).

Researchers have found that they can predict to a moderate extent the sentencing outcomes of judges by a number of such variables (that is, algorithms).[37] By and large, the most common and best predictors are the criminal's prior record and the seriousness of the offense for which she has been convicted. The scientists then draw up tables to show the average (sometimes displayed as a range) sentence given by all judges in the particular jurisdiction for each crime, and these are called "guidelines." Thus, when in doubt, the judge can refer to these guidelines to see how she is doing compared to the general practice of her colleagues. In this way, it is hoped that the judge's decisions will be regulated by the practice of her colleagues, that excessive or disproportionate punishments will be avoided[38] and eventually even become robotically managed.[39] However, recent research suggests that regardless of the existence or nonexistence of any type of sentencing guidelines, most variations in sentencing result from local, individual factors such as race and gender.[40]

Many judges have objected to the idea of sentencing guidelines because it is an oversimplification of the very complex task they face in deciding on the sentence. Both sides of this argument are right. The factors that the judge must weigh up are considerable in terms of the unique background of the offender. Unfortunately, the whole process is like a very bad joke, because the judge, after having gone through all the deliberations in deciding on the sentence, actually has only one simple choice of any consequence: in or out of prison, to which, if the answer is "in," is tacked on the number of years—which we know has only a vague link to the actual pains of prison to be experienced. It is like spending a month deliberating whether to call "heads" or "tails."[41]

The appealing quality of sentencing guidelines systems is that they solve the problem of matching the punishment to the crime by translating the practice of a group of "experts" (judges) into numbers (that is, statistical averages) that then justify the length of the sentence. The heavy assumption behind this approach is that types of punishments do not need to be changed. That is, it is assumed that the judge is (and always will be) faced by two decisions of any great importance when sentencing an offender:

1. In or out of prison?

2. If in, how much prison?

Why not consider other types of punishments, punishments that might better fit the crimes and allow for a more specific assessment of their numerical value? For example, most of the sentencing guidelines, after having gone through the complicated procedure of developing "salient factor scores" and various other scores that are used to reflect the offender's past record and seriousness of offense, then provide a "grid" (merely another way of saying that two factors are used) for computing the amount of prison. Yet prison is rarely expressed as a specific number but rather as a range (of three to five years, for example). Why is this? Is it to give the judge more discretion in deciding a sentence for a particular offender, or is it because the researchers do not know what the real (that is, amount of pain) difference is between say, three and five years of prison? At least it can be said that judges do have some guide as to the limits to which they should or can go. Yet is "three to five years" a sufficient guideline if people have little idea of the difference between three and five years' prison? For all we know, it might represent a difference similar to, say, cutting off one finger as against a hand!

We can see that we are still stuck with the same old problem of matching the punishment to the crime, even though sentencing guidelines have provided us with a very significant advance in procedure. But an advance in procedure does not really address the problem. Guidelines have worked miracles with the numbers, and indeed have made them more real than ever before. But that is why, in the long run, they actually extend the problem rather than solve it. We have to remember that they are numbers, and numbers only. Their reference to the actual pain of prison is tenuous at best. In fact one could argue that the numbers hide the true pains of prison; the numbers develop a life of their own. That is why the original federal sentencing commission and others at the state level that have followed them spend a lot of time fine tuning the gradations of crimes and matching them by numbers. There is no attempt to examine the quality of the punishment that is matched to the number, only the quantity.

The determination of the sentence rests on the numbers alone, without reference to the pain (whether chronic or acute) of punishment actually felt. By using guidelines, the judge refers to a superior source, that of collegiate practice with numbers. One can see why the pleas of reformers for less severe punishments have never been heeded.[42] It is very easy for commissions and legislatures to deal with numbers, ignoring the pains that they represent. Doubling a prison term from two to four is a simple computation. But how much actual pain does such a doubling represent? The problem is exacerbated even more when the reformers advocate less harsh conditions in prison, a reasonable attempt to focus on the quality of the pains endured in prison. Unfortunately, the perception of "soft" prisons, such as prison farms, as not really prison, makes the basic in/out of the prison decision much easier for the judge (and the public so represented), even though in most cases a judge has little say on what type of prison an offender sentenced to years of prison will actually endure. It is the "corrections department" that makes that decision, a decision made by a bureaucrat not directly accountable to the public.

Sentencing guidelines could be very useful if applied to moderate corporal punishment, especially a moderate corporal punishment such as electronic flogging. An initial step would be to provide estimates based on a formula derived from the quantification of prison terms, that is, how much prison equals how much electronic flogging. This would lead to guidelines of how much electronic flogging would match how much crime seriousness.

Administering Pain: Moderate Corporal Punishment

Even though electronic flogging is essentially a numerically based punishment, there is much diversity in the way it may be administered and manipulated. For example, as noted above, all sentencing guidelines that use prison as a punishment simply specify prison, along with the scale of the number of years, varying this according to the seriousness of offense and the offender's prior offenses. With the MCP of electronic flogging, it would be possible to vary the intensity of the shock (that is, how many volts) with the duration of the application of the shock (that is, apply the shock for so many seconds) and also vary the number of punishment "sessions." We can now construct a standard punishment unit (SPU) as follows:

$$SPU = V \times D \times I$$

Where
  V = number of volts
  D = duration of shock in seconds
  I = interval between shocks in seconds

These would be fixed by law, based on appropriate research. Sentencing may then vary the SPU as follows:

- Total number of SPUs to be administered
- Length of sessions in which the SPUs will be applied
- Number of sessions in which the SPUs will be applied
- Intervals between sessions

For example, if you receive 60 SPUs for your third burglary, the judge may sentence you as follows:

> Example 1, sentence completed in 12 months:
> Session length: 5 units
> Number of sessions: 12
> Frequency of sessions: 1 per month

> Example 2, sentence completed in 6 weeks:
> Session length: 10 units
> Number of sessions: 6
> Frequency of sessions: 1 per week

One can immediately see the broad range of choices that faces the sentencing judge, and here at last he or she will have some discretion worth using. Table 7.2 provides an example of what such a sentencing schema might look like.

After sentencing guidelines have been used with MCP, we may find that various levels of punishments would be agreed upon for various offenses. The limits of sentencing would thus be developed by collegiate practice, or fed back into a computerized system that would develop algorithms for administration of the punishment, in today's language, robotic assessment. More on this later in chapter 8.

As already noted, matching punishments to crimes is extremely difficult. Just glance at tables 9.1 and 9.2, which are rough comparisons between Western and Shari'a punishments and crimes in chapter 9. They are markedly different. Even comparing the punishments of crimes between the United States and European countries will demonstrate vast differences. Many of these differences are cultural, procedural, and even political. So we cannot hope to solve this huge problem of punishment simply by the introduction of MCP and OI, although their acceptance as a form of punishment would certainly mark a cultural change.

In an ideal world, punishment should be determined by the injury and harm done by the offender rather than the inherent wrongness of the act.[43] As the radical criminologist Jeffrey Reiman says, "Let the crime fit the harm and the punishment fit the crime."[44] The amounts of pain administered could then be more precisely adjusted to match the injury and damage of the offense, because they are quantifiable. This would require the rewriting of a lot of criminal codes, especially to remove the "mental element" that is so often part of the definition of crimes. Technically, this probably means

Table 7.2. Moderate Corporal Punishment Sentencing Schema

Crime seriousness	MCP (electronic flogging) Standard punishment units	Number of sessions	Length of sessions (minutes)	Time between sessions	Nonprison incapacitation Restraint Device	Induced coma
Infractions	1	1	1	N/A		
Mild misdemeanors	3	3	5	2 minutes		
Standard misdemeanors	4	4	6	2–3 minutes		
Serious misdemeanors	6	4–6	8	Daily or weekly		
Low-level felonies	8	6–10	8–10	Daily or weekly		
Standard felonies	10	10–12	10–12	Daily to monthly	Robotic tracking, stun belt	
Serious felonies	15	12–15	15–20	Monthly to yearly	Robotic tracking, stun belt, induced drug dependence	1–2 days
Very serious felonies	24	3	10	Monthly	Robotic tracking, stun belt, induced drug dependence	Months to years
The worst	30	3	10	Daily	Robotic tracking, stun belt, induced drug dependence	Life until death

- All misdemeanors may be mitigated by (a) punishment undergone by surrogates appointed by the court, (b) punishment exchanged for a monetary amount to be fixed by law, or (c) monetary punishment calculated according to offender's means.
- All serious felonies may be mitigated by voluntary donation of body parts of the offender.
- Those serious offenders currently serving prison time must exchange remaining prison terms for MCP, induced coma, or a combination of both, according to a formula to be established by law.

Source: Developed by the author.

converting many "felonies" into "misdemeanors" or infractions and punishing them according to strict liability, as is currently the case with many traffic offenses and other contraventions against various regulations, for example, sanitation and pollution regulations.[45]

But enough of fantasy.[46]

The acute pain of moderate corporal punishment could be managed under existing criminal codes. Most prison sentences, as currently prescribed in the criminal law, could be translated into their equivalents of MCP. All that would be needed would be to determine how much prison equaled how much corporal punishment, defined in terms of length of shock, intensity of shock, number of applications in one sitting, and even, in some exceptional cases, number of sessions over how many days or months. We can see that there is considerable variability in how to apply MCP (and even more when done robotically, as we will see soon), so that matching these to differing lengths of prison terms should not be difficult, especially as often sentences are prescribed as ranges. We can see that under such a system judges will have many more choices; at last their discretion will mean something.

But we have already seen in the first part of this chapter that determining the equivalence of different punishments can be very complicated. At first it seems rather simple: we have a scale of punishments graded according to their seriousness, and we simply match those to a scale of crimes graded according to their seriousness. The challenge is to match up the two scales. Where does one locate the center of these scales? How does one match the scale of MCP to the scale of crimes? This is an old problem that confronts all philosophers of criminal punishment. It is actually that nasty problem that will not go away: the limits problem. We have seen that sentencing guidelines offer a solution to matching the crimes to punishments by mandating that judges conform to its restrictions, though allowing for exceptions. Guidelines may be adapted to local jurisdictions, so we may assume that most judges will not make extreme departures from the guidelines. It is predictable, though, that some will. The question remains, therefore, how to avoid these excesses, even though they will be the exception. It comes down to a question of the principle of proportionality, that is to say, punishing by numbers. And as can be seen from the complicated guidelines produced in many jurisdictions (do a web search for "sentencing guidelines" to see for yourself), guidelines themselves are prone to excess, many becoming incredibly complex, requiring experts to interpret and apply them.

The problem of proportioning punishments to their crimes is largely a modern problem, or at least was first introduced by the utilitarians when they began to focus on the amount of punishment rather than the kind of punishment. Beccaria solved the problem this way:

> One punishment obtains sufficient effect when its severity just exceeds the benefit the offender receives from the crime.[47]

This sounds like a great solution, and the utilitarians have argued for a long time that it provides a rational answer to the essentially mystical question with which the advocates of retribution have had so much trouble. When asked how they figure the proportion of punishment to crimes, retributivists have had no real answer for a couple of centuries. They could once have replied that the question made no sense to them, because they did not think in terms of degrees or proportions of punishment, but rather in types of punishment: their main aim was to make the punishment express or fit the crime. In that classical system, there is only partial grading of offense seriousness; rather, the focus is on matching particularly colorful punishments to their crimes, reflecting as far as possible the crime in the punishment.[48] The same may be said in respect to Shari'a law. Strictly speaking, there are only half a dozen crimes defined as such in Shari'a law and a range of qualitative punishments that can be used to reflect them.[49]

Historically in Western criminal law, the classification of crimes into a hierarchy of seriousness was done only in a very broad sense (basically only two, it would seem, public and private, which later became felony and misdemeanor), so naturally there was a preoccupation with types of punishment. This is in addition to the fact that the amount of pain that resulted from punishment was not seen as entirely the measure of the crime's "seriousness," since the presumption that pain is a kind of evil as it is seen today was quite different. The link between such punishments as the pillory or stocks and the particular crime was absolutely clear because they were essentially public (as, in some ways, was prison in those days), and, besides, the description of the offense was often pinned to the pillory or even to the body of the criminal.

Today it has become a kind of magical act when a particular crime is transformed into a particular portion of prison, because the punishment has become an abstraction, a mere expression of numbers. The choice is so difficult that the US Supreme Court has historically ducked the issue, even in cases where the amount of punishment seemed to be clearly out of proportion by commonsense standards—such as the case of Mr. Rummel described in chapter 4. A sign that the court may be changing, though, was the case, in 2012, of *Miller v. Alabama*, where the court ruled that life without parole for a juvenile was unconstitutional. Commentators have interpreted this ruling as a finding that life without parole is "worse than death."

But don't hold your breath. In July 2017, a Virginia county court convicted Jason Brooks, thirty-eight years old, of six counts of grand larceny (of car tires and rims) and sentenced him to 132 years in prison—it was his third felony.[50]

The utilitarians are responsible for punishments like those of Rummel and Brooks, which are essentially deterrent (that is, utilitarian) and not retributive punishments. The utilitarians, following Beccaria, say that the evil of the punishment must outweigh the pleasure or gains of the offense. How does this translate into a measure of proportionality of prison? There is no way to do it except in terms of outcome. That is, one could apply more and more punishment until one had eradicated or reduced the incidence of the crime in question. Clearly, we cannot do this, or we run the risk of violating people's sense of justice, which, as Aristotle once said, is related to a sense of proportion.

Unless there was some limit imposed (which, one would have to admit, would be a kind of arbitrary or mystical limit, one that "felt right"), then there would be no barrier to increasing punishments to enormous proportions in order to achieve the desired level of compliance. At the extreme, for example, one could introduce five-year prison terms for parking violations and keep on increasing them until parking violations were eliminated. Such punishments would seem out of proportion—unjust—for such crimes of minimal seriousness. The reason we run afoul of such a problem of proportions here is the abstraction of the punishment into a numerical procedure that makes it possible to go to extremes without "feeling it."

It is now time to put to good use the quantitative approach to punishment and at the same time avoid, as far as possible, its negative effects, the abstraction of the punishment into numbers that have a life of their own. This requires the application of pain through MCP (a short sharp electric shock), robotically administered, applied at a level that invokes visible or audible painful reactions on the part of the punished. The next chapter first reviews the evidence and practice of how pain is felt, and why pain is, generally, a leveler, ensuring that all pain of punishment is felt the same for everyone. It then examines how machines and robotics may be used in administering the pain of punishment, showing why robotic punishment of MCP promises to be the most equitable, credible, least damaging, and most efficient punishment for most crimes.

Chapter Eight

Punishing without Bias

The True Pain of Punishment Is the Great Equalizer

As Ford, mastermind in the futuristic TV series *Westworld*, said to a
robot, "Never trust a human."[1] Humans are especially prone to indulge
in excesses of punishment even when, at the same time, they would rather
not actually do it themselves. How many of those who favor the death
penalty would personally do it? Could you really see yourself shooting or
hanging someone? Even administering a lethal injection? And the same with
corporal punishment. Who would personally want to flog an offender for
something they may have done to someone else? Punish "in cold blood"?

Prison separates people from punishment. It is why we have mass
incarceration. To most, prison is an abstraction, it serves the convenient
purpose of doing all kinds of bad things to offenders in isolation and
secrecy. Returning to MCP in public could alleviate this problem by making
us acknowledge once again the violent nature of punishment, making us
more accountable for what we do to criminals. The critics of this position
naturally complain that it will be only the bullies who would actually carry
out such corporal punishment and that it would only be a matter of time
before such punishments were moved behind doors, back inside prisons.
Furthermore, critics will argue forcefully that subjecting an offender to violent punishment dehumanizes him, treats him like an animal. We have also
seen that, historically, flogging itself reached an unacceptable point of excess.

Even those who have recently defended corporal punishment as a solution to mass incarceration find themselves having to deal with the problem
of whether or not corporal punishment is degrading, or more degrading than

other types of punishment.[2] Yet the point of all punishment is to degrade the offender, subject her to the power of another, and, in Western eyes, that other is the state. The good thing about corporal punishment is that it highlights this unsavory political fact of criminal punishment. But it also highlights the fact that the punishment process also degrades the punisher—even defenders of corporal punishment insist that it must be carried out in a "dignified" manner. When I was a student teacher, we were routinely taught that one should never punish a child in anger. Punishment should be carried out with precision and calm, that is, dehumanized.

So we reach the conclusion that MCP, if it is to be adopted as a policy, must be dehumanized, because it is unrealistic (and unreasonable) to expect that those who administer the punishment will do it calmly and without violence. Traditional flogging cannot be done calmly, and certainly cannot be done without violence, because it is a violent act in and of itself. It makes much more sense, therefore, to remove humans from the equation; to employ robots to administer the corporal punishment, and to choose a corporal punishment that can be administered with a minimum of violence. The solution is obvious: electronic flogging administered by the simple press of a button, and applied to an arm or a leg.[3]

However, a major objection is that, because pain is subjective, it would be felt so differently by each individual that it would be an inequitable punishment, even if administered by a disinterested third party such as a robot. Let us look at the evidence.

In general, studies show that individuals vary according to the threshold at which they report pain—that is, the point of severity in the painful stimulus at which they report that it "hurts" or request that it be stopped. The kinds of painful stimuli applied and measurement of subjects' responses to them are as follows:

1. Application of pressure to tissue or bone, such as the use of a blood pressure arm band with a hard object sewn into it

2. Application of electric shock that can be carefully calibrated

3. Application of heat to various parts of the body that can be calibrated in terms of skin temperature at the site of application

4. Asking patients who are in pain, either through chronic illness or postoperative pain, how they perceive and report upon their pain, and how often they request pain killing drugs

We should make an important distinction here between pain threshold and tolerance of pain.

Pain threshold refers to the point on the scale of severity of the pain stimulus (for example, heat) at which the person reports that he or she "feels" it as pain (burning or prickly heat). This may vary somewhat among individuals. However, this should not detract from the fact that all individuals feel pain as pain. As we increase the intensity of the painful stimulus, all persons will soon decide where along that scale to call "stop!"

An additional advantage in the administration of physical pain is that one does not need to rely exclusively on verbal reports to ascertain when it "hurts." Rather, there are physiological reactions, such as sweating and pupil dilation, not to mention jumping or flinching, that are good indicators that the stimulus is having a painful effect. In this way, we are able to eliminate at least one aspect of the complicated process of the person's perception of pain (that is, we do not have to depend on the subject telling us when it hurts). If you would like to see how people react to mild electric shocks, do a search on YouTube for electronic dog collars. There are many videos of people trying out these collars on themselves, whether for the fun of it or to see how bad it might be for their dog. Most even place the collar around their necks, but some have tried it on the thigh. Generally, the collars have five levels of shock intensity, so one can see how easy it would be to calibrate the shock for offenders in order to make sure it really hurt, but did not injure.

Tolerance of pain is not necessarily related to a person's pain threshold. While a person may call out "stop" relatively early in the application of a gradually increasing amount of pain, she may nevertheless be able to withstand certain levels of pain for quite some time. The tolerance of pain refers to the time element in pain. Again, people may vary in the extent to which they can tolerate pain over time, and it has generally been found that the variations in tolerance of pain are greater than the variations in pain threshold.[4]

Since pain in these experiments is almost always at a very low level of intensity, people will cry out or ask for it to be stopped long before it reaches a point where they can no longer take it, or where physical injury would occur. We would expect variations among individuals according to when they called "ouch!" However, if one were to administer a painful stimulus that was, say, twenty times that of the lowest pain threshold, the extent to which this pain was felt differently among individuals would be "leveled." That is, it would be felt the same (very painful) by everyone. And if we used a physiological indicator, we could be even more certain.

For example, suppose we have established from our experiments that the range at which people display a high sweat reaction is from a low of 5 volts to a high of 20 volts, with most people at about the middle, that is, 12 volts. We could safely administer 30 volts for a one second duration, and be sure that everyone felt the shock as very painful. This would have the effect of leveling the punishment, because we could be absolutely sure that the punishment really hurt every person to whom it was applied, and hurt them equally. This method of applying pain is of brief duration, but it is clearly painful.

Scientific studies have found that the variations in perceptions of pain are much greater for chronic pain (that is, drawn out pain) than for acute pain.[5] We are on much safer ground using temporary application of a painful stimulus that we know will really hurt every person who receives it than applying some other form of pain that, by its nature, requires application over long periods of time. The longer the time period, the more pain tolerance will override pain threshold. And the longer the time period, the harder it is to control the amount of pain administered and the way it is perceived.

With the application of acute pain, intensity depends much more on the amount of electric shock, the amount of heat, amount of pressure, or whatever pain stimulus is used. Only as a secondary technique need time be used to vary the amount of pain. Thus, we may apply 30 volts of shock for as brief a time as a fraction of a second. And, for some offenses, this may be sufficient. Some experimentation may also be necessary as to the appropriate parts of the body to attach the electrodes and the amount of voltage and current to apply without causing tissue damage or invoking other serious reactions, such as a heart attack.[6]

It would be necessary to avoid another phenomenon that occurs naturally in the body when pain is experienced over a long period of time, the body's defensive apparatus that manufactures substances interfering with the brain's processing of painful stimuli. It may be that people will adapt to the level of painful stimulus over time, and thus may not "feel" it as much as in the immediate and momentary onset of pain. Indeed, some torture victims have referred to this very phenomenon and even report in retrospect that the torture was not all that bad. This is why the best torturers make cunning use of time, and will vary torture sessions over some weeks or months.[7]

Does reaction to pain differ according to social and ethnic background? A number of studies by various anthropologists and psychologists claim to have found differential responses to pain and suffering according to religious and ethnic background. One well known study conducted in

the 1950s found that "old Americans" (that is, white Anglo-Saxon Prot-
estants) were more likely to tolerate pain for a longer period and of more
intensity without complaining than were Irish or Italian Catholics and
Jews.[8] There were a number of control problems with this study, so the
results are probably not definitive. Others have found that Eskimos will
tolerate more pain than whites, and that whites will tolerate more pain
than blacks. However, all these studies have been severely criticized on the
basis of their very small samples and their reliance on cultural stereotypes
to select their groups.[9] Although a few studies have found some support
for the claim of differences in response to pain according to religious background, other reviews of this research have generally concluded that, while
different cultural or social groups may be said to respond to and interpret
pain differently, there is every chance that they actually feel pain in about
the same way. The research simply suggests the obvious: that particular
ethnic or religious groups complain differently about pain. They do not
show that these groups feel the intensity of pain differentially. In fact, the
one evaluation of all research conducted into the cultural differences in
response to pain concluded as follows:

> There is no evidence suggesting that the neurophysiological
> detection of pain (i.e., pain threshold) varies across cultural
> boundaries.[10]

It is important, however, when assessing the cultural variations in
response to pain, to take into account exactly in what context the pain is
felt. For example, in some cultures, certain bodily mutilations and other
procedures (rituals, sport) result in injury and its accompanying pain. Such
practices range from boxing to circumcision in different societies. Tolerance
of pain therefore varies considerably. The sensation of pain, though, is universal. We may therefore conclude that pain sensation is not differentially
distributed in society according to social class or race. Certainly, if there
were any differences, these would be comparatively much less than are those
of fines or prison. Pain, like death, is a great leveler.

In sum, people's physiological reaction to painful stimuli is pretty
much the same. The way they deal with the pain varies according to the
way they have been brought up. In other words, all people feel pain as pain.
The ways they react to this pain may vary. But this conclusion only applies
to acute pain. It is a very different matter when we examine tolerance of
chronic pain, of which prison is the prime example.

There are drastic variations in tolerance of prison according to social and ethnic background. Not only do people (including inmates) perceive time differently (and it is time that is the quantitative element of the pain of prison), but inmates also experience prison life in widely differing ways. Some, indeed, see no difference between life on the inside and life on the outside:

> It's not a matter of a guy saying, "I want to go to jail or I am afraid of jail." Jail is on the street just like it is on the inside. The same as, like, when you are in jail, they tell you, "Look, if you do something wrong you are going to be put in the hole." You are in jail, in the hole or out of the hole. You are in jail in the street or behind bars. It is the same thing.[11]

Differences in tolerance of prison are also demonstrated by the fact that white males have the highest suicide rate (96 per 100,000 inmates) in prison,[12] followed by Latinos (30) and African Americans (16). It should be added that it will probably never be known the extent to which inmates of differing backgrounds experience the pain of prison differently, because it is impossible to measure the pain threshold of prison. This is because prison is such an abstruse and complex pain provider: it applies many different kinds of pain, such as restriction of liberty, time, diet, and space; denial of sexual gratification; enforced obedience; allows corporal mutilation (by self and others); and so on—all of which are mixed in together.

The Fairness of Moderate Corporal Punishment

As opposed to prison, one can immediately see the inherently attractive features of MCP using electric shock. It ensures that all persons receive the same amount of punishment. All people, rich or poor, black or white, will suffer the same amount of pain. This surely fulfills the requirements of equity and fairness. People will truly receive the same amount of punishment for the same crimes. No longer will it be possible to claim that the punishment favors the rich or poor, since we know that we have, by the scientific selection of an intensely painful stimulus, ensured that each individual will experience the same amount of pain. And to those purists who would insist that, no matter at what level of intensity of shock, each one will feel it differently, one may reply that, even if this is so (and it is not), it is demonstrably clear that, in comparison with the punishment of prison (or even whipping, for that matter), the application of physically acute, temporary pain of electric shock to the body is far more equitable, and far less susceptible to variations in effects. It achieves its object, then stops.[13]

Would minorities suffer more than they do now? In 2013, there were 1,574,700 inmates in state and federal prisons. As of December 31, 2013, according to the US Bureau of Justice Statistics, "3% of black male U.S. residents of all ages were imprisoned . . . compared to 0.5% of white males." The chances are that every African American in the US has at least one relative in prison, and probably more.[14] Furthermore, prisons create the opportunity and increase the probability of racial bias inside them, especially in regard to prison discipline, a fact that is well documented.[15]

The trouble is that these figures do not have much impact, because the ordinary person is not likely to be confronted by the silent process that keeps people of all colors in prison, though given that all African Americans are likely to have at least one family member in prison, they may feel the effects of prison more keenly than others. They are by far the biggest ethnic group to suffer from mass incarceration. Criminals can be funneled into this archipelago and forgotten about by the majority of people who are happy that someone will keep them locked up, and preferably silent. Only from time to time do prison riots break this silence, but after a brief spilling of blood, the silence returns, and we hear nothing more.[16]

Clearly, if MCP can become a viable alternative to prison, then African Americans stand to gain more than any other ethnic group. Critics constantly point to the destruction of the African American family that has occurred over the past thirty years or more, especially the absence of father from the home. It is surely obvious that prison contributes to this destruction by taking young males, many of them fathers, away from their families.[17] Prison is more humane than MCP?

It is impossible to publicize the tremendous suffering caused by imprisonment because it is by design administered in secret. If African Americans were punished in public with corporal punishment to the differential extent that they are currently punished with prison, there would be a public outcry. It would be too much. It would force us to be accountable for our excesses in punishment. Right now, we are not accountable for the excesses of prison, because it is a secret and silent punishment. The differential rate of black imprisonment is a silent statistic. It will take much more than the best-selling *The New Jim Crow* or the Black Lives Matter movement to bring about any change in this punishment.

What about women and children? Recent studies suggest that women have a lower pain threshold than do men and that this difference develops during adolescence.[18] Senior adults also have a higher threshold than young adults for some types of pain, though superficial pains such as pin pricks to the skin show less of a difference.[19] One need only watch children getting their shots to see that there is a wide range of pain tolerance in children, but that probably they have a generally lower pain threshold than adults, or at least that's what it sounds like! To further confuse the problem, it is likely that cultural stereotypes also affect how we attribute the response of others to pain, and affect the roles and expectations of certain groups to respond to pain differently.[20]

But there is evidence to show that women and children suffer at least as much or more than do adult men from the punishment of prison. Studies have shown that women suffer the separation from their families much more than do men,[21] and it is a well-established fact that the young who are sent to prison are those who are preyed on by rapists, and if they are not raped, they are turned into hardened criminals by older inmates.[22]

Administering simple sharp pains to the skin using MCP is likely to have less variation in its subjective experience by offenders according to gender or ethnicity, though it is uncertain about children, who, ironically comprise the class in society that is most commonly already subjected to corporal punishment. If we are to believe Murray Straus's surveys, it seems that over 90 percent of American parents at some time in their lives spanked their own children.[23] Some twenty states in the United States still allow corporal punishment of school children.[24] So this is not at all an "unusual" punishment for children. In the celebrated case of Michael Fay, the American teenager in Singapore who was caned for vandalism, some 49 percent of Americans surveyed actually approved of the caning.[25] What is unusual about the MCP proposed in this book is that it is advocated for adults.

It might reasonably be argued that punishing criminals with corporal punishment is treating them like children. This is a fair criticism. The solution, though, is to stop hitting kids, so that we can't any longer claim that corporal punishment is a children's punishment. In fact, the use of corporal punishment on children within the family is very dangerous, because the children have no recourse. It is punishment administered in secret (the sanctity of the home) and thus full of the same dangers of excess as found in the use of corporal punishment in prisons. There is no ready accountability, no "due process" one might say, within the traditional family household.[26] Corporal punishment is a painful punishment. It should only be used against those who have broken the law. There is no justification for its use otherwise.

There is an obvious exception to all this: selective unfairness. We still must keep prison because of the terrible few, the worst of the worst. We have seen that OI—open incapacitation without prison—can be applied to these few very, very serious offenders. Bodily incapacitation, in an open society, can be applied with differing degrees of intensity, that is, with or without severe pain or, more likely, suffering, since we envisage such incapacitation to be lived with for up to a lifetime by the worst of the worst. They are sentenced to bear chronic pain, unless, of course, the choice is for death in life—induced coma. The latter are deprived of consciousness; they are beyond pain. Should anyone, including the worst of the worst, be subjected to such punishment? Sometimes one must be unfair to be just.

Controlling the Pain of Punishment

Convicts are well aware of the ways in which prisons differ from each other, and these variations occur within prisons that are supposed to be of one type, such as "maximum security." Unlike MCP, it is difficult to vary both the intensity and duration of prison in a precise way.[27] Length of prison term obviously does it for duration, but even this solution does not suffice, because we have no control over the precise pains experienced as a result of prison, so there is no way to comprehend the real difference in pain of one year as against two years of prison. And it is even more difficult when we ask what the difference is between, say, twenty years and twenty-one years. Is the pain felt in each of these one-year differences the same? We can see in this example that duration and intensity of the pains of prison are hopelessly mixed up.

One way to vary the intensity of prison is to introduce various types or degrees of security—such as maximum security down to minimum security prisons. While such variations in intensity are not specific enough, they also affect the credibility of prisons as a punishment, since minimum security prisons are easily portrayed as "resorts for white collar criminals." "Perks," such as gym equipment, TV, or even libraries, convey the (mistaken) idea that prison is not that bad a place. Varying the intensity of prison in this way undermines its credibility as a punishment, paradoxically feeding the public's demand for more and more punishment, which under the present system can only be prison.

We can minutely control both the intensity and duration of the temporary pain of MCP. More importantly, by employing modern robotic technology, it is possible to eliminate the role of humans in administering the punishment. In fact why should not the judge who announces the sentence, actually administer the punishment, or if that is asking too much, press the button that does it? One might add that it would be a good idea for the judge to be able to see the punishment carried out via her laptop or tablet so that she does not lose sight of the fact that she has actually punished an individual with a prescribed dose of pain, that her sentence has been precisely implemented.

In contrast, if we are to control the intensity of prison, we must look closely at the types of pain that occur in prison—diet, hard labor, isolation cells[28]—and consider systematically grading these so that the intensity of prison may be adjusted to the punishment deserved by the crime.[29] None of these can be controlled in a precise way, but, worse, they occur within a secret enclosed environment, so are open to abuse and excess. The scandal of Abu Ghraib in 2003 is a prime example of such abuse. Varying pains within prison is not a realistic proposition. The distance of the pains of imprisonment from the punisher (that is, the judge) is vast.

It is clear that, where appropriate to the crimes, the use of MCP instead of the vague use of prison as punishment is preferable for all offenders except for the worst of the worst. For them, it is not painful enough and does not incapacitate. The application of MCP can be precisely controlled in terms of duration, frequency, and intensity. The physical sensation of pain is basically the same for everyone, although people may differ in the way they react to it. These variations are far fewer for MCP than reactions to prison where conditions vary so much that there is no reliable way to control their quality or intensity. The only problem in administering pain of MCP is that it may be subject to human error when administered.

Human error occurs constantly in every field of life. Humans typically confuse what they want with what is possible; what ought to be with what is. The scientific method was invented by humans specifically to remove human error out of the equation of research; avoid the constant temptation to support preconceived conclusions. The only way to remove human error in administering punishment is to eliminate humans from the process. Robots are the solution.

It may be argued that, by advocating the robotic administration of punishment, offenders are dehumanized. This is false. By comparison, real dehumanization is what happens to offenders when they are inducted into prison, and the rest of their lives subjected to the many pains and humiliations of prison. The slight, by comparison, dehumanization by robotic punishment is a reasonable price to pay for the many advantages it offers. Most importantly, robots eliminate human error from administering punishment. The major fact in the dehumanization of offenders in prison is that they are dehumanized by other humans—the guards, officials, administrators—and secondarily by the physical architecture of the prison itself. The humans who administer the punishment of prison are themselves dehumanized, as has been well demonstrated in the experiments of Zimbardo and others cited earlier in this book. (By "dehumanized" here, we mean descending into the use of violence and sex to degrade and humiliate the objects of the animal-like instincts of their captors.)

Robots avoid the dehumanization of the administrator of the punishment (eventually to become both judge and jury) and achieve what so far has been an impossibility in our criminal justice process (except in the most twisted ways), for the offenders themselves to administer their own punishment by pressing the button of the robot to apply the appropriate amount of pain. (The twisted way in which this already occurs is the self-mutilation by prison inmates.)[30]

Before you dismiss the idea of punishment by robot as outrageous, consider this. There are many media reports and accounts of the increasing possibility, even actuality of robots delivering sex to appreciative clients, dare we say partners.[31] A cursory search of the Internet will turn up many sources. If robots are used to make cars, chocolates, and appliances; clean the house; drive cars and planes; satisfy appetites for food and sex, then why not that other major human chore, punishment? Surely robots are perfect for the job, given that just and fair punishment must be delivered according to specific intensities, durations, and frequencies.

As a matter of fact, Jeremy Bentham, the great utilitarian and a contemporary of the father of criminal justice, Cesare Beccaria, thought of such a way of administering punishment back in the eighteenth century. Both of these reformers were, and still are (though Bentham has received some bad press for his panopticon design for a prison), viewed as reformers of criminal justice. Both of them favored the use of corporal punishment on criminals, though this is conveniently overlooked by modern historians of corrections.

Jeremy Bentham described his idea of a punishment machine thus:

A machine might be made, which should put in motion certain elastic rods of cane or whalebone, the number and size of which might be determined by the law: the body of the delinquent might be subjected to the strokes of these rods, and the force and rapidity with which they should be applied, might be prescribed by the Judge: thus everything which is arbitrary might be removed.[32]

Always ahead of his time, this was perhaps Bentham's anticipation of the mass production that would follow closely on the heels of the industrial revolution. As far as is known, his machine was never built, but a century or so later a number of designs were proposed (some in jest but others more serious). In general, the designer favored those machines that had the capacity to administer the strokes (usually a whip or cane of some kind) to a number of individuals (usually boys) all at once. C. Farrell describes other contraptions that were imagined or built during the nineteenth and twentieth centuries in Russia, Britain, Australia, Europe, and the United States.[33] The majority of the designs were for the application of corporal punishment on school boys, but a few for adults. Some were used in hazing.[34]

In the 1970s, a more serious, though never built, patent was taken out by German inventor Otto Tuchenhagen, with eighty patents to his name.[35] His design was for a cane to be self-applied, automatically producing a magnetic card that recorded the strokes, which the offender then lodged with an official as evidence that the punishment had been executed. There would be no persons present, thus avoiding humiliation, and, furthermore, he argued that it would be much cheaper than prisons. A simple search on Youtube will return a number of videos of individuals who have invented various contraptions for administering corporal punishment, usually a paddle of some kind. As noted earlier, there are many videos of individuals trying out electronic dog collars on themselves and others.

The advantages of robotic punishment are considerable. One of the major criticisms of the traditional use of corporal punishment is that its application depends entirely on the skill, strength, vigor, and motivation of the individual administering the punishment. As Bentham put it:

> In whipping not even the qualities of the instrument are ascer-
> tained by written law: while the quantity of force to be employed
> in its application is altogether intrusted [sic] to the caprice of
> the executioner. He may make the punishment as trifling or as
> severe as he pleases. He may derive from this power a source of
> revenue, so that the offender will be punished, not in proportion
> to his offence, but to his poverty.[36]

A robot can be preprogrammed to administer the punishment according to strictly controlled schedules, overcoming the major criticism often leveled against whipping, which is that it should never be applied in anger—the danger of using it to excess. In fact, once we accept this type of punishment, as Tuchenhagen showed, the person to be punished can be given complete control of the administration of the punishment, since the robot would be preprogrammed by the judge via the court computer. The robot is designed simply to accept the programmed card (or in modern electronics an algorithm that controls the robot, telling it how many applications of pain and of what intensity and frequency have been chosen by the judge).[37]

Let us compare two scenarios of punishment. The first, a typical case that occurs today all across America. The second, a case that could take place sometime in the future, hopefully soon, where robotics take over the distasteful process of punishing.

> The judge peers out over his glasses at the pathetic woman who sits across the courtroom. In a violent outburst the offender has just called him a heartless tyrant. The public defender and a courtroom guard restrain her.
>
> "Mrs. Washington," says the judge. "This is your third shoplifting offense. You leave me no choice . . ."
>
> He hesitates, expecting another outburst. Mrs. Washington's three-year-old daughter sits next to her, eyes wide and watery. The judge tries to avoid her gaze.
>
> "Mrs. Washington, it is the judgment of this court that you be sentenced to a minimum of six months in jail. Your daughter will be turned over to the care of the Department of Youth, since the presentence report indicates that you have no husband or relatives who could care adequately for her."
>
> The mother is led, crying, out of the courtroom. The child pulls at her mother's skirt, crying "Mama! Mama!" But the hands of the court are upon her, and an innocent child is about to be punished for the crime of having a guilty mother.

Every day, all across America many, many families and relatives of offenders suffer in this way. This means that literally millions of innocent people are punished for other people's crimes.

Now, an example of what punishment of the future could be like.

Twenty-year-old John Jefferson stands beside his lawyer, the public defender.

"John Jefferson," says the judge, "the court has found you guilty of burglary in the first degree. Because this is your first offense, but the damage you did was considerable, I sentence you to . . ."

The judge pushes a few buttons at her computer console. The average sentence for similar cases to Jefferson's flashes on the display.

". . . five shock units. You have ten days in which to visit the punishment facility to receive your units."

A card with an embedded chip emerges from the machine attached to the computer. The card contains the algorithm[38] for administration of the electronic flogging. The punishment clerk retrieves it and hands it to the defendant.

"Follow me to the punishment facility," says the punishment clerk. "I advise you to get it over and done with right now. The units are doubled if you don't take your punishment by the deadline."

Jefferson nods and mumbles, "OK. Let's get it over with."

The victim of this crime is sitting at the back of the court. She approaches the court clerk, who directs her to the punishment room where she will be able to watch the administration of the punishment if she wishes.

Jefferson's wife and child are ushered to the waiting room where they will await Jefferson's return after he has received his punishment units.

Meanwhile, in the punishment room, Jefferson chooses to stand rather than sit to take his punishment. As part of the prosecution procedure, he has already received a medical examination to establish that he was fit to receive punishment.

In addition to the victim, a few members of the press are seated on the other side of the glass screen. A medic is also present.

Jefferson approaches the machine. A robotic voice speaks. "When you are ready, please insert your card in the slot to your right."

Jefferson complies.

"You may choose an arm or lower leg to be shocked. Which do you prefer?"

"My leg." Says Jefferson.

"Right or left?"

"Left."

A robotic arm extends and clamps around Jefferson's leg.

"When you are ready, press the red button directly in front of you."

Jefferson grits his teeth and presses the button.

The robot was automatically programmed with the five units when the judge pressed the button on her sentencing laptop. Jefferson receives five painful jolts of electricity to his leg. He screams loudly, and by the time the punishment is over, he is almost crying with pain.

The robot releases the offender. "Stand and walk a little," instructs the robot.

Jefferson limps around, rubbing his leg. A shade drops over the spectators' screen.

"Do you still feel the pain?" asks the medic.

"Of course I do!"

"Would you like pain medication?"

"Oh yes!"

"Here you are then. There's a water fountain over there. Just sign here and you've paid your dues."

Jefferson sighs and asks, "Which way to the waiting room?"

"Straight down the passage and second left."

Jefferson enters the waiting room where his wife rushes into his arms, crying, "I'm so glad it's over! Thank goodness you weren't sent to prison!"

"Me too. It's such a relief to get it over and done with."

We see in this example that only the guilty person is punished (that is, there is no punishment overflow). The punishment administered is clean, simple, and, most importantly, convincingly painful. Pain medication is offered to ensure that the pain of the punishment does not last and become chronic pain. The punishment is over in a brief time, and the offender is able to return to his family and his job. Punishment is confined only to the guilty. The side effects of punishment are minimized. It is the robot that does the punishing and, importantly, it carries out the specific instruction input by the judge who has pronounced the sentence.

Could robots administer other kinds of punishment, besides corporal? Certainly one can imagine all kinds of horrible contraptions that would administer the death penalty, such as those already used historically such as the guillotine, the invention of the trap for hanging, the electric chair, and the gas chamber—not to mention the various methods of putting to death using medical technology. However, all of these machines require actual human administration that is proximate to the offender.

In respect to corporal punishment (that is, not capital punishment) the already existing types of "robotic" punishment are ankle bracelets and other kinds of tracking devices that are inserted into or attached to the offender. These are not so much corporal punishments as they are confinement devices. They deprive the offender of a certain degree of liberty by allowing for surveillance, albeit from afar. One could, however, imagine that such a device as the wearable bracelet could also be programmed as a corporal punishment device if it were to deliver an electric shock when the offender, for example, strayed out of his house, should he have been sentenced to house confinement. This would be a function of corporal punishment rather like a dog collar.

Perhaps the most horrible type of punishment one could imagine for the twenty-first century would be a completely robotic prison. Such a prison would house inmates in separate cells, completely programed with toilet facilities, automatic food delivery, and so on, the prison guards reduced to a tiny number. Of course, the most horrible characteristic of such prisons would be the lack of any human interaction at all, thus rendering inmates even more hidden away from society than they are now, making it even easier simply to put the offenders in the prison and forget about them—the perfect rendition of mass incarceration! In point of fact, it would amount to mass solitary confinement.

We can see from this brief scenario that robotic punishments are best confined to MCP: the application of short sharp shocks, carefully measured to apply the minimal amount of pain necessary to match the offense, as defined by the law and interpreted by the judge, and as far as possible open to public scrutiny.

It might be argued that the removal of all human involvement in administering corporal punishment will "dehumanize" the entire process, including the person punished. And, perhaps worse, allow us humans, adept as we are at self-deception, to avoid responsibility for doing the punishment, enabling us to blame the robots. It certainly does make it likely that the very human aspect of administering corporal punishment is completely removed. The human violence of whipping, for example, is nowhere to be seen when a robot administers, quietly and methodically, an electric shock, and, indeed, in the scenario described above, the robotic administration of the shock is in fact invoked by the one to be punished.

One supposes that engineers could design robots that screamed and moved in anger mimicking humans who have in the past administered corporal punishments or indulged in violent acts. We should avoid this temptation, because it is the violence that makes corporal punishments appear to be so awful. You might respond that this is a good thing, because it will scare would-be offenders from committing crime. But we have seen that deterrence does not work in most cases, as attractive as it may seem as a solution to stopping crime. Besides, we humans prefer not to acknowledge that it is violence that we administer to offenders. It is why we have built prisons, to cover up the violence that we do to criminals in the name of judicial punishment. Robots do, in fact, make it possible for us to administer the pain of punishment without the accompanying violence, but in a much more careful, consistent, focused, equitable, and limited way. It is a quintessentially civilized punishment!

Robots do not have to be massively ugly, overbearing machines. These images are the product of the many popular movies invented by Hollywood. In such movies, robots are made in the image of man or woman, not in the image of truly helpful and benign machines. Take, for example, the many machines, precursors of robots, that we depend on every day in Western civilization—washing machines, toasters, electric ovens. The list is endless. These are benign, enormously labor-saving devices that we all appreciate. They have improved the quality of life immensely for humans and will continue to do so. It is even likely that machines created the conditions for the abolition of slavery in the West.[39]

The doomsayers cry that we are almost at the point where robots may take over the world and make humans obsolete.[40] So say the likes of Bill Gates of Microsoft and eminent scientist Stephen Hawking.[41] But such a scenario is only a scenario. We are conditionally better off in our Western civilization having robots do our dirty work for us; "conditional," because the major ethical or moral issue at stake in our use of robots is our ever-present human characteristic of cleverly shifting onto others responsibility for the moral and ethical decisions we make, especially about those who break the law and are designated as criminal.[42]

Using MCP, we can blame the robots for the punishment, just as we now blame prisons for what we do to the inmates, dismissing the violence and other pains of imprisonment as somehow incidental pains that we did not intend, yet well know will occur when the judge pronounces a sentence of a prison term. At least with MCP there is no incidental violence. Any repressive or instrumental violence is totally under our control, carefully specified by the algorithms that govern the behavior of our robots. We can blame them, but it's obvious that they do our every bidding.

The Normal and the Spectacular

As I noted early in this book, the famed French sociologist Emile Durkheim argued at the beginning of the twentieth century that a certain amount of crime was "normal" and that the punishment that it necessarily demanded was also therefore "normal." Sociologists have argued ever since over what amount of crime would be normal, though they have not paid as much attention to what amount of punishment would be normal. From Durkheim's point of view, one needed just enough crime to invoke the passions of the masses, whose "solidarity" was reinforced by the punishment. That is, by punishing criminals, it made us feel good; as those who were not punished, we were part of the "good" noncriminals who ganged up on the designated criminals. "Us" against "them," as they say. Of course, for this process to work, the masses have to understand or know that punishment is being done; otherwise, there would be no point in punishing. Thus, the spectacle of punishing criminals is explained by Durkheim[43] and his followers, and looked upon as necessary for societal well-being, for maintaining the cohesiveness or solidarity of the society.[44]

However, I think that the true process of punishment in society is a silent process in which individuals grudgingly consent to be punished for infractions because they know that it is necessary for social order. If you have followed my argument throughout this book, you will immediately recognize my assertion as the good old Enlightenment idea of the "social contract," in which each individual citizen gives up a little of his own personal "freedom" in order for the state to exercise its essential strong arm to maintain law and order.[45] It is only in this sense that people are capable of governing themselves—and even then, as we see democracies or republics of various kinds rise and fall, there are no guarantees.

The trouble is that the spectacular aspect of punishment, the bloody violence upon which it is built, has dominated most regimes in Western and Eastern societies from time immemorial. This is because, as Foucault conveyed in one of his rare lucid moments, prior to democracies, or "government by the people and for the people," dictatorial regimes held sway, and it was through the spectacular punishment of public executions that the power of the minority (King, Queen, Czar, or what have you) was asserted, demonstrated, and viewed in awe as power absolute. We know, though, that absolute power holds within itself its own destruction ("power corrupts"), a truth understood by revolutionaries everywhere, until they themselves hold power.

In democracies and republics of various kinds, spectacular punishments are no longer necessary. What is necessary is the acknowledgement by their citizens of the day-to-day control that the state must exert in order to get the job of control done. It is the mundane activities of a modern state's bureaucracies that requires the submission of its citizens, not the spectacular violence of crimes and punishments. Spectacular violence, in fact, is old hat, eclipsed by the incredibly realistic, more than realistic—fantastic—violence now rendered in movies, TV and video games. There is nothing in twenty-first-century real life that can match it.[46]

The control that state bureaucracies hold over the little person is enormous, so well portrayed by Kafka's pathetic K in his novel *The Trial*, that ends with K mortally punishing himself. In modern-day life, it is impossible to lead one's life without getting punished by the state—this so well established by the rise of the state's department of motor vehicles. It is "normal" to get a traffic ticket of some kind or other. It is the venue through which the state effects its control over the everyday lives of citizens. Ask any cop who does traffic stops. These are fraught with danger. We, the "victims" of traffic stops, truly resent and fear it. Police must undergo special training on how to do traffic stops, avoid escalation into violence. And flourishing legal services make much money by representing clients who don't want to go to court and will grudgingly pay the exorbitant legal fees.

Enter robots. First, speed and red light cameras are now installed everywhere. These short circuit the entire criminal justice process. They avoid any confrontation between traffic cop and driver. The first one hears of it is a notice of infraction that arrives in the mail. Second, in many states of the United States and elsewhere, it is now possible, as it is in New York State, to "cop a plea" online, to plead guilty and pay the fine, circumventing "due process." The robot makes it easy for you to plead guilty. The pain of it is when one writes a check or charges the fine to a credit card—and, later, the insurance company makes additional money off of it by adding a surcharge to your insurance premium.

What we have here is the normalization of punishment. I will expand on this idea in the final chapter, where I speculate about the future of punishment in Western civilization.

In sum, robots can carry out the sentences of judges in an efficient, equitable, and humane way, thus reducing human error, both moral and instrumental. The administration of pain can be controlled precisely in respect to timing, intensity, and frequency, preprogrammed in such a way that even the offender can take charge and administer his own punishment. In this way, we shift the responsibility for the punishment to the offender, the robot simply provides the device and algorithm. The offender needs simply to pull the switch, press the button, or insert the card. The robot also avoids responsibility for punishing. Perfect justice: offenders bear the responsibility for their own punishment, the logical outcome of their offense. Is it not a small price to pay for liberty? Given that punishment seems to be everywhere, would it not enhance our freedom if we were allowed to punish ourselves on behalf of the government? Better that you can do it to yourself with robotic help than have a human, resolute, indifferent, nasty, enjoying every minute of it, smugly superior, standing over you with a whip or shoving you into a cell and locking you up?

Self-punishment with the aid of a robot—now there is a truly civilized way to punish!

Chapter Nine

Civilizing Barbarism

*Mass Incarceration Violates More Rights Than
Moderate Corporal and Shari'a Punishments*

If robots seem just too far-fetched and morally indefensible for administering criminal punishment, what about a way of punishing miscreants
that is the product of a civilization as old as Western civilization, Shari'a
law? It is a system that has practiced corporal punishment for centuries, by
comparison uses prison minimally, and is now making its way into Western
civilization.

The advocates of Shari'a law argue that it is superior to the criminal
punishment process of the United States on a number of counts, but its
American critics point out that it violates the US Constitution. Opponents
of a new system of criminal punishment incorporating MCP and OI might
also argue that the punishment practices proposed would violate the US
Constitution. Can either system stand the scrutiny of the American Constitution as applied by the Supreme Court? And could MCP and OI stand
up to a Supreme Court challenge?

In this chapter, I offer, hopefully, an objective account of the basic
tenets, justifications, and practices of Islamic punishment as expressed in
Shari'a law and assess it according to both international standards and that
of Western civilization, the latter reflecting more or less the principles of
the US Constitution. Finally, I ask whether the criminal punishment system
I propose in this book would stand the scrutiny of the US Constitution.

Shari'a Punishments

In 2015, Arafa and Burns systematically compared the punitive theories and practices of Islamic law to those of the United States, and Islamic theory and practice came out the winner.[1] The crux of the argument was the familiar one: America's over use of prison. Comparing different kinds of punishments is complicated and difficult, especially in respect to corporal punishments, as we saw in chapter 7. It is even more difficult comparing Western to Islamic criminal punishment practices, because there is very little data available assessing, even simply recording, the application of Shari'a law in everyday practice. Close to half the world's population lives under various kinds of Islamic criminal punishment principles and practice, so it would be a little arrogant (a common fault of those in the West) to dismiss it as "primitive" or even "barbaric." Of course, labeling criticisms as arrogant does not mean that they are wrong in substance. It would certainly be arrogant to write a book that deals with corporal punishment and ignores completely the major criminal system of Islam that has practiced it for a couple of thousand years, and continues to do so.

The defenders of Shari'a law claim that the mutilations and severe corporal punishments that are available in Islamic law are rarely used, that they are publicized by the West in order to vilify Islam, and that built into the system is the discretion of the judge (the sole arbiter of a case) to prescribe much milder punishments and, in conjunction with the victim, to work out a monetary substitute for the punishment (various forms of "blood money"). This defense is similar to that made by biblical scholars who argue that the law of Moses, an "eye for an eye," was never meant literally, and point to the many examples where far milder punishments were used in its place, including blood money.[2] The trouble is, we lack any dependable or reliable data on the extent to which the mutilating and violent punishments of Shari'a law are applied. The world is left only with the extreme and violent depictions of mutilation, stoning to death, beheadings, and so on that appear constantly on the mass and social media. But there is no research that counts the actual number of cases that receive such penalties as against those that do not. The United Nations collects data on crime and justice from all member countries, but makes no effort to reach out to the religious organizations that enforce and adjudicate Shari'a laws and punishments in most Islamic nations. The following provides a description of the Islamic crimes and their punishments, but be warned that these are just descriptions and do not relay the actual incidence, prevalence, or practice of these punishments.

Islam and the Judeo-Christian religions share a common geocultural point in human history: North Africa. It is half way between the east and the west, as defined by the ancient world, which is why we call it the "Middle East" (a Eurocentric term). Arguably, the prime movers of Western civilization, the Romans, imported many of the religious customs, gods, and social and economic arrangements from all the peoples they conquered, especially Egypt and surrounding kingdoms. And these Middle Eastern countries also were colonized and conquered by the Greeks before the Romans. So it is very difficult to claim that the two cultures, that of Islam and Judeo-Christianity, are completely separate.[3] The following is an extremely oversimplified review of Islamic crimes and their punishments. The complexities that lie behind them are immense.

Islam can generally be divided into two "sects" Sunni (containing four schools) and Shiite (two schools).[4] Roughly 70 percent of Muslims are Sunni. Within each of those schools there are further distinctions in terms of process and interpretations of the Qur'an. This account draws mainly on the Sunni version of Shari'a.[5]

There are only about half a dozen "crimes" specifically defined by the Qur'an that invite serious punishments, which must be carried out in public. They are crimes considered to be crimes against Allah, for which punishments will be received in Hell, but for which humans, being so weak, must also be punished here on earth. There is no discretion allowed in the punishment of these crimes. They are also described in the Hadith, a collection of writings by the prophets in the eighth and ninth centuries BCE, claimed to be verbatim reports of Muhammad. The crimes are as follows:

1. Murder. This crime is generally described as the purposeful slaying of a believer.[6] (Killing nonbelievers is permitted, and, according to some interpretations, it is a duty.) The punishment is death by the hand of the victim's family: "And slay not the life which Allah hath forbidden save with right. Who so is slain wrongfully, we have given power unto his heir, but let him not commit excess in slaying."[7] Note here the concern with punishment excess, the charge made against mass incarceration in the West today.

2. Theft. "As for the thief, both male and female, cut off their hands. It is the reward for their own deeds, an exemplary punishment from Allah."[8] This is perhaps the most colorful punishment to Western eyes, illustrating the combination of both reflective and educative aspects of punishment. It reflects an element of the crime in the punishment (that is, the hands that steal are cut off), and this reflection is seen as "teaching a lesson" to the thief or perhaps as serving the motive of general deterrence for those who witness the punishment.[9]

3. Adultery. "The adulterer and the adulteress, scourge ye each one of them with a hundred stripes . . . and let a party of believers witness their punishment."[10] We see here another example of an ancient collective punishment described in the bible: that is, a punishment in which the community takes part by witnessing it. This type of punishment was a practice of the ancient Israelites, who stoned offenders to death.[11] It continues to this day in Islamic countries, available for public view on YouTube and other web sites. Note also that the specific number of stripes is stated.

4. Unfounded Accusation of Adultery. "And those who accuse honorable women but bring not four witnesses, scourge them with eighty stripes and never afterward accept their testimony—they are indeed evil doers."[12]

To these have been added, depending on the sect:

- Unlawful sexual intercourse (including homosexuality), punished by one hundred lashes[13]

- Drinking alcohol, punishable by up to eighty strokes of a palm stalk

- Banditry, punished by flogging or banishment

- Apostasy, disrespecting Islam, punished by death (a *hadd* crime, explained below, depending on the particular country or local tradition)

To repeat, the above classification is greatly simplified. The trouble is that there are so many esteemed Islamic scholars dating from the sixteenth century and before who have developed their own classifications, most of these based on very detailed examples of specific cases tried by judges and the exegesis of the Qur'an and other religious texts. There have been some attempts to "codify" the laws, most of these conducted during the various colonial periods of the British and other European empires.[14] European and common law systems were superimposed on Islamic law, which nevertheless remained, though not so visible to the occupying authorities. It was "eclipsed," as Rudolph Peters in his careful book *Crime and Punishment in Islamic Law* observes, awaiting the opportunity to break forth. It did so, for example, in Iran in 1979.[15] The following countries have reintroduced Islamic criminal law and continue to embellish the "penal codes" and practices to reflect its Islamic basis: Libya (1969), Pakistan (1979), Iran (1979), Sudan (1973), and Northern Nigeria (2000). Saudi Arabia never gave in to Western criminal law, retaining the noncodified Shari'a law as the law of the land.

In any case, if we are to compare Islamic crime and punishment with that of the West, we should bear in mind that the reemergence of Islam is ongoing, and it may take on many different forms as different sects and schools of thought gain supremacy. There are some aspects of Islamic law that are highly innovative from a Western point of view, in particular the idea of victims playing an active part in the punishment of those who offended them. A retaliatory or compensatory response may be allowed from the victim or victim's family in the case of a murder, rape, or other serious assault. This is not an especially new idea—it derives not from the Qu'ran but from the feuding societies that existed from the beginning of time throughout North Africa (and still exist in some places),where there was no strong centralized state, so that all wrongs were righted by private agreement between just the two parties, the offender and the victim.[16] There are also examples of this private system of punishment reported throughout the Bible, though these refer only to property crimes, not murder.[17]

If we adopt the traditional distinction in Western criminal law between crimes against the person and property crimes, Islamic law divides crimes against the person into two kinds: those of retaliation (*qisas*) and those of financial compensation (*diya*). Since in most cases the victim or victim's family may specify the punishment and even carry out the punishment, there is considerable discretion allowed. These crimes and their punishments are those where "blood money" may be paid the victim's family if the family agrees. Or the family may instead demand retaliation and killing of the murderer.[18] The extent to which any of these options are applied in practice is unknown. Perhaps formal records are kept in some Islamic countries, but as far as can be determined there is no published source of such data. This is a huge contrast with Western crime and punishment that produces massive amounts of crime and justice records, files, and statistics.[19]

Another group of crimes is highly discretionary and may include any sinful or forbidden behavior as well as *hadd* crimes that (a) could not be punished for procedural reasons such as the victims did not demand any compensation or (b) are other acts not covered by the traditional crime definitions but which may, by analogy, be deemed so. Further, this category also includes crimes that endanger public order or state security (*ta'zir*). In practice, this is the category of crimes that is easy for state authorities to abuse,[20] with little protection provided the accused.[21]

Punishing Principles, East and West

Given their common origins, we should not be surprised that there is some commonality in the justifications and principles of punishment between the Islamic law of the Middle East and Western Judeo-Christian law, though their implementation differs, of course.[22] These justifications and principles are as follows:

Retribution—an "eye for an eye" (aka "just deserts" or "poetic justice"), the familiar justification that dominates the Old Testament.

Deterrence—even the distant threat of Hell is not enough to deter humans, so *hadd* crimes must be punished on earth as well. All punishments must be public, fulfilling one of the requirements of general deterrence, as we saw above. Also, Shari'a punishments are exemplary, as were most of the punishments described in the Old Testament.

Rehabilitation—the offender must be guided back to a straight path (aka "corrections").

Restorative Justice—the offender must make amends, compensate the victim.

Repentance—the offender is given a certain amount of time to demonstrate that he has committed to "going straight" (aka "probation").[23]

Incapacitation (confinement)—permanent imprisonment is allowed for those who persist in repeating their crimes.

Incapacitation (individual)—cutting off the hand of a thief prevents further thefts; no Western equivalent, except maybe castration for sex offenders. The death penalty also serves this preventive purpose.

The Old Testament of the Bible forms the basis of much of the above. It is true that Moses did not specify the exact means of putting people to death, though it is not clear whether the "eye for an eye"—often called the "law of Moses"—was meant to be taken figuratively or actually. However, what eventually separated Western law from Islamic law was that Judaic law was encapsulated by Roman law, which was essentially a secular system of law. The overwhelming force of Roman law came from its secular function to preserve and promote the Roman Republic (and later its Empire).[24] Roman law was a practical law, made to facilitate commerce, settle private disputes (including murder and rape), regulate slavery, and, most of all, enforce tax collection. This is why Roman law remains well entrenched in all legal systems that have been touched by Western civilization. Its justification is not religious, but practical. It evolved to administer empires. It formed the basis of canon law (the Holy Roman Empire), and eventually the system of Western law. It established law and procedure dealing with criminal punishment, including the presumption of innocence, an adversarial trial before one's peers followed by a prescribed punishment.

The types of punishments that are available in Shari'a law are broader than in Western criminal law, particularly with respect to the types of death penalty and bodily mutilations, as we can see in the simplified summaries provided in tables 9.1 and 9.2.[25] In this respect, the two systems are opposites. Islam formally defines far fewer crimes but has more varieties of punishment. Western law has many, many defined crimes but few punishment varieties.

These contrasts in punishments reflect different laws and cultures even though they have a common ancient history.

The Two Cultures of Punishment

The cultures of antiquity that surrounded the Mediterranean, common to both Islamic and Judeo-Christian criminal justice, in their dim beginnings practiced not only human sacrifice but a considerable range of corporal punishments and aggravated forms of the death penalty. Yet ask any Western

Table 9.1. Summary of Shari'a and Western Punishments: Noncorporal and Confinement

Noncorporal Punishments	
Shari'a	West
Reprimand—the least severe	Caution; suspended sentence
Fines—compensation to victims or to the state	Fines—"day fines" linked to the offender's income; sometimes compensation of various kinds
Confiscation of property	Confiscation of profits from drug or corporate crime
Exposure to public scorn	Few public punishments—community service and sex-offender registries
No formal equivalent	Probation and parole
Banishment—for banditry, unlawful sexual intercourse; men only	No equivalent
Prison	
Shari'a	West
Imprisonment—supposedly only for debtors, not a penal punishment; for *ta'zir* crimes	Mass incarceration; preventive detention in jails

Source: Peters, *Crime and Punishment*, 33–38.

person whether there is any similarity between the punishment of criminals in the Middle East and the West and the answer would be that there is a vast difference, that the West does not use corporal punishment against its criminals, especially cutting off hands or feet. Yet, as we saw in chapters 1 and 2, while the practice of corporal punishment ebbed and receded at various times since antiquity, it never fully retreated in the West until the campaigns against it arose in the nineteenth century, spawned by the Enlightenment thinkers of the eighteenth century who opposed the death penalty (but not corporal punishment). This "enlightenment" did not touch the Islamic cultures until it was imposed on them by Western colonialism, starting in the nineteenth century. Western civilization's imperial nations imposed Western commerce and laws along with their punishments, but

Table 9.2. Summary of Shari'a and Western Punishments: Corporal and Death Penalty

Corporal Punishment	
Shari'a	West
Flogging with a leather whip—stripes deposited all over the body excluding the head and genital area; exceptions or adjustments for health or sickness	Shock incarceration; solitary confinement
Amputation of the right hand or foot—cut off and cauterized in boiling oil	No equivalent
Cross amputation—four fingers and four toes (Shiite law)	No equivalent
Retaliation for injuries—amputation or blinding to one who has inflicted such injuries on others	No equivalent
Death Penalty	
Shari'a	West
Death penalty—mostly beheading by sword; for a pregnant woman, postponed until after birth	Death penalty (some states of USA and a few Western countries)—lethal injection, firing squad, electric chair
Stoning to death—with medium sized stones; first stones (according to some sects) thrown by significant witnesses	No equivalent
Crucifixion—sometimes after death; others first crucified then stabbed in chest; others (Shiite) crucified for three days and if still alive, the life is spared	No equivalent

Source: Peters, Crime and Punishment, 33–38.

took care (following the ancient Romans) to preserve and allow the indigenous traditions of law and punishment of Islam and other religious and cultural traditions of the occupied country. For a century or more, Western imperial countries absorbed some of the literature and art of the countries they colonized, but not criminal justice. And gradually they opened their doors for their colonized subjects to migrate to their "mother country," and the results of that migration are obvious all over Europe and the UK, including now the United States.

It is likely that this "tolerance" of foreign cultures (a clever technique of control) contributed to the continuation of corporal punishment in Middle Eastern countries that, over the last two decades have seen a resurgence of Shari'a law and its punishments, a "return" to the original practices and beliefs handed down by Muhammad. Islamic civilizations regard their law as sacred and untouchable, the literal word of Allah. They therefore cannot be "reformed" by an enlightened philosophy, because they are already perfect.

However, the Enlightenment thinkers of the West were motivated not so much to reform punishment itself, but to minimize the heavy hand of government on its citizens, and, even more importantly, to ensure equitable treatment by the rule of law: a government of laws not of men (a doctrine worshipped by the Romans, but implemented rather badly; a catch-cry for the American Revolution). The Fourteenth Amendment of the US Constitution enshrined the principle of equity in its rule of law.

While there are many statements in the Qur'an that echo this principle of equality before the law,[26] there are many that reveal the opposite, particularly in respect to actual procedures (witness testimony, burden of proof), and in respect to the rights of women, homosexuals, and nonbelievers.[27] We see here a familiar problem: there are no statistical data to back up either side of this disagreement as to how decisions are made in Islamic court procedures, the extent to which the alleged discriminations occur in practice. In other words, there is definitely a problem of transparency in Shari'a law and practice.[28] It contrasts greatly with the data provided by Western courts and procedural justice. Mind you, defenders of Islamic law would argue that there is no need for what the West calls transparency, because all trials and punishments of Shari'a are conducted in public, especially in local communities.

Before we leap to judgment about Islamic procedural law, we should note that for quite some time the US Constitution treated slaves and women as though they were not citizens. And some would argue that, while the Constitution says one thing, the everyday arrangement of social and economic life in America reflects its failure in practice, mass incarceration being one sore example.

The superficial and obvious difference between the Islamic and Judeo-Christian cultures that were both built on corporal punishment is that the West does not cut off hands and feet and has never done so, as far as can be determined, though a few hundred years ago, it did countenance branding and piercing, and sometimes cutting out the tongue. It did for a while, towards the end of the eighteenth century, sentence criminals to be dissected, but this was only after they had been hanged. In the two centuries before that, criminals could also be disemboweled as part of the death penalty. There is little idea of deterrence in the Old Testament, certainly none in the law of Moses, upon which both East and West uneasily sit. It was only when Christ and his followers put forward the promise of eternal life that a utilitarian structure in the justification of punishment emerged. That is, as the philosophers of punishment say, punishment became forward looking. Thus was established the moral justification for torture that reached its heights during the Roman Catholic inquisitions of the Middle Ages.

Shari'a and Liberty

There is a strong libertarian thread embedded in Islamic legal procedure. It has to do with the procedural law of Islam and is best reflected by the saying of the Ayatollah Khomeini, widely publicized following the Iranian revolution that deposed the Shah of Iran in 1979:

> Islamic justice is based on simplicity and ease. It settles all criminal and civil complaints and in the most convenient, elementary, and expeditious way possible. All that is required is for an Islamic judge, with pen and inkwell and two or three enforcers, to go into a town, come to his verdict on any kind of case, and have it immediately carried out.[29]

The procedure is essentially adversarial, in which the judge acts as referee and decides a case after the opposing sides have made their arguments and presented their evidence. In both civil and criminal matters, the case is essentially a private affair; that is, the state does not intrude. The judge, usually a mullah or Islamic scholar, well informed by decisions made in many past cases, decides the outcome. As noted earlier, victims or family of victims are very much involved in inflicting the punishment, including for murder, even inflicting the punishment themselves, or, if they so choose, to accept financial compensation in lieu of the punishment, or even accept a lesser punishment, showing leniency.

In sum, the finding of guilt and the punishment are essentially a local affair, the state remaining apart. This is a case of minimal government intrusion, where local families and citizens settle disputes. The judge is not a representative of the state but of Islam. It reflects the classic procedure of customary justice that prevailed in the deserts of Africa among the many tribes, particularly the Bedouin, and in other places in the world where there has been a weak or nonexistent state or central government.[30] The extent to which this procedure is essentially a product of custom rather than Islam itself is therefore in question, especially as we see today that Islamic countries are becoming more and more dominated by dictatorships and more and more there is the attempt to create the Caliphate, in which the state and religion are one. There has long been dissatisfaction submerged in Iran that the mullahs have grabbed too much political power, that power has been transferred to a central state rather than left to local groups and mosques.[31] As we have already seen, Shari'a law is essentially a decentralized system, oriented particularly to the needs of small local communities.

The idea of all disputes being handled in the simple way, as the ayatollah describes, is no doubt attractive. It even resembles the romantic image of justice of the Wild West in America. But it also reproduces exactly the famous last sentence in Beccaria's *On Crimes and Punishments*, quoted with approval by past and present penologists of liberal and conservative persuasion alike:

> So that every punishment should not be an act of violence of one or many against a private citizen, it must be essentially public, prompt, necessary, the minimum possible in the given circumstances, in proportion to the crimes, and dictated by the laws.[32]

There is, obviously, no way that modern Western criminal justice procedure meets any of these exhortations expressed by Beccaria. Punishment is not public, certainly never prompt, and rarely minimal; it is grossly disproportionate, and, taking plea bargaining into consideration with the uncontrolled punishments that occur within prison, is decidedly not dictated by the laws. A libertarian could point the finger at the Western state, the colossus that has invented a machinery of criminal justice that moves at a snail's pace, achieving little except mass incarceration.

When the sacred justification of law is combined with the secular justification, there arises a very powerful, doctrinal legal system that dominates every minute of every life: the theocratic state. This is because when the origin of law is sacred, it cannot be questioned, only interpreted. Such is the case with Islamic law, which spawned many very intelligent scholars who have over the centuries produced volumes of interpretations and applications of the few hints at criminal law, such as adultery and theft, provided in the Qu'ran and the companion volumes that have expanded on them. The West, following the Romans, has developed law in two directions: (1) the construction of legal codes (beginning with Justinian's Twelve Tables) that systematize offenses and their respective punishments and (2) the assembly in formal archives of common law that preserves cases and precedent. The relationship between the state and the law is therefore crucial and pivotal.

We hear often how important is the "rule of law." The United States is unique in this respect. Its founders created out of argument and debate a Constitution upon which the entire country's rule of law rests. Without it, the country would fall apart. This is why, until this century, the Constitution became almost sacred, why the Founding Fathers made it so difficult to change. Paradoxically, the founders recognized the danger of a religious state, which is why they enshrined the idea of separation of church and state in the Constitution. Yet it is this secular concept of government that is its Achilles's heel: for if enough dissatisfied citizens can get together and convince others that the republic, via its constitution, is "rigged" against them, then there is nothing really to stop them from attacking the "rule of law"—that is, the words (and they are only words) of the Constitution—and declare it irrelevant. In a religious state, there is no such weakness in the law so long as enough people believe in the sacred origin of the society (whether Islam or some other religion).

Radical Islamists today are fighting to establish a caliphate, a totally dominated society of Islam, with certainly no distinction between church and state.[33] Iran is probably the one country in the world that has achieved this condition. Yet it is a puzzle that most Islamic countries do not have a theocracy where Islam is the major religion. They are mostly governed by dictatorships (and only in Iran is the dictator a mullah) of one kind or the other, rarely are there any democratic governments. The possible exception is Indonesia, though Aceh province now enforces Shari'a law and there are signs that the rest of Indonesia will follow.[34]

There are signs, ISIS notwithstanding, that judges in Iran are trying to move away from whipping as a punishment, much to the disapproval of Sayyid Mahmoud Hashemi Shahroudi, chief of the Iranian judiciary until 2009:

> Our judges, unfortunately, influenced by some malignant world publicity, do not accept whipping. In my view, whipping is one of

the best, most just and fairest punishments. Because it's inflicted
only to the offender and the offender's family are immune from
side effects. This is especially so when it is accompanied by public
shaming, because it is more of a deterrent.[35]

This statement was made in the context of the complaint that prison was
being used far too much in Iran as a serious punishment. So it would seem
that the Western solution to serious crime—prison—is even seeping into
Shari'a law. Yet, as noted at the beginning of this chapter, a survey of attitudes to Shari'a law in Iran showed that the majority of Iranians approved
of Shari'a law, and this was fairly standard across all demographic groups.[36]
It is difficult to believe that so many would find Shari'a law so acceptable
if the mutilating and violent punishments that we see so much of in the
media were in fact inflicted so often.

To Western eyes, Shari'a law not only embraces corporal punishment
as part of its "rule of law" (more accurately "rule of life"), it does so without
much formal consideration as to what punishments serve society better. It
is a blunt instrument, and its legal process violates many human rights,
from a Western point of view. Yet the growth of Shari'a courts in the UK
is considerable.[37] Perhaps this is because it can be defended on Western
grounds as well. It has an appeal to many—a kind of libertarian appeal, as
suggested earlier—for it advocates a very simple, highly localized form of
justice, stripped of the baggage of bureaucracy that comes with any Western
legal system. It promises a swift process of justice in which the finding of
guilt is followed immediately by the punishment, even at times involving
the victims with infliction of the punishment. Paradoxically, procedures
such as these are often advanced as the hallmarks of Western criminal
justice, but they are never implemented in practice. Perhaps the reason is
that they would violate various parts of the US Constitution, as we will
consider shortly. Of considerable interest, though, is the qualitative aspect
of Shari'a punishments. In some respects they strike a balance between the
quantitative approach (strokes of the whip)—an approach that dominates
Western criminal sentencing, as we have seen in previous chapters—to a
qualitative effort derived from early biblical times to match the punishment
to the crime.

In the West, we are not quite ready to start cutting off hands, though
we have seen in chapter 6 that, in the case of the worst of the worst, bodily
incapacitation of various kinds is worthy of serious consideration, especially

if these can in any way contribute to the eradication of prison, the most barbarous punishment of all. We can learn from Shari'a that corporal punishments can be an important part of any culture that is based on punishment, which includes both Islam and the West. The direct, forthright, and uncomplicated (by comparison) administration of punishment is an element of Islamic criminal justice that we in the West should acknowledge. It is hard to deny that, until very recently, the corporal punishment of Islam has kept at bay the horrible and excessive punishment of the West, mass incarceration.

I ask you to keep this in mind when you consider the arguments urging the adoption of MCP and OI. Carefully controlled and wisely administered, it promises to rein in the dreadful Western punishment of mass incarceration. Some in the West fear Islam's encroachment. But like our Roman forbears, we should take from Islam what benefits us. It *is* possible to civilize corporal punishment. You may argue that, even if MCP were demonstrably more humane than current practice, introducing it would be impossible because it would be forbidden by the US Constitution. Maybe, maybe not.

Cruel and Unusual?

No US court has ever found whipping as a sentence (that is, judicial corporal punishment) to be unconstitutional according to the cruel and unusual clause of the Eighth Amendment to the US Constitution.[38] In fact, it was clearly considered constitutional on the very day the cruel and unusual clause became part of the US Constitution in 1791. At that time, it was a widely used punishment, so was not unusual.[39] In fact, both George Washington and Thomas Jefferson successfully petitioned Congress for its use in 1776 and in 1778, respectively.[40]

It is important to note here that we are considering judicial corporal punishment, not corporal punishment used as a means of prison discipline. This is an entirely different issue, although, if we were to expand the definition of corporal punishment to include everything done to the offender's body while in prison, such cases would become relevant. Expert opinion on Supreme Court adjudication of corporal punishment as a prison discipline is split.[41] However, the 2011 case of *Brown v. Plata* indicates that the court has at last tilted towards the view that the abominable conditions in overcrowded prisons together with excessively long prison terms may be cruel and unusual punishment.[42] But is prison itself corporal punishment? As we have seen throughout this book, a strong case can be made for it.

The classic case of judicial corporal punishment was decided by the Supreme Court in *Weems v. United States* on May 2, 1910.[43] Weems had been convicted of falsifying official records of the United States Coastguard, defrauding the government of 612 pesos (the crime occurred in the Philippines). The Philippine criminal code mandated fifteen years in prison with hard labor for this offense, plus the punishment of *cadena temporal*, which required him to be kept constantly in chains. In addition, he lost all political rights during imprisonment, was subject to permanent surveillance after his release, and was fined 4 thousand pesetas.

The Philippine Constitution contains the same clause concerning cruel and unusual punishment as does the Eighth Amendment to the US Constitution that was adopted in 1791:

> That excessive bail ought not be required, nor excessive fines imposed, nor cruel and unusual punishments inflicted.

Luckily for Weems, the Supreme Court struck down the sentence as cruel and unusual. However, the reasons it gave for this decision remain the subject of debate until this day. Because the *Weems* decision defined *cadena temporal* as corporal punishment, it was widely assumed that if a state were to enact a corporal punishment statute, it would be found unconstitutional. But this is far from certain. There are a number of reasons for this, many turning on the ambiguity and disagreement concerning the meaning of the phrase "cruel and unusual."

A number of legal scholars and historians argue that it is a fallacy to believe that the phrase "cruel and unusual," lifted from the English Bill of Rights of 1689, was included in that act specifically to exclude barbarous bodily punishments.[44] It is quite certain that this could not have been the intent of the framers of the English Bill of Rights, since barbarous punishments were used for at least another hundred years after 1689. What is clear is that their intent was to forbid the abuse of governmental power. This was the preoccupation of the English in the seventeenth century (they fought a civil war over it, after all). In this light the clause could apply to any kind of punishment, and the phrase "cruel and unusual" may be taken to mean something closer to "arbitrary and capricious" (akin to the Fourteenth Amendment guarantee of due process—more important in respect to Shari'a law, as noted previously).

It is true that the court in Weems did consider the interpretation of abuse of governmental power as a factor in the intent of the framers of the English Bill of Rights. But the court also found it necessary to go further in justifying its decision, especially that part focusing on proportionality: that is, the idea that fifteen years' prison was too much compared to the seriousness of the offense. This point opened the way for subsequent appeals against excessive prison terms for minor crimes such as that of Rummel, mentioned earlier in this book, who received a life sentence for stealing a total of $229.11. It also established a precedent for the arguments in the 2011 case of *Brown v. Plata* that life in prison was an excessive punishment both in amount and quality (deplorable prison conditions). This conclusion came after many cases in which the Supreme Court refused to rule any prison term as excessive. In fact, in 1991, the court even refused to overturn a sentence of life in prison without parole for possession of 672 grams of cocaine.[45] So it would appear that, while the Supreme Court introduced the notion of proportionality, it had never taken the rule very seriously, and therefore the only way to explain its decisions prior to *Brown v. Plata* is to conclude that it was the "extras" of *cadena* (the corporal punishment) that were enough to make the Philippine law cruel and unusual.

Why did the court even bother to address the proportionality question in *Weems*? One can only speculate on this. It is likely that its reasoning was wholly limited to a quantitative conception of prison as a punishment, because, as we have seen in previous chapters, it is a punishment that is traditionally thought of in terms of "amounts." It is the amount of punishment that is linked to proportionality, not the type of punishment.[46] But the framers of the English Bill of Rights could not have had the quantitative notion of proportionality in mind, because there was no conception of the numerical base of punishment until the utilitarians, such as Beccaria and Bentham, introduced it in the late eighteenth century. Before that time, one was not sentenced to a certain number of lashes, but merely to be whipped. Before the utilitarians, the reflective view of punishment held sway. That is, the concern was for reflecting or matching of the punishment to the crime, not its proportionate amount; quality of punishment, not quantity. By the time the Americans came to frame their Constitution, the utilitarians had reached the height of their ideological power, and there is good reason to believe that Beccaria's thought had penetrated the minds of the framers of the American Constitution.[47] So the chances are that they believed "cruel and unusual" included the quantitative notion of proportionality that the court later reflected.

Notwithstanding the different interpretations of the framers of the Constitution, most decisions on cruel and unusual punishment have pretty much assumed that the Eighth Amendment "expresses the revulsion of civilized man against barbarous acts—the 'cry of horror' against man's inhumanity to his fellow man" (*Robinson v. California*, Justice Douglas concurring).[48] Other interpretations have made similar pronouncements referring to the "traditional humanity of modern Anglo-American law." Clearly, this "humanity" is assumed, or defined, merely in terms of the absence of corporal punishment, since the court had consistently failed to rule as cruel and unusual a number of prison terms that were clearly out of proportion and excessive by anyone's standards. The prime examples are those of *Rummel*, already noted, and more recently *Ewing v. California* (2003), where the Supreme Court decided that Eighth Amendment rights are not violated by California's three-strikes law, in which the defendant was sentenced to twenty-five years in prison for stealing three golf clubs. A quote from the dissenting opinion of Justices Scalia and Thomas reads, "Ewing's sentence is, at a minimum, 2 to 3 times the length of sentences that other jurisdictions would impose in similar circumstances. That sentence itself is sufficiently long to require a typical offender to spend virtually all the remainder of his active life in prison."[49] Earlier cases, some of which were cited in the *Ewing* case, included a life sentence for stealing $310,[50] and a life sentence for sale of drugs.[51]

Until *Brown v. Plata* and other Supreme Court decisions following it, not only did the Supreme Court consistently refuse to overturn excessive prison sentences, it also refused to rule on the question of whether particular conditions in prisons violated the cruel and unusual clause.[52] For example, in 1979, the court overturned a lower federal court decision that found that numerous practices and conditions in a New York City detention center were cruel and unusual. These conditions included the following: the inmates were defendants awaiting trial, they were subject to unannounced searches, strip searches were conducted of friends and family, and Christmas packages were refused.[53]

The court made a similar decision in June 1981 when it rejected the opinion of a federal district court that double-celling in an Ohio state prison in cells designed for one constituted cruel and unusual punishment. The majority of the Supreme Court Justices concluded that

> the constitution does not mandate comfortable prisons, and prisons of [this] type which house persons convicted of serious crimes, cannot be free of discomfort.[54]

The court also refused to rule that brutality and violence in prisons constitute cruel and unusual punishment. In *Ingraham v. Wright* the court noted that, although prison brutality is part of the total punishment that an individual is subjected to for his crime and, as such, is a proper subject for Eighth Amendment scrutiny, nevertheless, the protection afforded by the Eighth Amendment is limited after incarceration; only the unnecessary and wanton infliction of pain constitutes cruel and unusual punishment.[55]

One might agree with the court that there is no compelling reason to make prisons comfortable. But the clear irony of the court's position was that it seemed to affirm the infliction of harsh conditions, especially violence, upon the inmates largely because they are by-products of prison itself, whereas if we specifically chose to apply a violent or harsh punishment on a criminal, then this would be unconstitutional, because it would be an act of "barbarous punishment." Is not the brutality of neglect just as barbaric as brutality with a purpose?[56] Furthermore, it is very clear that the actual pains suffered by inmates vary enormously from one to another.[57] That inmates undergoing the same prison terms have vastly different experiences of the pains of imprisonment is well established.[58] This means that offenders are punished differently for the same crimes.

The court's failure to conceive of the variety of possible punishments is well demonstrated in its assumption that all corporal punishments are the same, and that they are all synonymous with torture. We see this thinking expressed in the case of *Jackson v. Bishop*, decided December 9, 1968.[59] The case concerned an injunction brought against the superintendent of the Arkansas State Penitentiary to cease using the strap against prisoners for disciplinary purposes. The Court of Appeals held, among other things, that any use of the strap (even when due process of the Fourteenth Amendment was demonstrated) violated the Eighth Amendment of the Constitution that prohibits cruel and unusual punishment, simply because it was cruel. A final observation made by Justice Blackmun appeared to extend this decision to judicial corporal punishment as well as to its use in prisons:

> Neither do we wish to draw, in this context, any meaningful distinction between punishment by way of sentence statutorily prescribed and punishment imposed for prison disciplinary purposes. It seems to us that the 8th Amendment's proscription has applicability to both.[60]

The court ordered the superintendent of the Arkansas State Penitentiary to cease use of the strap.

Justice Blackmun's extension of this decision to include judicial corporal punishment is questionable for two reasons. First, the court itself, in arguing the same case, actually recognized that

> there is authority, some of it recent, with seemingly contrary indications. Certain of these cases rest on the presence of specific statutory provisions for corporal punishment for crime. [61]

In other words, the principle governing the right of states to establish their own laws and punishments was upheld, and certainly it was the main reason why the Supreme Court has been reluctant to find the excessive prison terms in cases described earlier to be cruel and unusual; it did not (could not?) interfere in the states' rights to legislate their own crimes and punishments.

Second, the court reviewed a lot of evidence against the use of corporal punishment, but none, it would seem, in favor of it. It referred to two "expert penologists" whose testimony "clearly demonstrated" that the use of the strap "in this day is unusual and we encounter no difficulty in finding that its use is cruel."

Yet the arguments that the court trotted out against corporal punishment were virtually the same as those used in the British Home Office study of 1938 and that by Caldwell in the 1940s, the many biases we encountered in chapter 5. Here is a summary of the court's arguments that are listed in the Blackmun commentary along with my responses to them:[62]

1. "Whipping creates penological problems and makes adjustment to society more difficult." There is no evidence to support this claim. Indeed, compared to prison, the difficulties of societal adjustment and penological problems created by corporal punishment pale into insignificance.

2. "Corporal punishment generates hate toward the keepers who punish and toward the system that permits it." Administered within a prison setting, no doubt this has occurred. But is it not the prison setting itself that generates the hatred, rather than corporal punishment?

3. "It [corporal punishment] is degrading to the punished and to the punisher alike." There is no evidence to support this view, especially concerning the punished. In fact, the British Home Office study found that, if anything, it added to the

pride of the prisoners who could demonstrate their manliness at being able to "take it."[63]

4. "Corporal punishment is easily subject to abuse in the hands of the sadistic and the unscrupulous." So is any other punishment. As a sentence, however, it cannot be abused in this way. The British Home Office study candidly noted that there was no evidence of excessive use of the birch or lash when used as a sentence.

5. "There can be no argument that excessive whipping or an inappropriate number of whippings or too great frequency of whipping or the use of studded or over long straps all constitute cruel and unusual punishment. But if whipping were to be authorized, how does one (or any court) ascertain the point that would distinguish the permissible from that which is cruel and unusual?" Agreed, this is a problem. But it applies to prison even more so, does it not? And although the Supreme Court had until *Brown v. Plata* recognized the difficulty in drawing the line between what is and is not an excessive prison term, it nevertheless has not been a problem of sufficient magnitude to justify finding prison per se cruel and unusual. Therefore, why apply this rule only to corporal punishments?

6. "Public opinion is obviously adverse." The court cites as evidence for this assertion the fact that only two states still permit the use of the strap and that a few states have expressly outlawed it. But public opinion polls show a sizable majority consistently supports corporal punishment.[64] The majority of people favor it in schools and at home in disciplining their children. So if it's OK for children, why not for criminals?[65] And in the polls conducted in regard to the Michael Fay case (see further below), a majority supported his corporal punishment.

In the mid to late nineteenth century, a number of American states affirmed the use of corporal punishment: whipping for wife beating in Maryland; sixty lashes for cattle stealing in New Mexico; flogging not unusual in Virginia.[66] And, in 1963, the Supreme Court of Delaware unanimously upheld the constitutionality of whipping, noting that punishments are only cruel and unusual if so designated by the will of the people expressed through the legislature.[67] The abolition of judicial corporal punishment was effected not by the courts but by legislation, both federal and state. However, it is quite clear that corporal punishment was not abolished because of legislation enacted to abolish it, but rather it began a steep decline, and only after it had become less commonly applied did legislatures act to abolish it, following, in most cases, the apparent "public will."

Coinciding with the steep decline of corporal punishment was an incredible increase in construction of monolithic prisons. There may be other reasons why legal flogging declined at various points and places in the United States, but it is likely that the early prison binge contributed considerably to it.[68] The overall decline in corporal punishment also coincided with the Civil War and abolition of slavery. The history of corporal punishment in relation to those two factors is yet to be written, though Michael Meranze provides an excellent analysis of the persistence of corporal punishment, whipping especially, on slaves, even as mass incarceration was under way.[69]

To get a clearer idea of the potential legality of MCP and how it compares to prison, let us look briefly at the main rules that various courts have used in deciding whether a particular punishment was cruel and unusual. These rules have mostly been derived from those stated in *Weems*, although a few decisions have tended to "modernize" them, adding a couple of new standards. This applies especially to the California courts. There are basically four rules.

First, the punishment must not be disproportionate and the courts adopted three criteria for assessing proportionality:

1. *It must not be out of proportion to the particular crime.* Since life terms have been held as OK for seemingly insignificant crimes, we must conclude that the Supreme Court, at least until *Brown v. Plata*, has not seen this rule as being all that important. It has, however, ruled that the *kind* of punishment may be excessive to the crime, as it did in *Coker*, where it ruled that the death penalty was excessive for the crime of rape.[70] If this is so, one may ask whether corporal punishment of a moderate amount would be deemed excessive for the crime of rape? Or not punishment enough?

2. *It must not be excessive in and of itself.* Since the Supreme Court has held that the death penalty, which is the ultimate

in corporal punishment, is not cruel and unusual when administered by states that guarantee due process, it is hard to see how corporal punishment of a lesser amount would be cruel and unusual, provided it were administered fairly and in proportion to the crime. The court's decision in *Bishop* was not justified. In fact, its decision amounts to a mere assertion that corporal punishment is "cruel." How can it find corporal punishment as cruel but not the death penalty?

3. *A punishment is considered excessive if it serves no penal purpose.* In the light of the vast amount of research on prisons concerning their lack of deterrent effects, it would appear that they perform no penal purpose beyond incapacitation, or at least their current purpose is much obscured. What is the penal purpose of corporal punishment? The essential purpose is clearly to inflict pain on the offender in retribution for an offense. The courts have recognized that retribution is a legitimate penal purpose.[71] MCP can achieve this far better for many crimes. Its penal purpose is clear and unequivocal. This certainly cannot be said of prison today, where it isn't even clear anymore whether offenders are being treated or punished.

Second, the punishment must not allow for the unrestrained use of power. In *Bishop*, the court painted a grim picture of the punisher standing over the punished, punishing to excess, often for minor infractions. It also noted that there was no way to prevent the unrestrained use of the strap by low-level personnel in such a setting, and that when the prison system had introduced rules for its application, they were often broken. Thus, corporal punishment, the court concluded, was too open to abuse of power.[72] But the court had it around the wrong way: because of its (necessarily) totalitarian structure, it is prison that is too open to abuse of power, such that any disciplinary methods used inside—whether it be solitary confinement, bread and water rations, or corporal punishment—is open to abuse by those who have the power. The fault does not lie in corporal punishment, as such; it lies in prisons, as such. Scandals of bodies being dug up in prisons have been rife at least since the beginning of the twentieth century. Yet the courts have consistently failed to link the "cruel and unusual" clause of the Eighth Amendment to prisons, preferring instead to dump it on corporal punishment. The bias rests on a serious historical fallacy: the court has assumed that, because the bloody punishments of the seventeenth century occurred at the same time as did the abuse of power by government officials, it was the bloody punishments that caused the abuse of power! Surely it is the other way around.

Third, the punishment must not be barbaric, cruel, or applied as torture. Prison, because of its totalitarian structure and capricious use of time, comes much closer to the definition of torture than does MCP. Yet the courts have consistently confused torture with corporal punishment, apparently on the blind assumption that any punishment that causes immediate bodily pain is "torture." We have seen that this is not the case. Torture essentially involves a process, one in which the notion of "due process," as stated in the Fourteenth Amendment, is absent, because interrogation, judgment, and punishment are all combined into one. Corporal punishment when used under conditions specified in this book, is not torture.

Is it cruel? Compared with prison, it is difficult to see how anyone could claim that corporal punishment is cruel, even though the Supreme Court seems to assume as much. Here again, one must distinguish carefully among the kinds of corporal punishments. All corporal punishments are certainly not the same, as we have seen. Two hours in the pillory being pelted with rotten eggs is vastly different from having one's hand cut off. Yet it is the bloody punishments of the seventeenth century that the courts have assumed to be typical of corporal punishments.

If corporal punishment can be shown not to cause any lasting damage to the body, except that it hurts (as we saw in the previous chapters), then how can one conclude that this punishment is cruel? When one adds up the special advantages MCP has over prison—that is, it is quicker, has fewer side effects, is easier to calibrate, and has many other humanitarian advantages—how could one claim that it is cruel?

Is it barbaric? The court has assumed all corporal punishments to be of the kind that were used in the seventeenth century, the bloody kinds of punishments. These, they say, are barbaric. But if this is so, are we to conclude that we have only risen from the state of barbarism in the last two hundred years, given that such barbaric punishments were used up until the end of the nineteenth century? Has "civilization" only become civilized so recently, and for the other 2,500 years we were in a state of barbarism? And, since almost all parents use corporal punishment at some time on their children, are they also barbaric?

It is convenient to simply hang a label on a punishment and claim that it is barbaric. As we saw in chapters 1 and 2 it is much more difficult to say why it is barbaric. The only way to do it is to claim that civilization is progressing towards some greater goal, and that what has gone before is, therefore, not as enlightened as what we do today. One need hardly mention that there are respectable theories about the relationship between progress and history that deny that civilization has made any progress at all![73] To label past punishments as barbaric in this sense is arrogant to say the least. It is the bias of modernism. Perhaps mass incarceration is more barbaric than a whipping post in every town square?

Fourth, punishment must conform to evolving standards of decency. In *Weems*, two ways of making this assessment were adopted. First, a comparison was made across different jurisdictions to see whether the same offenses were punished in about the same way. Presumably, if the majority of the states did not prescribe *cadena* for the offense at issue in *Weems*, then one could say that the Philippine law was out of step with evolving standards, and in this sense unusual. Similarly, one could compare the punishment for the offense with punishment for different offenses within the same jurisdiction, and if it seemed to be out of step or exceptional, then one could conclude that the punishment did not fit the crime.

One can, however, play games with these criteria, as did the court for *Rummel*. It found that many other jurisdictions prescribed life sentences for repeating felons. But the question it did not ask was: do other jurisdictions hand down life terms as punishment for the theft of $200? The notion of felony was assumed, in a magical way, to make comparisons across jurisdictions the same. But what constitutes a felony, and what does not, has been the subject of much argument for many years, so that many of the in-between crimes (which are the bulk of crimes) may be felonies in one jurisdiction and not in another.[74] The court's legal reasoning presumes that common practice represents, somehow, the peak of past progress. We have seen that this cannot be demonstrated. Second, it assumes that the laws of a particular time represent evolving standards of decency, when in fact there may be quite a gap between the public's views and those embodied in the law.[75]

It is a matter of options. The lobbying of twentieth-century reformers has eliminated the option of corporal punishment. If it were brought back, the chances are it would be welcomed by a majority of the people. Indeed, if the polls taken during and soon after the Michael Fay case are any indication, there was a substantial 50 percent of the American public in favor of corporal punishment of the type Fay received,[76] even though that type of punishment leaves scars on the body, which, by the way, would probably be sufficient for the Supreme Court to rule it as "cruel and unusual."[77]

The Supreme Court's tilt in *Brown v. Plata* towards a finding that excessive prison is cruel and unusual, introduces considerable complexity in trying to guess what it would do if faced with a case of judicially prescribed MCP, assuming, of course, Fourteenth Amendment protections. One hopes that the court will be forced eventually to examine more closely the specific kinds of corporal punishments that may be legally inflicted on an offender and compare these to those that are currently inflicted under the cloak of prison.

The introduction by the states of laws allowing MCP no doubt would be subject to careful scrutiny by the courts. However, because the Supreme Court is so unwilling to interfere with the states' rights to enact their own crimes and punishments, the chances are that such statutes would be upheld, provided the following guidelines, in addition to those required in any sentencing, were followed:[78]

- It must be demonstrated to have a sound penological purpose.

- It is authorized by legislation, but is not mandatory.

- Public opinion supports it.

- Extreme cruelty in execution of the punishment is prohibited (scarring, breaking of the skin, prolonged application of pain).

- It allows for alternative punishment or cessation, if the offender becomes physically or mentally unfit to receive the punishment.

- It is delivered by robot, eliminating the danger of human error and cruelty.

- It is medically supervised by a physician who is empowered to suspend the punishment if she deems it necessary.

- Fourteenth Amendment rights are protected along with other "human rights."

Incapacitation

If we take prison as the typical mode of incapacitation of criminals, we know that it so far has not been found cruel and unusual by the Supreme Court. However, the complaints of mass incarceration have forced the fact of its excessive use out into the open, and now the Supreme Court has given hints that too much prison may be cruel and unusual. Note, though, that the court has found that it is the excess (that is, disproportionality) that is unconstitutional, not mass incarceration (sometimes referred to as over-crowding) that is unconstitutional. So the chances of prison going away any time soon are very slim. Furthermore, it has been argued convincingly that embedded in the history of the Supreme Court's decisions on the excessive use of prisons has been the presumption of the court that the rehabilitative ideal—that criminals can be rehabilitated by prison—justifies its excessive use.[79] We see here the utilitarian ethic at work.

In any case, there are ways to incapacitate the terrible few without resorting to prison (OI), as we have seen in chapter 6, such as various kinds of physical restrain or incapacitation. What constitutional challenges would this innovative practice present?

This is entirely new territory. The closest cases and regulatory laws concerning use of physical restraint concern devices and techniques that are used in the following settings:

1. In mental institutions to restrain violent inmates[80]

2. During transportation to restrain violent criminals[81]

3. In schools or institutions to restrain disabled children or adults[82]

4. During a trial in the courtroom to restrain violent or poten-tially disruptive offenders[83]

Most cases focus on the equal protection clause of the US Constitution, that is, denial of due process. There have been no cases, as far as can be determined, that have examined whether the use of bodily constraint *as a punishment* would be unconstitutional. In fact, in the court cases, the restraints have generally been taken as necessary to protect restrained individ-uals from self and others (the caregivers, attendants, transportation officers, court bailiffs) from violence, and, in the case of criminals, to prevent their escape. Typical methods of restraint of offenders in transportation are hand and leg shackles, and in the courtroom a stun belt, a device not supposedly visible to the court, that the bailiff can monitor wirelessly and deliver some fifty thousand volts for up to five seconds. The California Supreme Court found that the use of the stun belt did not interfere with the defendant's

Fourteenth amendment right to a fair trial (his courtroom demeanor was not affected by wearing it—the device was not activated), though other state courts have banned their use.[84] The US Supreme Court has yet to rule on this issue.

The stun belt has been manufactured and in service in the US since the 1990s. In 1996, Amnesty International designated it as a torture device that was "in direct contravention of international standards on the treatment of prisoners," a violation of human rights. But what are human rights?

Bodily Punishment and Human Rights

Supposedly human rights, as a collection of principles that transcend nation states, apply universally to humans everywhere. They are enshrined in various statements and conventions of the United Nations. As such, however, they are subject to the manipulation and interpretation of those countries that may at particular times in history dominate the conventions of the United Nations. It is only very recent that the UN has condemned the United States practice of mass incarceration as a violation of human rights.[85] The UN pronouncements on the extent to which or whether at all corporal punishment violates basic human rights is limited, though as we saw in chapter 3 it has had a lot to say about torture and often confused torture with corporal punishment. Further, since judicial corporal punishment is deemed not to exist in the United States, one must presume that its condemnation by the United Nations as a human rights violation applies to countries that currently use corporal punishment, which means, generally, Islamic countries, particularly those that follow Shari'a law. A number of human rights violations typically brought against Shari'a law, would arguably apply to the United States if it introduced judicial corporal punishment. The two most common are the ban on cruel or degrading punishments and the death penalty.[86]

The International Covenant on Civil and Political Rights and other international conventions and treaties outlaw degrading or inhuman and cruel punishment. However, the definitions vary considerably across conventions. The UN Convention against Torture even avoids defining what degrading, cruel, and inhuman punishment is. This leaves the door open for advocates of Shari'a law to claim that its punishments do not violate this human rights principle. Further, in 2003, the UN Commission on Human Rights redefined this principle, making it considerably softer: "Corporal punishment, including of children, can amount to cruel, inhuman or degrading punishment or even to torture."[87] The infliction of the death penalty, cruel punishments, or life imprisonment of children is forbidden by various international conventions on human rights, but the United Nations has failed to achieve its abolition, managing to pass only a moratorium on use of the death penalty, a resolution that was most recently reaffirmed in 2014.[88]

Rudolph Peters in his book *Crime and Punishment in Islamic Law* identifies a number of basically procedural issues that are related not so much to the use of corporal punishment but to the system of law followed by Shari'a.[89] The tendency, however, has been to emphasize these claimed violations of human rights as somehow the product or expression of the barbarity of corporal punishments applied in Shari'a law. The procedural human rights violations—the products of Western principles—he identifies as applied to Islamic law are as follows:

- *No punishment without law*—an enshrined principle embodied in all Western legal systems that requires that no person can be punished without having been found guilty of a crime, that is, a crime clearly legislated by the state. This is a *sine qua non* for any criminal procedure. However, crimes are not defined by the state in Islamic countries unless they have been codified under previous imperial rule. They are defined by legal scholars (via the Qur'an and other religious texts) who may also be mullahs (priests) interpreting the word of the Qur'an or *hadd*. So one can argue that "no punishment without law" does not apply under pure Islamic law, since the word "law" means something quite different in Islam.

- *Due process.* The Fourteenth Amendment of the US Constitution demands that all people regardless of race, gender, or any other attribute are equal before the law. Under Shari'a law, however, the testimony of a man is worth twice as much as that of a woman; in retaliatory offenses, such as *hadd*, testimony by women is not admitted at all. When women report rape, in some jurisdictions this report is simply interpreted as a confession of unlawful sexual activity on the part of the woman. In respect to homicide, a woman is worth half that of a man if blood money is chosen as the punishment. Finally, a husband is expressly permitted to kill his wife and her lover if he catches them in the act. Different rights also pertain to

Muslims and non-Muslims. Testimony of non-Muslims is not permitted in court, and generally non-Muslims are treated similarly to women.

- *Freedom of religion.* The Qur'an does not permit freedom of religion or free speech. Apostasy, that is, practicing a religion other than Islam, is generally punishable by death. A big problem with this "crime" is that it is vaguely defined and may be inferred from "utterances."

Defenders of Shari'a law bristle at these criticisms, arguing that they represent an imperialist view of crime, punishment, and law, and that they reflect the double standard of the West. They argue forcefully that the United States and other Western nations are in clear contravention of the cruel and inhuman punishment prohibition, as evidenced by their excessive use of incarceration, the existence of such places as the Guantanomo Bay prison, the retention of the death penalty by some Western countries, including its application to juveniles, and the shocking number of persons incarcerated without trial (awaiting trial), throughout parts of Europe, particularly France.[90]

The important point to understand is that the procedural violations of human rights should not be confused with the actual types of punishment administered. Any punishment, whether corporal or not, may be exacerbated by procedural injustices. Yet it is also very clear that certain types of punishment, especially the vague, uncontrollable types of punishment, like prison, are much more likely to invite procedural injustices and abuse. The simple, clean, uncomplicated administration of MCP, accompanied by swift implementation by robot, offers far superior procedural human rights safeguards compared to prison.

In sum, not all corporal punishments or bodily incapacitations are cruel, though the US Supreme Court has never addressed the latter issue. An enlightened view reveals that there are many different kinds of corporal punishments and incapacitations, some cruel, some not, but that all corporal punishments, in fact all punishments, are always prone to excess, hence cruelty. Their careful legal regulation is certainly necessary to avoid such abuse. In Brown v Plata, the US Supreme Court has at last signaled that excessive use of punishment is probably cruel.[91] If and when legislatures and courts comprehend the distinctly humane and economic advantages of MCP, perhaps it will begin to address the greatest human rights violation of the past fifty years, mass incarceration.

Shari'a law is fast becoming more visible to the West as the massive migration of Muslims from North Africa and elsewhere to Western countries continues with no sign of abatement. It is foreseeable that there will come a day when Islamic punishments are no longer "unusual" in Western societies that contain large Muslim populations, opening the door to a more flexible view of corporal punishment's role as a response to crimes. There is, of course, a long way to go, given the accusations of human rights violations of Shari'a law, as outlined in the preceding discussion. Though, as we have seen, those accusations are easily turned back on the accusers, who must defend mass incarceration, which is the product of the Western system of criminal justice.

As for the terrible few, we would do well to note again the very low (by comparison) prison rates in Islamic countries. Are we to assume that there are fewer of the worst of the worst criminals in Shari'a law countries? Or do we conclude that most of them have been punished and are living among ordinary citizens? Or killed by the death penalty? Or joined a terrorist group where killing is encouraged and rewarded? If the latter, though, we would expect the worst of the worst to join the army in Western countries, would we not?[92]

Chapter Ten

The End of Punishment (as We Know It)

Punishment Redistributed in a Century of Surveillance

In the twenty-first century, we live in a surveillance society, that surveillance conditioned on economic activity, especially markets. And more and more, it is algorithms and robots that drive this dynamic. We should view crime and punishment within that context. The literati of the twentieth century criticized Bentham for designing a prison, the Panopticon, where all prisoners could be watched day and night. Indeed, many blamed Bentham's model for the growth of state surveillance. A deep state perhaps comes close to that. But twenty-first-century society is anything but that. People no longer care about their privacy, as they did in the twentieth century. Social media has demonstrated that, as has reality TV (a star of which is now a US president).

What the enlightenment thinkers did not count on was that the surveillance of individuals would appear on two fronts: the state and the private, or, more precisely, the corporate sector. The twenty-first-century fear is that these two may combine to create a massive surveillance capability. The attempt in 2016 by the FBI to force Apple to give up its encryption of a cell phone is indicative of this trend. The demands of various US government agencies on Google, Facebook, AT&T and Verizon, and others to open their extensive files of their customers also point to the danger that, while individuals have given up much of their privacy to make their lives easier (shopping, communicating, expressing themselves, amusing themselves), the question remains whether governments will be able to restrain themselves—or be restrained by their subjects, the people who are highly ambivalent about what they want. Further, as I write this, the balance of power to control may be shifting away from government and into the hands of enormously powerful giant information collectors who use their troves of information and media reach to censor or control what information its users receive. It is no accident that the first object of any revolution is always to take over the media.

It is against this vast sea change in the structures and mechanisms of governmental powers that we must view the future of criminal punishment. Our robotic capabilities and surveillance techniques are far greater in this century, able to track and control all individuals who have committed crimes and who are undergoing punishment. We no longer need to bunch them up in a prison. We have many other options, including embedding criminal punishment within market economies, disentangling it from the state, bringing it back to the people—by which I mean all individuals, separately, acting on their own volition.

This is a radically different view of criminal punishment. Does it have a future?

1984 Redux

At the dawn of the twenty-first century, much of the context of George Orwell's *1984* surrounds us. Newspeak dominates the airwaves, political correctness mimics the strict thought control overseen by Big Brother, individual or independent thought is called hate speech, and deep state, in collusion with social media, collects private information of its citizens. One could go on. But perhaps the most horrible scene of *1984* was where Winston's fear of rats was used to torture him. Big Brother knew all of Winston's secret life, including his nightmares about rats. His captors strapped a cage around his head and threatened to release rats to eat his face off. Note of course, that this was a torture, not a punishment. The aim was to break his will, reduce him to a docile, thoroughly obedient believer in the Party. And as we saw in chapter 3, the threat was more than enough to do the job. Winston was defined as one of the terrible few, and it took a terrible threat of torture to "cure" him. This was a clever literary device, of course, used to convince the reader that it was Winston who was "right and moral" and the Big Brother society that was evil and wrong. It was Winston's sacred right to privacy that was destroyed; his most cherished idea of who he was. Torture destroyed him as a person; he became, one might say, a mere robot, no longer able to think for himself: the classic function of torture.

Much of this worrisome picture of society appears to ring true today—except for one thing. The advent of social media has revealed one puzzling truth: many people actually seek to display their most private lives to all. Privacy is not as sacred as those who bought the Orwellian scenario assumed.[1] While we complain that Google, Facebook, Amazon, and other major digital companies collect more and more information about our everyday lives, we happily go along with all this. It makes our shopping choices more interesting, more efficient, people appear to enjoy having Amazon suggest to them what they might like, remind them what they bought months ago. Mind you, customers are offered the option to opt out of being tracked. One suspects that most do not.

Furthermore, the market economies in which we lead our daily lives provide us with a freedom that Orwell could never have imagined. The fear engendered by Orwell was that we would all be turned into unthinking robotic slaves of the state, unable to think for ourselves. The crass moral arrogance of social media and fake media notwithstanding, none of us will be turned into robots by the state, as happened to Winston, whose brain was subdued by torture of the worst kind. On the contrary, we should see that we can indeed make use of real robots to do our bidding, to be our slaves, if you like, to do our punishment for us. And we should allow individuals to administer this punishment on themselves, at their discretion, controlled by algorithms developed by government in conjunction with the private sector.

In sum, we do not need a prison to administer punishment and keep criminals under surveillance.[2] Robots can now do that, and they can do it by embedding criminal punishment within our everyday lives, lives that are themselves embedded in market economies. This perspective introduces us to a radically different way of viewing criminals and their punishment, one to which I briefly alluded in chapter 8.

Normalizing Punishment

For the majority of offenders, MCP should be applied with the aim of making MCP an everyday occurrence, something like paying a speeding fine. The spectacle and ritual of punishment as it has long continued should be left to the movies, theater, and video games. Taking one's punishment should be like writing a check, or perhaps like "taking one's medicine" (when medicine tasted something awful).

In his wonderful science fiction book *Erewhon*, first published in 1872, Samuel Butler describes how the professional punishers ("straighteners") in this imaginary world, make house calls when called upon by the those suffering from an illness. In *Erewhon*, crime was viewed as an illness, and illness as crime. Following the logic of this mischievous dichotomy, doctors behaved like law enforcers whose job was to administer prescribed punishments for those who had suffered the sickness of committing a crime. The offenders (the morally sick) would call on the "straighteners" to come to their home, diagnose their crime/illness, and then carry out a regimen of punishment that invariably involved a good flogging and, for serious crimes/illnesses, bread and water diet. The flogging was administered in the offender's home, typically in a room reserved for the punishment, sometimes the offender's bedroom. These punishments were treated as "normal" and the offender's friends and family would call on him to see how he was doing. He in turn greatly enjoyed their visits and well wishes.

Viewed in this light, who among us has not suffered the punishment of a traffic or parking fine? Various studies have shown that, at a minimum, one in three persons who drive a car will get a ticket at some time in their lives. The average number of people who receive speeding tickets in the United States per day is 112,000 and the annual number of people who receive speeding tickets, as of 2015, is 41,000,000.[3] Furthermore, philosopher and legal scholar Douglas Husak has shown that more than 70 percent of all people have committed an offense for which they could be jailed![4] It is likely, wouldn't you say that everyone has broken the law at some time in their lives? Think about it. Be honest, now!

In modern society a traffic stop is a "normal" occurrence, a great nuisance, and often a costly one. Those with the money may call a lawyer, who will make the charge go away or plead it down to a lesser offense, one that does not include "points." In many jurisdictions, those who do not want the stress of standing before a judge in the banal chaos of traffic court, may plead guilty online and pay the fine with a credit card or a check. Ancillary punishments may follow when insurance companies then raise one's insurance premium. Here we have three very important characteristics of modern punishment. First, it is possible to pay a surrogate (a lawyer) to basically bear part of the punishment by appearing before a judge. Second, private parties such as insurances companies may piggyback on the punishment by levying additional "fines" (fees). Third, with the modern deployment of traffic cameras, the actual confrontation between offender (you or I) and the state (traffic cop) disappears. Instead, the confrontation appears when one receives an infraction notice in the mail. The punishment has been bureaucratized. Why not make all crimes, except the absolutely most serious, like this?

The bureaucratic state is, of course, the quintessence of civilizations— invented by the Romans as they learned to administer their sprawling empire. Unfortunately, while traffic crime has been well bureaucratized, regular crime has not, except in one very serious respect. Prisons have become monoliths of bureaucracy. All developed countries of the world have huge prison systems, usually referred to as departments of corrections, or, made infamous by Solzhenytsin, gulags. Social scientists have long observed that one overriding feature of bureaucracies is that they serve first and foremost themselves. They develop a life of their own. Thus it is with prisons. Which is why, in the long run, reducing them in size or proportions is very unlikely. The only solution is to replace them with a different kind of bureaucracy, one that mimics that for collecting traffic fines. One that treats most crime as "normal"—that is, "There but of the grace of God go I."

We must understand that criminal laws are legislated with the expecta- tion that they will be broken. They are made on the assumption that anyone in society may break them, not just a terrible few. The majority of crimes that we legislate are there for ordinary people to commit. The majority of offenders are not sick or deranged. They simply break the laws when they see (mistakenly or not) advantage for doing so, or when provided with an opportunity that is difficult to pass up. Automobiles are manufactured and marketed as having great acceleration, high maximum speeds. Yet it is against the law in most countries to drive them at their maximum speed. We manufacture many very powerful drugs. Yet it is against the law to consume them as one wants. The most wonderful and lethal guns are manufactured. Yet there are many laws restricting their ownership and use. Opportunity causes most crime, not evil disposition. And the legislation of crimes creates the opportunity for breaking the law. I know this seems cynical. But one cannot escape the formidable logic of law making and law breaking.

It follows that for the majority of crimes, a dose of pain, depending on the legislated severity of the crime, is enough, so long as it is prescribed and administered carefully, with as much control as possible, but, more importantly, can be self-administered in the privacy of one's own home. Many people have their own blood pressure device, treadmill, or exercise machine. Why not also have a punishment machine that is linked to a monitoring center (yes, surveillance, already occurring with exercise machines of various kinds) that can keep track of the punishment administered and report this accordingly to the bureaucratic punishment system? Call it a corrections department if you like. So long as it does not administer a prison system.

There is one caveat here. We know in the case of traffic cameras that politicians have been unable to resist the temptation to use them as a revenue raising tool. The result is speed traps and other techniques that create opportunities for infraction to multiply so that the revenue from fines soars. It is important to understand that this criticism of speed cameras (on the part of us citizens, not on the part of politicians who love them) is a criticism that is specific to this type of punishment—monetary fine. Politicians can do lots of things with big pots of money. They can do little with big pots of MCP.

Admittedly, there is always the danger in any bureaucracy of going to excess, especially if that bureaucracy is not held accountable for its actions. And we have already seen that there is a universal tendency to take all kinds of punishment to excess, if its administrators are not held accountable. The secrecy of the punishment of prison feeds irresponsibility and leads to excess. If punishment is applied by the offender on himself in his own home, it is unlikely that this will lead to excess (with some individual exceptions, perhaps). A prison is part of a bureaucracy. A private home is not (not yet, anyway). Admittedly, under the robotic system, the private home is under surveillance, but this type of surveillance is not more than that incurred by having a telephone account or Internet connection. Strictly speaking, in the postmodern world, there is no privacy.

Transition: Body for Prison

Regular criminals incarcerated (those not in solitary confinement or super-max prisons) should be removed from prison and corporally punished by robot to the commensurate amount as indicated by their prison sentence, reduced by the amount of time they have already served. Scales of intensity and frequency of MCP would need to be constructed, of course. A criminal with ten actual years left to serve (taking into account the various reductions that may apply) would need to be matched by a set number of shock units, one sitting a week, for, say one month or less, depending on the intensity and number of shocks administered in each sitting. In comparison, an individual with just one year left to serve may receive MCP accordingly and be freed immediately. In general, the rule should be that increasing the intensity of the shock (that is, how much a one-time application hurts) should reduce the length of time over which punishment units are administered. Some experimentation would be needed. Again, a general rule could be that the criminal may elect to shorten the time over which his punishment is received by increasing the severity of the punishment applied in each punishment session.

Using the formula we developed earlier for administering a standard punishment unit (SPU), conversion of a prison term would look something like this:

> 1 month in prison = 1 SPU
> 12 months = 12 PSUs
> 5 years = 60 PSUs

The sessions could be administered daily, weekly, or monthly at judicial discretion, tailored to meet each individual case. A sentence of five years in prison could, in principle, be converted into a day of, say, five sessions of 12 SPUs, or spread out to a year of five sessions per month. By "judicial discretion," of course, I mean whatever algorithms inform the robot that will be making the decision and calculation.[5.]

The New Normal

If we continue the line of thinking to normalize punishment, we are led to some amazing and maybe shocking possibilities. If we take the idea of "normalizing" seriously, what, then, is the "new normal" that we may apply? Here, I offer, partly in jest, but also seriously, ideas that in some cases reflect the normality (including hypocrisy, the base element of civilized punishment) of society's application of criminal punishment.

Consider crime insurance. The socialist government of New Zealand offers crime-victim insurance to all its citizens, though the insurance covers the person victimized, not the offender. In varying degrees, compensation by the governments of various states of the United States and other developed countries is offered to victims of crime. The criteria for coverage, of course, depend on the facts of the case, especially an assessment of the relationship, if any, between the victim and offender (some crimes may be victim precip-itated). Note here, though, that Shari'a law already allows victims to play a direct role in the punishment of the offender for most personal crime.

But why not provide offender insurance? Corporations in many ways already have this when they insure against a wide range of risks, many including the costs of government regulation of their activities, their costs of doing business. Why should not individuals also be allowed to take out crime insurance to cover them when they commit a crime?[6] Think carefully about this. Insurance does, of course, turn every risk into money. Which leads to the next outrageous idea.

Think of punishment as a commodity. Given the transformation of punishment into shock units according to the formula I outlined in chapters 7 and 8, why not allow people to trade in punishment units as they do any other commodity? There are two fascinating options here. Punishment units could be traded as bitcoin and other private (nongovernment) monetary systems. Privately owned and operated courts could deliver sentences to offenders. Or, a government entity could supervise and fix the initial value of the shock unit. A sentence issued by a court, therefore, would in point of fact be like printing money, except the value created would be shock units. In the punishment commodity market, punishment units would be bought and sold like any other commodity. At some point, though, as with every commodity, the shock unit would have to be consumed. In the case of criminal punishment, the units are attached to the individual offender who committed the crime. What I am suggesting here is something similar to the market-based system used to regulate environmental pollution by corporations.[7] You may think I am nuts. But if it is okay for regulating what many call corporate crime (willful pollution) why not for common crime? Note that the actual punishment that the offender may eventually experience will depend on the value of the shock units at the time of punishment. A punishment trader may be able to get a very good price or a bad price, depending on the market. If this sounds ridiculous, how does it compare to the current punishment horse-trading done between lawyer, prosecutor, judge, and client, better known as "plea bargaining," the outcomes of which are mostly fixed in favor of the prosecutor, the trading conducted within a market that is fixed in the prosecutor's favor in most cases. While I am not an economist, I also think that a market approach to punishment would work against punishment excess, because the more goods you put on the market, the cheaper they become, that is, their value drops.

A few hints for offenders or would-be offenders. Consider buying up punishment in advance either on the market or taking punishment in advance just in case you need it. If you are lucky enough to be arrested for a crime, you may do well to plea up and bank the excess to use next time, should you happen to offend again. If you bank up a lot of punishment units you could also consider a part-time job as an independent contractor to act as a surrogate for someone else's criminal punishment.

Allow surrogates. Those who have money may hire the best defense attorneys; those who do not, get the court appointed one. Is that fair? Especially when the punishment is going to be painful? In a market-based punishment system, there is no prosecutor or defense attorney and preferably no judge. It is all robotic, trial included. Algorithms rule. But let's be serious here. We have seen that all people, whether rich or poor, black or white, experience pain about the same. Yet, I am guessing that there may be some people who, for whatever reason (maybe they're poor, maybe they like getting punished, experiencing pain) will volunteer to be punished on another person's behalf. Rich people (or those who can afford it) could hire them for such a purpose, and these would take the punishment on the offender's behalf. And if the offender had no money, perhaps those who wish to do good for crime could donate their services and undergo the offender's punishment for him (dare I suggest that this would be the quintessential Christian solution to punishment?). Of course, the value of the punishment units received on behalf of the offender, would be tax deductible as a charitable donation. Finally, in the case of penniless offenders who are much loved by their families, another family member may, if he or she so desired, take the punishment on behalf of the family member. Perhaps parents may prefer to take the punishment instead of their children, or even vice versa.

Share the punishment. Some (Durkheim, for example) argue that punishment is a necessary force to keep society from breaking apart—not a commodity but a shared resource, such as water and air.[8] If this is the case, it doesn't really matter who is punished or for what, so long as it is carried out. Some would add that it should also be shared equally and justly. We can see here a problem with the relationship, or lack thereof, between equality and justice. If equality is the dominant principle, then all people, regardless of what they have done or regardless of whether they "deserve" it, should cop some punishment. Yet justice is not served, because knowing people as we do, some deserve punishment more than others, do they not? If justice is demanded, then the punishment should be distributed randomly, so that all have a chance to participate, and fate (roll of the dice) is the judge. This scenario forms the basis of the well-known short story *The Lottery*, by Shirley Jackson. Codified criminal laws are designed to counteract fate, but both scenarios of punishment depend on elaborate ritual.

What about a punishment score? If you want to take out a mortgage or lease a car, your credit score suddenly becomes important. Many resent the infringement on one's privacy that the credit scores represent, and they are often looked on as being more insidious because they are constructed and tracked by private companies. But because Western society is founded on debt (unlike Islamic societies that build capital without charging interest, the latter a crime of usury under Shari'a law) it is inevitable that such massive accumulations of information upon the economic behavior of every individual who wants to participate in Western society becomes absolutely necessary, as is the inevitable demise of cash, the last bastion of the anonymous buyer and seller. Finally, the paying of taxes of many kinds to many state and federal entities also creates a massive trove of information accumulated on each individual's financial life. In fact taxation (seriously pioneered by the Romans) is the lifeblood of Western civilizations, maybe all civilizations. The Internal Revenue Service of the United States is feared by many, especially those who dutifully pay their taxes. The IRS has few legal constraints on what it can do to spy on and punish individuals who do not pay their taxes. Due process exists, but in a withered form.

Recent legislation in the United States has denied or made it very difficult for companies to use the criminal record of an applicant for a job as a reason to deny employment. Law enforcement agencies maintain records of criminal offenses for their own purposes, usually to help solve crimes on the assumption that once a person has committed a crime the chances are that he will commit another. Those records, however, are notoriously incomplete, mainly because they depend on information that must be collected from a wide variety of disconnected agencies: police, courts, prosecutors, corrections departments, all of these existing as different entities at the federal, state, and local levels.

Under the proposed system of robotic punishment, administered like any other economic transaction, the self-administration of robotic punishment can be easily tracked, and punishment dossiers in the form of an accumulated score of punishment units could be easily computed. How a prospective employer would view a punishment score is a matter of conjecture. On the one hand, that a person has taken on a lot of punishment might indicate that he is a dutiful and obedient citizen. On the other hand, a high punishment score may indicate a propensity to commit too many infractions. But given that punishment units are tradable and marketable, there is no way to use someone's punishment score either for or against the individual. Surely, this is a good thing as far as individual liberty is concerned. The punishment score is therefore a source of information to an individual to show her progress as a citizen, just like a bank account or credit score. This is no longer a figment of the imagination. China (predictably) has announced that it will construct social credit scores of all its citizens and punish them accordingly by denying them use of various public utilities such as transportation, when their credit score falls to an unsatisfactory level.[9]

Incapacitation

I have argued for the adoption of techniques of incapacitation that do not depend on prison. These were mainly forced addiction on a drug similar to heroin (but not heroin) for which the horrible criminal must depend on the authorities for constant maintenance. This is done without a prison, the offender maintained in his own home, as the case may be. The second, equally controversial, was induced coma for whatever number of years, according to prevailing criminal laws.

Both these methods of incapacitation will be expensive to maintain. Induced coma would probably cost as much as currently it costs to house the terrible few on death row or in maximum security prisons. And if prison is any example, the risks of escalation are real and would need to be countered by making the homes of those subjected to incapacitation open to public scrutiny. Members of the public would be allowed to view these persons by appointment, and an open house scheduled on a regular basis. The importance of public scrutiny cannot be overstated: it will prevent excess and work against the natural inclination to ignore the plight of these terrible few, making sure that they are treated with respect and care. The punishment is incapacitation and only incapacitation. Every effort should be made to minimize the side effects or overflow effects of the punishment. Should the offender's family want to do all the caregiving of the offender, this should be allowed, once the family members or close associates have received the necessary training to do so.

Admittedly, this ultimate solution of substituting open incapacitation for prison begins to look a little like "treatment" instead of punishment. One may ask, where is the pain in induced coma? This solution to prison runs counter to my argument in this book that the central ingredient of punishment is and must be pain, and only that. It is a paradox of sorts, but it does have a solution for those who are inclined to intensify the punishment side of incapacitation by coma. For example, why not wake the terrible criminal up and let him see for a short period (the length of the punishment would have to be determined according to the seriousness of his offense) what he's missing?

I have argued also throughout this book that the utilitarian justification for punishment that justifies incapacitation is a dangerous one, always tilting to excess, often hidden behind what might be called "good intentions" such as treatment. I do not make this exception to my argument lightly, but I cannot see any other way around the problem of what to do with the terrible few. As it is, we are constantly faced with the even more challenging defect of the utilitarian ethic, which will be (and already is) the tendency to define more and more offenders as the worst of the worst. The only solution I can see in this would be to legislate a maximum number of the terrible few beyond which we cannot go. However, cost does not seem to be a problem in dealing with this class of offender, so I acknowledge that this would be very difficult to achieve.

Today, the terrible few are housed in supermaximum prisons that have flourished for the last few decades, at enormous cost to the taxpayer. The supermax prison, of course, is totally and completely out of public view, drawing occasional articles in magazines and newspapers, but rarely under scrutiny. As I have repeated many times, making the punishment open to scrutiny is the only way to ensure that some limit will eventually be placed on the punishment of the terrible few. Unfortunately, the supermax demands the opposite.

The increased use of the supermax is certainly cause for worry, since it would suggest that the numbers among us who are dangerous, the terrible few, are growing, though it's impossible to tell. In any case, I can't claim to solve all the problems of our criminal justice system and can only hope that eventually good sense will prevail and that, at least when we decide to incapacitate the body of an individual for his or her terrible crimes, that the form of incapacitation may in whole or in part be reversed should it turn out that wrongful conviction occurred or some other mistake was made. A stretch of prison can never be taken back. Admittedly, losing a few years of life in an induced coma can't be made up for either, in the case of wrongful conviction, but at least the individual will not have the horrible memories of the violence and shame of prison to weigh him down for the rest of his life.

In sum, this book has established general rules as to the limits to which we may go in trying to match crimes to their deserved punishments, including the limits on punishment when it is used to deter future crimes. The uncompromising moral demand, in the name of compassion, that we exclude all harm from punishment comes at a great price: the separation of the actual facts of punishment from its legislative, judicial, and public comprehension. The real effects of modern-day punishment are unavoidably destructive, in many cases violent. Prison is the product of this compassionate morality, leading inevitably to mass incarceration.

The application of MCP by robot, an acute temporary corporal punishment, is an ideal mix of the concrete elements of retribution and the civilizing process of using precise, numerically based punishments. There is the possibility that MCP may in some cases even deter criminals and potential criminals from committing future crimes. The robotic administration of MCP reduces both human error and eliminates the violence that historically has accompanied the administration of corporal punishment.

The ultimate aim should be the complete abolition of prison, for even if prisons are retained for the terrible few, their very nature, as we have seen, will inevitably lead to their expansion and mass incarceration all over again. This means that, even for the worst of the worst offenders, incapacitation without walls should be introduced, varied according to the dangerousness of each case and severity of the offender's criminal record.

A great deal of experimentation and research will be needed in order to completely abolish prison. There will be the strong temptation to retain it at least in the form of local jails for particular criminals, such as child or spouse abuse, where there may be a real need to incapacitate the offender so that he can do no further harm. Ways of restraining such individuals will be needed, particularly in respect to tracking their locations. In general, also, these offenders are not the terrible few, though they are dangerous to particular individuals. In these cases a combination of MCP and incapacitation may, regrettably, be necessary. There are already laws available that allow restraining orders. Incapacitating and confining technologies should be applied and used for as long as it takes, and jails avoided at all cost.

The bad press that traditional corporal punishment has received as a result of the mass and social media portrayals of the horrendous punishments of Shari'a law and the abuses of Abu Ghraib prison make it very difficult for any sane solution to criminal punishment of the twenty-first century to gain acceptance. Those who are outraged by my proposal to use MCP by robots no doubt will call it "electrocution," which commonly conjures up an image of the electric chair, the dreadful killing of a person by an outrageous amount of electricity, enough to "fry" the offender. This book does not advocate any such punishment and argues strongly against the excessive use of any punishment.

Mass incarceration is a cancer on our society and a clear violation of human rights. Robotic MCP, while it may violate the body (minimally), does not violate human rights by any stretch of the imagination, especially compared to prison. Like washing machines and automobiles, the chores of criminal punishment can be assumed by robots, freeing us from this horrible burden of violent punishment that has undermined civilizations East and West since the beginning of time. Furthermore, the use of modern technologies of bodily incapacitation and surveillance make it possible to punish even the worst of the worst in a humane way, without the torture of maximum incarceration and solitary confinement.

If we think of criminal punishment in terms of markets, one would have to admit that in the United States and similar Western countries we are experiencing hyperinflation of punishment. The prison bureaucratic complex is a monopoly that needs to be broken up so that there will be more competition in types of punishment on offer, so that individuals may gain control of it for their own use, avoiding bureaucratic excess, taking on direct responsibility for the punishment that is applied to those who have broken the law.

The key to humane and restrained criminal punishment is to normalize it, make it less of a big deal, more of a nuisance rather than a catastrophe, have it intrude on the individual lives of people as little as possible, to empower people to apply the punishment to themselves. To keep, as far as humanly and socially possible, a third party out of the punishment equation. And if there must be a third party, let it be a robot.

I can understand the frustration, even anger, of those readers who will see that the logic underlying my argument to abolish prisons and replace them with MCP and OI is unassailable yet absolutely unacceptable. The logic of my argument is the same as it is for holding automobiles responsible for some 37,000 deaths in the United States every year in car accidents. There is no call for the abolition of automobiles. We have a deep attachment to automobiles and rarely acknowledge that it has such a price. And, as with prison, there is an obsessive concern with car safety (that is, prison reform, rehabilitation, prisoner reentry), ignoring the fact that, although injury and death may be reduced somewhat through car safety, it is their very existence that causes so may deaths. The attachment to cars, however, is only about one hundred years old. We have an even deeper attachment to punishment, so will very likely not give it up for a long time. Technology holds the key. Very soon there will be many driverless cars, hopefully one day no cars with humans driving them, which will result in a substantial reduction in road deaths (by elimination of human error).[10]

The analogy to the history of the automobile is instructive. The automobile in its infancy, especially in the middle of the twentieth century, came to be seen as an icon of liberty, the idea of driving off into the unknown, the wind blowing in one's hair. Free at last! Novels such as Kerouac's *On the Road*, movies such as *Thelma and Louise*, and the steadfast resistance to seat belts signified this feeling of liberty. Not anymore. With GPS, EasyPass, speed cameras, car registration, drivers' licenses, insurance requirements, and increasingly restrictive speed limits, that liberty has gone. We have seen over the past fifty years or so a steep increase of state control over people's lives through substantial regulation in all areas of life.[11] The argument in favor of all this regulation is that it keeps us safe, saves lives. Or, to recall the Enlightenment thinking, each of us gives up a little of our liberty in order to enjoy it in a safe society. This contrasts with Durkheim's view that we punish the few in order to feel safe ourselves. The logic of this idea of punishment is that the more we punish the few, the safer we will feel. But we can see the serious flaw in this idea of punishment: humans are a weak lot. They will punish others as much as they can in order to feel safe themselves, all the time justifying it as in the name of society (you will recognize this as the utilitarian ethic of general deterrence). Thus, we have mass incarceration.

If we think of punishment as a form of moral capital, perhaps its redistribution might be in order, at least in terms of each of us taking on the responsibility for bearing a small amount of punishment, rather than heaping all of the punishment on to a statistical few who are locked up and out of sight. It may not come in my lifetime, but maybe by the end of the twenty-first century, we will be able to normalize punishment by (1) shifting the responsibility for its administration primarily to robots, thereby reducing the amount of damage done by criminal punishment that reveals the darkest side of humans, prison; and (2) shifting responsibility secondarily to us, individually, in our homes, thereby acknowledging the actual effects of punishment on ourselves and others in everyday life.

Finally, let me offer twelve steps that will bring us closer to just, fair, humane, nonincarcerating criminal punishment:

1. Understand that criminal punishment is the intentional infliction of pain by the state on an offender for an offense.

2. Accept that humans are an obstreperous, recalcitrant, and disobedient lot—at least, that is how they are depicted

in the Old Testament and the Qur'an—so infractions are inevitable.

3. Understand that rules, in the form of prohibitions and criminal laws, are made to be broken, literally. That is, they cannot exist without their concomitant punishments. Punishment makes the rule of law possible.

4. Acknowledge that forgiveness, as depicted in the New Testament, is not possible without the prior existence of defined wrongs; otherwise, there would be nothing to forgive.

5. Believe that punishment induces shame in both the punisher and the punished, because forgiving and hurting are the two competing motivations that condition the satisfaction of punishment.

6. Understand that matching a punishment to a crime is a hazardous undertaking for humans, especially as the history of punishment shows that hurting far outweighs forgiving, leading to a tendency to the excessive use of punishment.

7. Confine the violent spectacle of punishment to movies, video games, and contact sports by normalizing real punishment as a mundane everyday occurrence.

8. Abolish prison as a punishment, because it hides the pain of punishment from public view, thus avoiding accountability, and is imprecise in its application of pain to offenders.

9. Replace prison with MCP, a corporal punishment that can be applied with a minimum of violence, and with OI, incapacitation without walls, for the terrible few.[12]

10. Assign the administration of electronic flogging to a robot in order to remove human error.

11. Allow the offender to self-administer the preprogrammed sentence of moderate corporal punishment in the privacy of his or her own home.

12. Find a balance between the competing demands of retribution and deterrence. That is, the punishment should never exceed the seriousness (injury and damage) of the crime by even a tiny amount.

Appendix A

Debating Points

Common Criticisms and Their Rebuttal

Criticism: Corporal punishment and bodily incapacitation, no matter how moderate, would be a violation of the Eighth Amendment of the US Constitution against cruel and unusual punishment.

Reply: Corporal punishment of the carefully controlled type described in this book has never been found to be cruel and unusual by the US Supreme Court. The case that comes closest is that of *Bishop*, in which a leather strap was used. But this concerned the use of corporal punishment in a prison, and it is argued by some interpreters of that case that corporal punishment was found unconstitutional because of the way it was used in the system (several rules were broken) not because it was corporal punishment per se. The finding was also a dictum, not a controlling precedent.

If the court can find that a life sentence in prison for possessing 672 grams of cocaine is not a disproportionate sentence and that it is not cruel and unusual to use corporal punishment on innocent (as against criminal) school children (*Ingraham v. Wright*), there would seem to be plenty of room for maneuver. Given that the court is reticent to interfere in the states' rights to enact their own crimes and punishments, there is every chance, provided that a law was carefully written, that it would pass the test of constitutionality. Some states had corporal punishment statutes as late as 1972. The case of *Brown v. Plata* at last addressed the issue of the excessive punishment of prison as cruel and unusual, a finding that surely supports its replacement by a far more controllable moderate corporal punishment.

Bodily incapacitation is widely used in schools and other institutions. Most Supreme Court cases concerning its use refer to the amount of force that is allowed to restrain violent individuals and the context in which physical restraints are applied. In no case has it been ruled that bodily incapacitation in itself is unconstitutional.

Criticism: Moderate corporal punishment and bodily incapacitation will unleash a kind of fury of the masses and get out of control.

Reply: Criminal punishment is already out of control in the form of mass incarceration. Close to two million lives of inmates right now are being ruined by the excessive use of prison as a punishment, to say nothing of the secondary punishment of millions of their family members. It is not the vengefulness of people that has caused prison to get out of control. Rather, it is its separation from the people, its loss of credibility, and the failure to take direct responsibility for this punishment that has caused its use in barbaric proportions. Robotically applied corporal punishment offers the chance to get punishment under control, reduce the excesses of prison, and get punishment out in the open, no longer an embarrassing secret.

Criticism: Moderate corporal punishment and bodily incapacitation will be added on to prison, and the prison population will not decrease.

Reply: Corporal punishment must never repeat the mistake of the past by using it in conjunction with a prison term, since this would defeat the whole purpose of temporary corporal punishment and subject it to the same criticisms now made against prison. The combination of these two punishments is therefore morally indefensible. It is possible that moderate corporal punishment could take the place of probation, since it would cost less, because probation requires more expensive personnel to administer it. In any case, probation has lost its credibility as a punishment. Because corporal punishment is a credibly painful punishment, it is more likely to offer a genuine alternative to prison, so that the chances of it becoming an add-on to prison are much less. Given the historical coincidence of the rise of prison populations in conjunction with the abolition of corporal punishment, reintroduction of corporal punishment may reverse this trend.

However, the dangers of bodily incapacitation, especially induced coma, are real: we know the strong temptation within institutions to drug inmates to make them easy to manage. Legislation would be essential to forbid the application of induced coma within institutions of any kind, including hospitals. The trading of body parts for release from prison will also reduce the prison population.

Criticism: Corporal punishment and bodily incapacitation will encourage violence by setting a bad example.

Reply: This is probably the most common criticism. In spite of claims to the contrary, an unbiased review of the research shows that whether or not children learn aggression from watching others do it is still unclear, and, in cases where it has been shown to affect children, these are not long term effects. Just in case, we should not let children watch the corporal punishment of criminals unless this experience is accompanied by a clear explanation of the crime and why the individual is being punished. This criticism, and much of the research used to back it up, fails to examine carefully the context in which corporal punishment is used, which is essentially (properly administered) in the context of discipline. It is not wanton violence. If a delinquent says, "I beat up this little old lady, but so what, the cops use violence too?" then one must point out that violence is clearly not deserved by the old lady, but it may well be deserved by the delinquent. He is fortunate that we are sufficiently civilized not to visit on him harm that is anywhere near the amount of harm he has caused his victim—even when we use moderate corporal punishment. Finally, robotic corporal punishment removes the human essence of any violence that accompanies administration of corporal punishment, thus considerably eliminating violence that could occur in administration of the punishment. Essentially, robotic punishment removes the violence from corporal punishment.

Criticism: Corporal punishment and bodily incapacitation amount to a return to torture.

Reply: Torture is a process that requires total control of the individual's body and mind over an extended period of time, with the goal of extracting confession, proving guilt, and punishing, all at the same time. Moderate corporal punishment has no interest in such matters. The control of a person's mind, which was indeed the horror of Orwell's *1984*, is exactly what prisons try to accomplish. Therefore it is prison that is more like torture, not corporal punishment. Another feature of torture is excessive use of pain. This book makes clear that the programmed use of corporal punishment ensures against excessive use of any punishment by demanding the highly controlled application of pain as punishment. This is not torture by any stretch of the imagination.

Criticism: Plea bargaining over the number of electric shocks to be administered would amount to a sick joke.

Reply: Every day American lawyers and prosecutors callously bargain away years of an offender's life. Bargaining over the number of shock units that may involve only a couple of hours of the person's life is a far more humane and sensitive approach to the offender's plight. As well, the introduction of robotics into judicial sentencing may show the way to abolition of plea bargaining, which, in the long run, denies the offender a fair trial.[1]

Criticism: Corporal punishment and bodily incapacitation have severe negative side effects.

Reply: There is little research to support this assertion. In fact, in regard to use of electric shock as punishment, while some mild negative side effects have been observed (such as aversion to the mechanism that delivers the shock) the positive effects far outweigh the negative effects. Once again, compared to the punishment of prison, the negative side effects of corporal punishment are negligible, especially if delivered in accordance to the guidelines suggested in this book, and especially if delivered robotically. There are essentially no side effects.

Criticism: Corporal punishment humiliates and degrades the offender.

Reply: There is no evidence that it humiliates or degrades any more than any other severe punishment, especially prison, whose requirement of total subordination of the inmate for reasons of prison control humiliates and degrades the offender twenty-four hours a day, seven days a week. Opportunities to humiliate an offender in prison begin from the very first moment of admission, when inmates are routinely made to remove their clothes and are subject to physical examinations, without privacy. In fact the currently popular shock incarceration is essentially founded on the infliction of humiliation on the offender. Such humiliation is a far cry from the corporal punishment advocated in this book. We should remember that all punishment potentially degrades and humiliates. It is a question of whether corporal punishment is more prone to doing so than other punishments. We have seen clearly that moderate corporal punishment degrades much less than any other punishments. In fact, in many ways, it may be seen as uplifting to the offender who can be proud that he or she "took the punishment as deserved," rather like taking bad tasting medicine.

Criticism: Corporal punishment and bodily incapacitation degrade those who administer it.

Reply: Indeed, it may for those who enjoy whipping someone or otherwise intentionally hurting others who have no way of defending themselves. Fortunately, this criticism does not apply to robotic corporal punishment, because it is not administered by a human. One cannot degrade a robot. It might be argued that, in the robotic use of punishment, where the judge presses the button to begin the moderate corporal punishment and can see the results of this in action, the judge becomes the punisher and therefore is degraded by setting a robot on to the offender. If this were to happen, it would probably be a good thing, since it ensures that the judge is aware of what she is doing, becomes more accountable for her actions of sentencing someone to be hurt. When sentencing an offender to prison, the judge has no such direct information or even comprehension of what she is doing to the offender when she delivers a prison sentence.

Criticism: Corporal punishment and bodily incapacitation are a return to barbarism.

Reply: What is barbaric? This is a position of cultural arrogance. It is also hypocritical. Injury to the body of the accused already occurs in uncontrolled proportions within prisons, through rape, beatings, and protection rackets. Robotic corporal punishment, as described in this book, makes sure that we are publicly accountable for the punishment we administer and any injury that occurs to the offender. This is not what happens with prisons that are secret, allowing many hidden punishments for which society avoids responsibility because these injuries were "unintended" (though predictable). If there is any barbarism in punishment, the label surely applies to prison, where the uncontrolled, irresponsible, and excessive pain of prison is wantonly inflicted on offenders and coincidentally their family members. And some have argued that they destroy whole neighborhoods.

Criticism: Corporal punishment and bodily incapacitation are out of step with modern sensibilities.

Reply: David Garland made this observation in his excellent book *Punishment and Society*. It is not really a criticism, since it does not challenge the argument, only its timing. If sensibilities change—and they might, given the encroachment of Shari'a law on Western culture—presumably Garland would not argue against it. Garland uses the word "sensibilities" as though it is synonymous with "manners" or "taste." For example, he reviews the work of Norbert Elias on the history of manners and tries to apply it to the history of punishment. This fascinating work attempts to explain why we abide by everyday habits of behavior, such as using a knife and fork and not defecating in public or urinating at the dinner table (which Elias shows were quite common not too long ago). Would the use of corporal punishment be like eating one's cereal with one's fingers at the dinner table? On closer analysis, we see that this criticism is actually the same as the "barbarism" criticism that imposes "civilized" rules upon human habits, such as using a knife, fork, or spoon. We in the West eat hamburgers and french fries with our fingers, so the rules are not that strict, as Elias and Garland imply. Anyway, whose sensibilities was Garland thinking of? We know the answer to that, don't we?

Criticism: It's fascism plain and simple.

Reply: Talk about the pot calling the kettle black! Liberal penologists deny the basic force that drives Western and Middle Eastern culture: punishment. By denying that force, liberal penologists who will not punish, simply create a greater demand for it. Reformers blame the excesses of prison on all kinds of woes, such as the tyranny of the state, inequality, racism, class conflict, capitalism—the list goes on. But the responsibility for the excesses of prison today lies squarely with the reformers themselves, who have undermined the punishment processes in society, all in the self-righteous name of "doing good."

The reformers of the nineteenth and twentieth centuries created prisons as we know them today. Ashamed of punishing, they have swept punishment behind the secret walls of prison. There it has grown and festered like a huge ulcer. Guilty about punishing, they have invented programs to negate the punitive might of prison. Deeply concerned with control, they have invented community programs of nonpunishment to add on to prison. All the forms of criminal punishment in use today in the West have been invented by such reformers. The only exception to that historical fact is the death penalty. And even there, their efforts to abolish it have contributed to massive incarceration, because life in prison without parole has been a price paid by reformers in return for abolition of the death penalty. Not to mention in jurisdictions where the death penalty still holds, it has been turned into a long and lengthy form of torture that combines long prison terms with a final, tantalizing possibility of being put to death. Until prison took over as the price paid for the abolition of the death penalty in Britain and Europe, the excessive use of the lash made up for the big gap in punishment severity left by its abolition. Robots can manufacture and drive cars, guide airplanes and drones. They can administer corporal punishment without the violence of the lash, and—without the intemperate interference of humans—will punish within reason, without excess.

Criticism: If robots took control of corporal punishment and bodily incapacitation they would end up taking over the world.

Reply: Could they do any worse than humans?

Criticism: Only a fascist would advocate corporal punishment of criminals.

Reply: This is an old trick, popular in politics. When you can't beat the logic of the argument, you attack its advocate. But worse, the argument expresses an oversimplification about the personality of individuals popularized by famed psychologists such as Theodore Adorno and his colleagues (*The Authoritarian Personality*) and Hans Eysenck (*The Psychology of Politics*) in the aftermath of World War II. Adorno invented the "F scale" (F for fascism), which ranked individuals according to how authoritarian their personalities were. One of the many items of the scale was whether the individual supported the death penalty or not. Eysenck constructed a scale that divided people's personalities into extroverts and introverts, the extroverts, of course, being the authoritarians. This gross oversimplification of peoples' personalities set the basis (and academic justification) for calling anyone who exercised authority or discipline a "fascist." In the twenty-first century, the word is now used in a much broader sense to refer to any person who says or does anything one does not like.

Criticism: Using electric shock to punish criminals is disgusting, because it treats them like dogs.

Reply: The fact is we treat our dogs far better than we treat criminals, though admittedly our stray dogs do not fare so well. Have you ever been to the local lost dogs' home? You can see how they suffer. Putting animals behind bars is cruel, isn't it? Why are zoos closing, many replaced by free range animal farms? Putting masses of criminals in prison, many overcrowded, a significant number in solitary confinement, is far more cruel than a short sharp shock or two, even if it resembled a dog's collar (which it wouldn't).

Criticism: Moderate corporal punishment or bodily incapacitation are fantasies that will never happen.

Reply: While it may not be robotic, electric shock is already widely used in the courtroom as an instrument of incapacitation. Stun belts are applied to unruly offenders in the courtroom, who, significantly, are not yet guilty of the crime for which they will be punished. If we can apply severe electric shock to those who are not yet guilty—and the amount of shock delivered by these stun belts, sometimes causing defecation and urination, is far greater than recommended by moderate corporal punishment—surely moderate corporal punishment is acceptable for those who have been found guilty of a crime?

Criticism: Is there no compassion?

Reply: The same question should be asked of those who support, directly or indirectly, the continued use of mass incarceration. The very structure of a prison leaves no room for compassion or forgiveness. The prisoner is reminded every day of the relentless application of its cruelty, all the while his family and loved ones suffering the overflow of his punishment, all the while his body suffering from the violence of prison, the dreaded enforced boredom of prison life, the incessant authoritarian imposition of the harsh discipline that a prison demands, all of this dumped on him by his fellow man. Talk about fascist regimes! Prisons are exactly that!

Reformers may respond, "We offer rehabilitation, teach them a trade in prison, offer parole, and help with reentry, so they can lead a better life after release." These compassionate solutions for punishment are not what they seem. It's a stark case of "doing bad by doing good." It's Munchausen syndrome by proxy—we put them in prison in order to treat them later for the harsh effects of the prison that we put on them in the first place!

Christian conservatives may complain that corporal punishment or bodily incapacitation leave no room for compassion or forgiveness. However, one sect of Christianity, the Quakers, in 1829 advocated solitary confinement of prisoners, there to be given a bible and time to reflect on their sins. Very good intentions, don't you think? The actual outcomes of this punishment were described by Supreme Court Justice Samuel Freeman Miller:

> A considerable number of the prisoners fell, after even a short confinement, into a semi-fatuous condition, from which it was next to impossible to arouse them, and others became violently insane; others still, committed suicide; while those who stood the ordeal better were not generally reformed, and in most cases did not recover sufficient mental activity to be of any subsequent service to the community.[2]

Moderate corporal punishment and bodily incapacitation offer a truly conservative solution to criminal punishment. They preserve the liberty of those punished by keeping them within their local communities and, where necessary, in protective nonprison settings. Those receiving the punishment are treated with respect, with the aid of robots, their punishments are inflicted by themselves for themselves. They are not subjects of rehabilitation or some other social experiment. The cruelty of physical punishment is kept to a minimum, equally applied.

Finally, by ensuring that punishment is normalized in the ways described in this book, we make it much easier for all of us to identify with the plight of the offender, just as we do when we see someone pulled over by a police car. "There but for the grace of God go I." Now that is real compassion!

Criticism: And what about forgiveness?

Reply: Again, we must question the submerged motives of those who righteously advocate various reforms as a substitute for punishment, and question the actual outcomes that result. Restorative justice, for example, is based on forgiving. It underestimates just how hard it is to forget, which is the only way to forgive, don't you think? How does one forgive especially terrible crimes such as genocide, which, if forgotten, probably make it more likely that such crimes will be repeated? In fact it asks far too much of the victims. Jesus set a very high standard of perfection to which no human could ever come close. "Forgive them Lord, for they know not what they do." Really? Need one give examples of the dreadful crimes of genocide that beg forgiveness? Forgiveness comes *after* the punishment. As the German poet Heinrich Heine famously observed, "One must, it is true, forgive one's enemies—but not before they have been hanged."[3] Pope John Paul II forgave Mehmet Ali Ağca, who shot him in an attempted assassination. But this occurred only after he had been punished.

Criticism: But what about mercy? How can you advocate such cruelty?

Reply: To repeat yet again, this question should be asked of those who support any kind of punishment, especially mass incarceration (which most support by default, because they never provide credible alternatives to it).

Strained or not, there is no place in criminal justice for mercy, at least while mass incarceration reigns. Commuting a death sentence to life in prison might be taken as a great act of mercy. But a life in prison is hardly a gift from Heaven. In fact, even commuting the death penalty to five years is hardly merciful. One must again question the motives. The release of several hundred criminals from prison by Presidents Obama and Trump on the grounds that their crimes were nonviolent or to alleviate mass incarceration, was not an act of mercy. The fact that reasons had to be given to justify the act demonstrates that. For an act of mercy is an arbitrary, emotional act, independent both of what punishment the offender's crime deserved or its effects on the victim. At bottom, therefore, an act of mercy is a selfish act—no more, no less—and its effects may or may not be good, more than likely bad. As shown in *The Merchant of Venice*, only the powerful (Shylock) can be merciful.[4] And only the powerless need plead for it, preferably on their knees.

Criticism: You purposely overlook the good things that prison can do. What about all the inmates who earn college degrees in prison?

Reply: "Today, prisons are schools for crime. They must become schools for citizenship." Thus spoke a passionate advocate of the Bard College program for inmates.[5] Who could disagree with this statement? Advocates recount many examples of the great successes of these programs, a number of individual lives enriched and even, one might say, saved. But consider this. It costs a lot of money to send your kid to Bard College. It's very competitive and hard to gain admission. The banner of these programs is, quite simply, "Commit a crime and go to college for free." Facetious, you might say. In fact, as shown throughout this book, the overall statistics on the rehabilitative effects of prison show that they continue to be schools for crime and, I would add, always will be until they are abolished.

Appendix B

A Chronology of Civilized Punishments

8th century BCE	Old Testament punishments defined; law of Moses, "eye for an eye" pronounced. Maximum number of lashes of forty, reported in Deuteronomy 25:3.
71 BCE	Crassus crucifies six thousand slaves in retaliation for their revolt.
30 CE	Jesus whipped, crucified.
622	Muhammad flees to Medina. Qur'an and the Sunnah, along with their prescribed punishments, gain acceptance in North African countries.
800	Shafi'i systematizes judges' cases and introduces reasoning (and therefore punishment) by analogy. Handbooks on Islamic law follow.
1207	Pope Innocent III issues definition of heresy, ushering in the era of inquisitions and their tortures.
1478	Start of the Spanish Inquisition.
1530	King Henry VIII passes the Whipping Act.
1693	Witches hanged in Salem, Massachusetts.
1757	Drawing and quartering of Damiens in Paris.
1776	General George Washington petitions Congress to increase strokes of the lash in military from thirty-nine to one hundred.

1785	Russian Charter to the Nobility exempts nobles from corporal punishment.
1786	Public whipping post discontinued in Philadelphia.
1822	Martin's Act in Britain forbids cruelty to animals.
1829	Eastern State Penitentiary opened, October 25.
1832	Anatomy Act ends dissection of murderers in UK.
1853	The Penal Servitude Act establishes prison as a punishment in itself in the UK, not as a holding facility, as traditionally used.
1854	Martin's Act extended to include causing mental suffering to animals.[1]
1868	Last public hanging in UK.
1872	Public corporal and capital punishment abolished in Philadelphia, signaling the beginning of mass incarceration.
1874	First US military prison opens at Fort Leavenworth, Kansas.
1906	First US Federal Prison for civilians opens in Leavenworth County, Kansas.
1910	Revolt of the Whip in Brazil.
1936	*Brown v. Mississippi*, in which US Supreme Court holds a defendant's coerced confession violates the due process clause of the Fourteenth Amendment.
1950s	Mass incarceration begins in earnest.
1952	Last public whipping in the United States.
1965	Death penalty abolished in UK.
1968	*Jackson v. Bishop*, in which Corporal punishment is formally banned in Arkansas prisons, signaling the formal end of corporal punishment in US prisons.
2011	*Brown v. Plata*, in which US Supreme Court rules excessive prison term to be cruel and unusual according to the Eighth Amendment.

Notes

Introduction

1. In Latin, *exitus acta probat*, the motto of George Washington's coat of arms.

2. Shakespeare, *Hamlet*, act 3, scene 4.

3. Matthew Pate and Laurie A. Gould, *Corporal Punishment around the World* (Santa Barbara, CA: Praeger, 2012).

4. This in spite of the fact that there are plenty of legal decisions arguing that prison officials have a duty to protect inmates from the violence of other inmates, that "being violently assaulted in prison is simply not part of the penalty that criminal offenders pay for their offenses against society." Farmer v. Brennan, 511 U.S. 825, 832, 834 (1994). The fact that these cases continually appear demonstrates that prisons are themselves generators of violence, certainly providing the opportunities and conditions in which inmate on inmate violence is guaranteed to occur. Otherwise, why is there any need to have legal rules against it?

5. Emile Durkheim, *The Elementary Forms of Religious Life* (New York: Free Press, 1965).

6. For an excellent analysis of the nonsense language that pervades criminal punishment and criminal justice, see Robert A. Ferguson, *Inferno: An Anatomy of American Punishment* (Cambridge, MA: Harvard University Press, 2014); also reviewed by Erik Luna in *Criminal Justice Ethics* 34, no. 2 (2015): 210–47.

Chapter One

1. Such visual violence, now produced in spectacular color and 3D, even drawing the viewer inside the spectacle through virtual reality and video games, may provide a much appreciated cathartic substitution for committing real violence. This well-established Freudian principle, originating with the ancient Greek philosophers, no doubt plays an important part in this sublimation of violence. See, for an excellent analysis and assessment of this phenomenon, Mark Pizzato, *Theatres of*

Human Sacrifice: From Ancient Ritual to Screen Violence, Psychoanalysis and Culture (New York: State University of New York Press, 2004).

2. Samuel P. Huntington, *The Clash of Civilizations and the Remaking of World Order* (New York: Simon and Schuster, 2011).

3. If a master was murdered by a slave, all the slaves were put to death. The range of Roman punishments included: for theft (*furtum*) of various kinds, being whipped then thrown over the Tarpeian Rock, and being whipped then reduced to slavery; for evasion of the census or military service, penal servitude, loss of citizenship, and being sentenced to road making. Forms of execution included beheading by sword (*ad gladium traditio*), crucifixion, burning, gladiatorial combat (lasting three years might get a pardon). See W. W. Buckland, *A Text-Book of Roman Law: From Augustus to Justinian*, 3rd ed. (London: Cambridge University Press, 2007); C. E. Brand, *Roman Military Law* (Austin: University of Texas Press, 1968).

4. Matthew Pate and Laurie A. Gould, *Corporal Punishment around the World* (Santa Barbara, CA: Praeger, 2012); G. Geltner, *Flogging Others: Corporal Punishment and Cultural Identity from Antiquity to the Present* (Amsterdam: Amsterdam University Press, 2014). For an extensive history, with colorful descriptions of forms of the death penalty, see George Victor Bishop, *Executions: The Legal Ways of Death* (Los Angeles: Sherbourne Press, 1965).

5. Dorothy E. Roberts, "The Social and Moral Cost of Mass Incarceration in African American Communities," *Stanford Law Review* 56, no. 5 (2004): 1271–1305. See also Michael C. Campbell and Matt Vogel, "The Demographic Divide: Population Dynamics, Race and the Rise of Mass Incarceration in the United States," *Punishment and Society* 21, no. 1 (2019): 47–69; Michael C. Campbell, "Varieties of Mass Incarceration: What We Learn from State Histories," *Annual Review of Criminology* 1 (2018): 219–34; "Are All Politics Local? A Case Study of Local Conditions in a Period of 'Law and Order' Politics," *Annals of the American Academy of Political and Social Science* 664, no. 1 (2016): 43–61; Michael C. Campbell, Matt Vogel, and Joshua Williams, "Historical Contingencies and the Evolving Importance of Race, Violent Crime, and Region in Explaining Mass Incarceration in the United States," *Criminology* 53, no. 2 (2015): 180–203. Even the Romans did not use prison as a punishment (though they did use it to temporarily detain individuals, see Buckland, *Text-Book of Roman Law*).

6. Zachary R. Morgan, *Legacy of the Lash: Race and Corporal Punishment in the Brazilian Navy and the Atlantic World* (Bloomington: Indiana University Press, 2014).

7. In 1873, the US Army began the use of large-scale prisons to replace corporal punishment, with the opening of the first military prison at Fort Leavenworth, Kansas, in 1874. Stanley L. Brodsky and Norman E. Eggleston, eds., *The Military Prison: Theory, Research, and Practice* (Carbondale: Southern Illinois University Press, 1970). The mission of these prisons was, predictably, "restoration

training." In 1968, Private Bunche attempted to escape from the army Presidio Stockade and was shot. Twenty-seven prisoners sang freedom songs in protest. They were charged with mutiny and received sixteen years' hard labor. In Britain a similar change occurred. In 1825, it was estimated that one man in every fifty-nine army recruits was flogged. In 1868, flogging was abolished in peacetime, and finally, in 1881, abolished completely. Scott Claver, *Under the Lash: A History of Corporal Punishment in the British Armed Forces* (London: Torchstream, 1954).

8. George Washington to President of Continental Congress, February 3, 1781. Cited in, John Dewar Gleissner, "Prison Overcrowding Cure: Judicial Corporal Punishment of Adults" *Criminal Law Bulletin* 49, no. 4 (2013): 711–55.

9. Myra C. Glenn, *Campaigns against Corporal Punishment: Prisoners, Sailors, Women, and Children in Antebellum America* (Albany: State University of New York Press, 1984), 150–51. For a time, naval commanders also introduced other kinds of corporal punishments to replace whipping, such as keel-hauling, placing hands, arms, and legs in irons of varying kinds, the latter a form of incapacitation.

10. Abby M. Schrader, *Languages of the Lash: Corporal Punishment and Identity in Imperial Russia* (Dekalb: Northern Illinois University Press, 2002), 15–151. Schrader makes a strong case that incarceration was used in a number of locations throughout Russia and also in other parts of Europe as a substitute for corporal punishment.

11. Michel Foucault, *Discipline and Punish: The Birth of the Prison*, trans. Alan Sheridan (New York: Pantheon, 1977). See also David J. Rothman, *The Discovery of the Asylum: Social Order and Disorder in the New Republic*, rev. ed. (New Brunswick, NJ: Aldine Transaction, 2002). Rothman adds a more substantial empirical basis to the argument.

12. Academics, generally following Foucault, have seized on this moment as the shining example of the monolithic State sneakily hiding away its coercive authority behind prison walls. Having a firm grip on the obedience of the masses, especially the rabble, quietly disciplined now behind prison walls, it has no need to display its power and authority by the spectacle of violence of corporal punishment or aggravated death penalty. See, generally, Michael Ignatieff, *A Just Measure of Pain: The Penitentiary in the Industrial Revolution* (New York: Pantheon, 1978); Rothman, *Discovery of the Asylum*; Foucault, *Discipline and Punish*.

13. Michael Meranze, *Laboratories of Virtue: Punishment, Revolution, and Authority in Philadelphia, 1760–1835*, 2nd ed. (Chapel Hill: University of North Carolina Press, 1996). In his excellent book, Meranze describes the transformation of public corporal and capital punishment through forced labor, reduction of the death penalty, and finally imprisonment in solitary confinement. However, the major types of punishment he describes historically are capital punishments, with few descriptions of corporal punishments, excepting that of penal labor, which would seem itself to be a form of corporal punishment, as is solitary confinement in prison.

14. Graeme R. Newman and Pietro Marongiu, introduction to their translation of Cesare Beccaria, *On Crimes and Punishments* (New Brunswick, NJ: Transaction, 2009).

15. Marcus Tullius Cicero, *The Political Works of Marcus Tullius Cicero: Comprising His Treatise on the Commonwealth; and His Treatise on the Laws*, trans. Francis Barham, vol. 1 (London: Edmund Spettigue, 1841), http://oll.libertyfund. org/titles/546; Andrew Lintott, *The Constitution of the Roman Republic* (London: Oxford University Press, 2003).

16. For what it's worth, I am against capital punishment, but not always. I try to stay away from the death penalty debate in this book, because it has a way of taking over the entire argument, introducing issues not directly relevant to corporal punishment, even though, of course, the death penalty, depending on how it is administered, is supposedly the ultimate form of corporal punishment (also depending on how it is defined, as we will see later in chapter 3).

17. Meranze, *Laboratories of Virtue.*

18. Kevin J. Murtagh, "Is Corporally Punishing Criminals Degrading?," *Journal of Political Philosophy* 20, no. 4 (2012): 481–98.

19. There have been few serious histories of corporal punishment. Geltner, *Flogging Others,* offers a critique of the common criticism that corporal punishment is barbarous, a critique that was offered in Graeme R. Newman, *Just and Painful: A Case for the Corporal Punishment of Criminals* (New York: Macmillan, 1983) some thirty years ago. Geltner's claim that prison did not necessarily rise as a result of the abolition of corporal punishment is misleading. While prison was used at various points in antiquity and later, it is difficult to deny the fact of its rise as a universal punishment in every country of the world, beginning in the eighteenth century. Contrary to Geltner's claim, we have the Enlightenment thinkers to thank for that. There are, of course, many other factors that contributed to the rise of prison as a universal punishment. The detailed history of abolition of corporal punishment and its contribution to the rise of prison is yet to be written.

20. The book, interestingly, was published as part of a series, the Library of Modern Sex Knowledge, running to eleven volumes, ranging from venereal disease to the "mysteries of sex," most of them written also by Ryley.

21. And it explains why Muslim women (mostly the objects of sex, after all) must be kept wrapped up and out of sight.

22. Center for Security Policy, "Poll of U.S. Muslims Reveals Ominous Levels of Support for Islamic Supremacists' Doctrine of Shariah, Jihad," June 23, 2015, https://www.centerforsecuritypolicy.org/2015/06/23/nationwide-poll-of-us-muslims-shows-thousands-support-shariah-jihad/.

23. Promoters, like the Muslim Brotherhood, of the spread of Islam and the eventual establishment of a Caliphate, call it "civilization jihad." See Center for Security Policy, *Shariah: The Threat to America, an Exercise in Competitive Analysis,* Report of Team B II (Washington, DC: Center for Security Policy, 2010), https://www.centerforsecuritypolicy.org/2010/09/13/shariah-the-threat-to-america/.

Chapter Two

1. See generally, Leon Radzinowicz, *A History of English Criminal Law and Its Administration from 1750*, vol. 1, *The Movement for Reform 1750–1833* (London: Stevens and Sons, 1948).

2. Eli Sagan, *Cannibalism: Human Aggression and Cultural Form* (New York: Harper and Row, 1974).

3. We should understand that this "progress" is not necessarily related to a progression in our moral sensitivity, as much as it is related to progress in medical science. With the discovery of pain killing drugs, we have developed a more acute perception of the horror of pain than people had prior to the widespread use of these drugs.

4. Where Western civilization begins and ends is a bit difficult to identify. Until the advent of radical Islamic extremists at the beginning of this century, it was widely assumed that the countries of the "Middle East" had become Westernized in their economic system, including commercial law, industries, and urban structure that existed side by side with an Islamic legal system, that is, Shari'a criminal justice.

5. Norman O. Brown, *Love's Body* (Berkeley: University of California Press, 1966).

6. Much has been written on this complex topic. For a scholarly description of the age of "psychological man," see Philip Rieff, *The Triumph of the Therapeutic: Uses of Faith after Freud* (New York: Harper, 1966). And on narcissism, see Norman O. Brown, *Life against Death* (Middletown, CT: Wesleyan University Press, 1959); Jean M. Twenge, *Generation Me: Why Today's Young Americans Are More Confident, Assertive, Entitled—and More Miserable Than Ever Before* (New York: Atria, 2014).

7. Indeed, the "entitlement culture" is identified as a symptom of the extreme narcissism of the twenty-first century, explaining also the application of the term "microaggression" to any behavior or speech perceived as even slightly threatening, and the demand for "safe spaces" on college campuses. Jean M. Twenge and W. Keith Campbell, *The Narcissism Epidemic: Living in the Age of Entitlement* (New York: Atria, 2010).

8. In the twentieth century, the major proponent of this view was Harry Elmer Barnes in his *The Story of Punishment* (Boston: Stratford, 1930). His view is perpetuated in modern textbooks on corrections. Today's view of the history of punishment is that its history reflects a "sense of greater compassion"—Mary K. Stohr and Anthony Walsh, *Corrections: The Essentials* (Los Angeles: Sage, 2011), ch. 3—a view that reflects the morality of the eighteenth-century Enlightenment, when the West *really* became civilized.

9. Graeme R. Newman, *The Punishment Response*, 2nd ed. (New York: Routledge, 2017), chs. 2–3; Folke Ström, *On the Sacral Origin of the Germanic Death Penalties* (Stockholm: Wahlström and Widstrand, 1942); Hans von Hentig, *Punishment: Its Origin, Purpose and Psychology* (Montclair, NJ: Patterson Smith, 1973).

10. Douglas Hay et al. *Albion's Fatal Tree: Crime and Society in Eighteenth-Century England* (New York: Pantheon, 1975).

11. Here are some other analogical examples:

Blasphemy was punished either by cutting out the tongue or by piercing a hole in it and pinning it to the cheek with an iron pin.

The hand was cut off the counterfeiter or false coiner.

The most common form of the death penalty was hanging, but arsonists were burnt to death.

"Scolds" (women who talked too much and spread gossip) were thought to have fiery tongues and hot spirits, so their bodies were cooled off by dunking in cold water on the ducking stool.

In Germany, the kidneys were removed with red-hot pincers, because they were thought to be at the seat of the criminal's wicked disposition.

12. Murray A. Straus, *Beating the Devil Out of Them: Corporal Punishment in American Families* (New York: Lexington, 1994). Currently twenty of the fifty states in the United States allow the corporal punishment of school children, according to Matthew Pate and Laurie A. Gould, *Corporal Punishment around the World* (Santa Barbara, CA: Praeger, 2012).

13. See, for example, Newman, *The Punishment Response*, ch. 4; Zachary R. Morgan, *Legacy of the Lash: Race and Corporal Punishment in the Brazilian Navy and the Atlantic World* (Bloomington: Indiana University Press, 2014); Scott Claver, *Under the Lash: A History of Corporal Punishment in the British Armed Forces* (London: Torchstream, 1954); Joseph K. Taussig, *Military Law* (Annapolis, MD: United States Naval Institute, 1963).

14. These extreme punishments have been reported in Newman, *The Punishment Response*, but to provide the flavor of what went on, here are a few examples:

In the Navy, one William Brennan received 500 lashes for mutinous behavior (1781).

James Allen received 100 lashes for insolent and mutinous behavior (1792).

Thirty men received 50 to 500 lashes for desertion and drunkenness (1782).

15. Newman, *The Punishment Response*.

16. An example of such a sentence was that passed by the House of Lords under James I on Mr. Edward Floyde for "irreverent observations" and "being a papist": ". . . sentence of life imprisonment, preceded by branding on the forehead and whipping at the cart's tail from Fleet to Westminster Hall." The number of strokes was not counted. Whipping continued until the cart completed its circuit of the village. "Edward Floyd," *Wikipedia*, https://en.wikipedia.org/wiki/Edward_Floyd.

17. Affirming the primal horde model: Sigmund Freud, *Totem and Taboo*, trans. A. A. Brill (New York: Random House, 1946); Konrad Lorenz, *On Aggression*, trans. Marjorie Kerr Wilson (New York: Bantam, 1967). Against the model: Ashley Montagu, *The Nature of Human Aggression* (London: Oxford University Press, 1976); Erich Fromm, *The Anatomy of Human Destructiveness* (New York: Holt, Rinehart and Winston, 1973); Petr Kropotkin, *Mutual Aid: A Factor of Evolution* (Boston: Extending Horizon Books, 1914).

18. See, for example, Stanley M. Garn, ed., *Culture and the Direction of Human Evolution* (Detroit: Wayne State University Press, 1964).

19. Corporal punishment is probably still extensive throughout South Africa, a civilized country, though no sound account of its use has been written since the excellent paper by James Midgely. See James O. Midgely, "Corporal Punishment and Penal Policy: Notes on the Continued Use of Corporal Punishment with Reference to South Africa," *Journal of Criminal Law and Criminology* 73, no. 1 (1982): 388–403.

20. Strictly speaking, they didn't invent crucifixion (the Persians did, around 500 BCE), but they made extensive use of it. Recent scholarship has also suggested that Roman civilization was not as violent as traditionally believed. See Adrian Goldsworthy, *Pax Romana: War, Peace, and Conquest in the Roman World* (New Haven, CT: Yale University Press, 2017).

21. See Newman, *The Punishment Response*, preface to the second edition.

22. In relation to parental use of corporal punishment, Straus, in his *Beating the Devil Out of Them*, argues that corporal punishment, even the slightest use of it, leads to escalation of violence, and all sorts of other societal and psychological ills. Straus certainly shows that probably over 90 percent of all Americans have at some time been hit by their parents. Whether or not this is a good thing, in the abstract, I leave aside. What I argue is that precisely because most people have experienced corporal punishment, they are much more likely to accept it as a credible punishment. They can identify with its pain.

23. The popular and politically correct punishment of "time out" that parents and teachers use against children is perhaps a very light taste of what prison is like. The parental use of slapping or the use of paddles, straps, birches at school obviously provide a much more concrete taste of what corporal punishment of the lash is like.

24. That punishment is an irrational force that drives society has been recognized by punishment scholars, though with different orientations. Karl Menninger's polemic against punishment, *The Crime of Punishment* (London: Penguin, 1977), does at least recognize its irrational element. See David Garland, *Punishment and*

Modern Society (Chicago: University of Chicago Press, 1990), in which punishment is recognized as fulfilling both irrational and rational functions.

25. Adapted from *Albany Times Union*, August 9, 1981.

26. James E. Robertson, "The Old and the New Prison Overcrowding: The Legacy of *Rhodes v. Chapman*," *Correctional Law Reporter*, December/January 2017. See further, for the dreadful conditions in jails and lockups, James E. Robertson, "Conditions of Confinement in Lockups," *Correctional Law Reporter*, October/November 2017.

27. Madden v. Parnell, No. 5:16CV-P23-GNS, 2016 WL 4543484 (W.D. Ky. Aug. 30, 2016).

28. Madden v. Parnell, 2016 WL 4543484, at 1.

Chapter Three

1. Matthew Pate and Laurie A. Gould, *Corporal Punishment around the World* (Santa Barbara, CA: Praeger, 2012), xvi.

2. "Corporal Punishment," *Wikipedia*, accessed November 2, 2015, https://en.wikipedia.org/wiki/Corporal_punishment.

3. Uwe Streinhoff, *On the Ethics of Torture* (Albany: State University of New York Press, 2013). In his otherwise illuminating and very down to earth book, Streinhoff makes this error with his overly broad definition of torture: "Torture is the knowing infliction of continuous or repeated extreme physical suffering for other than medical purposes" (7). However, he does not use the word punishment at all, let alone corporal punishment. The closest he comes to it is what he calls "punitive torture," which he describes as the process of extracting confessions (114–16).

4. In an excellent review and analysis of the Roman Catholic doctrine on torture, corporal punishment is included within the title of the article, but in fact is a very minor part of the review, except to be mentioned in the final summary and conclusion in respect to the corporal punishment of delinquents (probably permissible), in contrast to his certain position that torture is now not approved under *any* circumstances. Brian W. Harrison, "Torture and Corporal Punishment as a Problem in Catholic Theology, Part II," *Roman Theological Forum* 119 (2005), http://www.rtforum.org/lt/lt119.html.

5. Peter Suedfeld, ed., *Psychology and Torture* (New York: Taylor and Francis, 1990), 1.

6. The definition of torture itself is very difficult. Wisnewski and Emerick list several procedures that might be called torture and are very critical of the UN definition from which I here quote. It is certainly often difficult to separate it from "wanton cruelty," though I think it easier to separate out corporal punishment from that. All punishment, including torture when it is used as a punishment, should be viewed as a process, not an object in itself. J. Jeremy Wisnewski and R. D. Emerick, *The Ethics of Torture* (London: Continuum, 2009).

7. Barbara Chester, "Because Mercy Has a Human Heart: The Centers for Victims of Torture," in *Psychology and Torture*, ed. Peter Suedfeld (New York: Taylor and Francis, 1990), 165. My italics.

8. For a catalog of these horrors, see Amnesty International, *Report on Torture* (New York: Farrar, Straus and Giroux, 1975).

9. ISIS (Islamic State in Iraq and Syria).

10. Suedfeld, *Psychology and Torture*, 3.

11. Malise Ruthven, *Torture: The Grand Conspiracy* (London: Weidenfeld and Nicolson, 1978).

12. Henry Charles Lea, *The Inquisition of the Middle Ages* (New York: Harper, 1979).

13. W. W. Buckland, *A Text-Book of Roman Law: From Augustus to Justinian*, 3rd ed. (London: Cambridge University Press, 2007).

14. Cited in Frank Graziano, *Divine Violence: Spectacle, Psychosexuality and Radical Christianity in the Argentine "Dirty War"* (Boulder, CO: Westview Press, 1992), 102.

15. See Frantz Fanon, *The Wretched of the Earth* (New York: Grove, 1968), for a moving analysis of the process during the French occupation of Algeria. And, for the psychological processes of tortured and torturer, see Ervin Straub, "The Psychology and Culture of Torture and Torturers," in *Psychology and Torture*, ed. Peter Suedfeld (New York: Taylor and Francis, 1990), 49–76.

16. Amnesty International, *Torture in 2014: 30 Years of Broken Promises* (London: Amnesty International, 2014. https://www.amnestyusa.org/sites/default/files/act400042014en.pdf.); *Report on Torture* (New York: Farrar, Straus and Giroux, 1975).

17. It is not only herself that the accused must betray by confession (false or otherwise). It is also widely documented in the annals of torture that, in times when torture has reached its height, she must give up the names of accomplices. Malise Ruthven in her informative book *Torture: The Grand Conspiracy* has noted that this is probably the most serious consequence of torture, since it is the ultimate betrayal, it destroys what is social in the accused, destroys the relations among individuals. This means that torture necessarily dehumanizes its victims, takes away their honor and dignity, makes them into something less than human. Thus it is no small surprise that sadistic rituals often play a major part in the actual process of torture. In the torture establishment analyzed by Graziano in his insightful book *Divine Violence*, concerning the Argentinean "Dirty War," he shows how psychosexuality dominated virtually every facet of the "war" right from the torture table to the language of political ideology. The sexuality that historian G. Scott Ryley most wanted to uncover is very much to the fore in torture.

18. Graziano, *Divine Violence*; Michel Foucault, *Discipline and Punish: The Birth of the Prison*, trans. Alan Sheridan (New York: Pantheon, 1977).

19. Adam Nossiter, "Boko Haram Militants Raped Hundreds of Female Captives in Nigeria," *New York Times*, May 18, 2015.

20. Stanley Milgram, "Behavioral Study of Obedience," *Journal of Abnormal and Social Psychology* 67, no. 4 (1963): 371–78; Philip G. Zimbardo, "The Human

Choice: Individuation, Reason, and Order versus Deindividuation, Impulse, and Chaos," *Nebraska Symposium on Motivation* 17 (1969): 237–307.

21. Willard Gaylin, *Partial Justice: A Study of Bias in Sentencing* (New York: Vintage, 1975).

22. It is also clear that to punish with pain for utilitarian purposes (that is, to change the offender's behavior through such techniques as behavior modification) is a process closely akin to torture since there is no way of letting up until the offender gives in—which may be early for most, but nevertheless after much suffering for some. This is another important reason why the classic retributive position, to be discussed further in chapter 4, is morally superior to any other justification of punishment, especially that of corporal punishment. Under a retributive system, the punishment is administered briefly and quickly, and that's that. The offender is viewed as a person of integrity, and there is no attempt to change him; only to punish him. The only aim is to hurt the offender. The utilitarian goal is not only to hurt the offender, but to subjugate him as well.

23. Graziano, *Divine Violence*, 67.

24. This was true in the 1990s in the United States. See John Irwin and James Austin, *It's About Time: America's Imprisonment Binge* (Belmont, CA: Wadsworth, 1994). And, twenty-five years later, even more so: Jonathan Simon, *Mass Incarceration on Trial: A Remarkable Court Decision and the Future of Prisons in America* (New York: New Press, 2014).

25. The 1976 Committee on Incarceration claimed that the pain that people feel as a result of corporal punishment was so subjective that it was impossible to control it. We review in more detail in chapter 4 how the committee came to this erroneous conclusion. Andrew von Hirsch, *Doing Justice: The Choice of Punishments*, report of the Committee for the Study of Incarceration, preface by Charles Goodell, chairman (New York: Hill and Wang, 1976).

26. See, for example, Harold Merskey, *Pain: Psychological and Psychiatric Aspects* (London: Baillière, Tindall and Cassell, 1967); J. P. Payne and R. A. P. Burt, eds., *Pain: Basic Principles, Pharmacology, Therapy* (Baltimore: Williams and Wilkins, 1972); Harold G. Wolff and Stewart Wolff, *Pain*, 2nd ed. (Springfield, IL: Charles Thomas, 1958); Richard A. Sternback, *Pain: A Psychophysiological Analysis* (New York: Academic Press, 1968).

27. The galvanic skin response (GSR) is a measure of the electrical conductance of the skin, thought to be affected by increases or decreases in moisture of the skin surface, often associated with various experimental stimuli, including pain stimuli. It is also claimed to be a measure of emotional arousal.

28. See Graeme R. Newman, *The Punishment Response*, 2nd ed. (New York: Routledge, 2017), for a review of these punishments.

29. Jon Ronson, *So You've Been Publicly Shamed* (New York: Riverhead Books, 2015).

30. See Merskey, *Pain*. Also, Hans W. Kosterlitz and Lars Y. Terenius, eds., *Pain and Society* (Berlin: Verlag Chemie, 1980).

31. Philosophers have also identified two types of pain. The eminent philosopher C. S. Lewis in his little book *The Problem of Pain* identified "A" pain and "B" pain. "A" pain is "a particular kind of sensation probably conveyed by specialized nerve fibers, and recognizable by the patient as that kind of sensation whether he dislikes it or not." And "B" pain is "any experience, whether physical or mental, which the patient dislikes." His definition of "A" pain solves the riddle of the masochist. Pain is pain. The masochist must first sense the pain as pain, in order to like it. That is, how people react to or value pain is separable from its definition. While pain in the "B" sense could conceivably include all the pains in the "A" sense if they were severe enough, pains in the "A" sense would appear not to include those of "B" sense. By making this distinction, Lewis has shown how it is possible to classify anything at all that one disvalues as painful ("B" pain). We must reject this use of the word as far too broad. C. S. Lewis, *The Problem of Pain* (London: Macmillan, 1973), 78. Some authors have described the lives of the working class as "worlds of pain." The word "pain" in this context is used simply to make a value judgment as to the quality of life among the working class, which is assumed to be "bad." The word "pain" should not be used to convey this value judgment because pain cannot be assumed to be in and of itself evil or even bad (though as we have already seen, the Enlightenment thinkers doggedly held to this assumption). Yet there is a sense in which a lifetime may be described as painful. The Christian religion is one among many that reveres pain in this sense. The lives of the Prophets such as Job and many Christian Saints were replete with pain and suffering—seen paradoxically as experiences that no one should have, yet at the same time to be treasured. The important point for us to observe is that this religious tradition views pain as something to be endured over time. It is essentially a view of pain as *chronic*. This, taken together with Lewis's "A" pain ("a particular kind of sensation") suggests that the religious and philosophical spheres recognize the distinction between acute and chronic pain, though they may value each of them differently. See, generally, Kosterlitz and Terenius, *Pain and Society*, especially part 1.

32. It might be argued that such physical punishment brings with it the pain of humiliation, which may last a lifetime. Murray A. Straus, *Beating the Devil Out of Them: Corporal Punishment in American Families* (New York: Lexington, 1994), claims lots of scientific evidence that corporal punishment (even the tiniest amount) has long term effects on children, causing them as adults to become criminal, violent, prone to spouse abuse, suicide, and depression. Needless to say, these are incredible claims, none of which are true. Straus has recently taken his argument further, raising it to the level of a universal truth: Murray A. Straus, Emily M. Douglas, and Rose Anne Medeiros, *The Primordial Violence: Spanking Children, Psychological Development, Violence, and Crime* (Abingdon-on-Thames, UK: Routledge, 2014).

33. The classic monograph on this topic was Lee H. Bowker, *Prison Victimization* (New York: Elsevier, 1982). See also Daniel Lockwood, *Prison Sexual Violence* (New York: Elsevier, 1981). For a survey of its extent in the 1990s, see Michael Braswell, Reid H. Montgomery, and Lucian X. Lombardo, *Prison Violence in America*, 2nd ed. (Cincinnati: Anderson, 1994). And, in the twenty-first century, James M. Byrne, Faye S. Taxman, and Donald Hummer, *The Culture of Prison Violence* (New York: Prentice Hall, 2007); Roger Smith, *Prison Conditions: Overcrowding, Disease, Violence, and Abuse*, Incarceration Issues (Washington, DC: Mason Crest, 2015).

34. There have been many books written on this question, but the classic is probably by George Bernard Shaw, *The Crime of Imprisonment* (New York: Philosophical Library, 1946).

35. See, for example, Malcolm Braly, *False Starts* (London: Penguin, 1976); Craig Haney, *Reforming Punishment: Psychological Limits to the Pains of Imprisonment*, Law and Public Policy (Washington, DC: American Psychological Association, 2005).

36. "Solitary Confinement Is Cruel and All Too Common," editorial, *New York Times*, September 2, 2015. The suit in question is *Ashker v. Governor of California*, No. C 09-5796 CW (N.D. Cal. Jun. 2, 2014).

37. *Oh, God!*, a popular 1977 movie, starring George Burns in the role of God.

38. Lewis, *The Problem of Pain*, 109.

39. See, for example, Sissela Bok, *Lying: Moral Choice in Public and Private Life* (New York: Vintage, 1979).

40. Lewis, *The Problem of Pain*, 86.

41. Kosterlitz and Terenius, *Pain and Society*.

Chapter Four

1. Graeme R. Newman, *Just and Painful: A Case for the Corporal Punishment of Criminals* (New York: Macmillan, 1983), 1. Adapted from *New York Times*, April 14, 1981.

2. Rummel v. Estelle, 63 L. Ed. 2d 382 (1980). The good news is that Mr. Rummel again appealed, not on the grounds of a disproportionate sentence, but on the grounds of ineffective assistance of counsel. He finally managed to plead his case down to theft by false pretenses and was sentenced to time served, which was three years. Rummel v. Estelle, 498 F. Supp. 793 (WD Tex. 1980).

3. Death Penalty Information Center, "Arbitrariness: In the Leading Execution State, Many Receive Probation for Murder," November 19, 2007, http://www.deathpenaltyinfo.org/node/2217.

4. There are some hopeful signs of change, as we will see in chapter 9. See also Richard S. Frase, "Excessive Prison Sentences, Punishment Goals, and the Eighth Amendment: 'Proportionality' Relative to What?," *Minnesota Law Review* 89 (2005): 571–651.

5. Jon Wool, "The Eighth Amendment: When Is a Sentence Disproportionate?," *Think Justice Blog*, May 24, 2010, Vera Institute of Justice, https://www.vera.org/blog/the-eighth-amendment-when-is-a-sentence-disproportionate.

6. Fair Sentencing Act of 2010, Pub. L. No. 111-220.

7. The science is settled as to the effectiveness of prison as a means of crime control: "The most sophisticated analyses generally agree that increased incarceration rates have some effect on reducing crime, but the scope of that impact is limited: a 10 per-cent increase in incarceration is associated with a 2 to 4 percent drop in crime." Don Stemen, *Reconsidering Incarceration: New Directions for Reducing Crime* (Washington, DC: Vera Institute of Justice, 2007). To continue with this policy, he concludes, is not cost effective.

8. L. F. Lowenstein, "The Genetic Aspects of Criminality," *Journal of Human Behavior in the Social Environment* 8, no. 1 (2004): 63–78; Frank A. Elliott, "A Neurological Perspective of Violent Behavior," in *The Science, Treatment, and Prevention of Antisocial Behaviors: Application to the Criminal Justice System*, ed. Diana H. Fishbein (Kingston, NJ: Civic Research Institute, 2000), 19/1–19/21.

9. Pat Carlen and Jacqueline Tombs, "Reconfigurations of Penality: The Ongoing Case of the Women's Imprisonment and Reintegration Industries," *Theoretical Criminology* 10, no. 3 (2006): 337–60. These researchers argue that, because the primary function of prison is to confine offenders against their will, rehabilitation within the same institution is not feasible.

10. See David J. Rothman, *Conscience and Convenience: The Asylum and Its Alternatives in Progressive America* (Boston: Little, Brown, 1980). Also Willard Gaylin et al., *Doing Good: The Limits of Benevolence* (New York: Pantheon, 1978).

11. See, in particular, Francis T. Cullen, Cheryl Lero Jonson, and Daniel S. Nagin, "Prisons Do Not Reduce Recidivism: The High Cost of Ignoring Science," *Prison Journal* 91, no. 3 (2011): 48s–65s; Robert Apel and Daniel S. Nagin, "Deterrence," in *Emerging Trends in the Social and Behavioral Sciences*, ed. Robert A. Scott and Stephen Michael Kosslyn (New York: Wiley, 2015), 1–10.

12. Norval Morris and Michael Tonry, *Between Prison and Probation: Intermediate Punishments in a Rational Sentencing System* (New York: Oxford University Press, 1991). Norval Morris was dean of the University of Chicago Law School, 1975–1978.

13. Rachel Porter, Sophia Lee, and Mary Lutz, *Balancing Punishment and Treatment: Alternatives to Incarceration in New York City* (Washington, DC: Vera Institute of Justice, 2002).

14. Norval Morris, in his *Between Probation and Prison*, did his best to convince the reader that these "intermediate punishments" were real punishments. However, on the occasional page, he slips up, when he actually refers to these intermediate punishments as "treatment": "As intermediate punishments become part of a comprehensive sentencing system, their efficiency must be critically evaluated so that, in time, *an effective treatment classification* may emerge." Morris and Tonry, *Between Probation and Prison*, 12. My italics.

15. See Horacio Fabrega and Stephen Tyma, "Culture, Language and the Shaping of Illness: An Illustration Based on Pain," *Journal of Psychosomatic Research* 20, no. 4 (1976): 323–37. Scholars have traced the word back to about 400 BC when it referred to a penalty, specifically a fine. Around 500 AD, it meant to inflict suffering, and in another sense the opposite of pleasure. Not until 1100 did it come to mean suffering in a general sense (that is, the suffering in hell), and eventually in 1400 to mean suffering of mental as well as physical pain (this, no doubt, coinciding with the mental tortures of the Inquisition). The modern meaning of any mental or physical suffering, or that one specifically "had a pain," did not arise until after 1600.

16. In his groundbreaking monograph, Leslie Wilkins, a pioneer of sentencing guidelines research, noted that it was not possible for his staff to agree upon what the difference between these sentences really meant. See Leslie T. Wilkins, *Principles of Guidelines for Sentencing: Methodological and Philosophical Issues in Their Development* (Washington, DC: National Institute of, 1981).

17. Many kinds of pain occur in our prisons. However, they occur by default rather than by design, and this is essentially what is wrong with them. See, for example, Michael Schwirtz and Michael Winerip, "Violence by Rikers Guards Grew under Bloomberg," *New York Times*, August 13, 2014, http://www.nytimes.com/2014/08/14/nyregion/why-violence-toward-inmates-at-rikers-grew.html?_r=0. The eminent historian David Rothman of Columbia University in 1981 claimed in his book *Conscience and Convenience* that this state of affairs existed in prisons because of lack of money. The 2014 review of the Rikers Island jail confirmed that money continues to exacerbate the problem. But, while an important factor, this explanation fails to penetrate the veneer of excuses we in the West have invented during the course of a couple of centuries, for the failures of our "correctional" system.

18. See Graeme R. Newman, review of *Conscience and Convenience: The Asylum and Its Alternatives in Progressive America*, by David J. Rothman, *Crime and Delinquency* 27, no. 3 (1981): 422–28.

19. Andrew von Hirsch, *Doing Justice: The Choice of Punishments*, report of the Committee for the Study of Incarceration, preface by Charles Goodell, chairman (New York: Hill and Wang, 1976), 111. The retributive thesis of this committee is again repeated in von Hirsch, *Deserved Criminal Sentences: An Overview* (Oxford: Hart, 2017), in which he considers a more detailed range of sentencing alternatives (but not corporal punishment) and replies to a number of standard criticisms made against the retributive thesis.

20. These comparisons are fraught with all kinds of methodological difficulties, making them highly questionable. See Gregory J. Howard, Graeme R. Newman, and William Pridemore, "Theory, Method and Data in Comparative Criminology," in *Criminal Justice 2000*, vol. 4, *Measurement and Analysis of Crime and Justice*, ed. National Institute of Justice (Washington, DC: National Institute of Justice, 2000).

21. Shari'a law countries included Afghanistan (74), Brunei (129), Iran (290), Iraq (133), Mauritania (44), Pakistan (43), Qatar (53), Saudi Arabia (161), and Yemen (53). There are many other Islamic countries that have varying degrees of Shari'a law in operation. Saudi Arabia has had a sudden increase in prison population in recent years, probably because of increased crackdowns on suspected terrorist groups. Matthew Pate and Laurie A. Gould, *Corporal Punishment around the World* (Santa Barbara, CA: Praeger, 2012), found Islamic countries significantly used corporal punishment more than non-Islamic countries and used prison far less. See also Laurie A. Gould and Matthew Pate, "Discipline, Docility and Disparity: A Study of Inequality and Corporal Punishment," *British Journal of Criminology* 50, no. 2 (2010): 185–205.

22. Fred Cohen, "U.S. Leads World in Women in Prison," *Correctional Law Reporter*, December/January 2017. These are 2010 US census data.

23. "United States of America," *World Prison Brief,* http://www.prisonstudies. org/country/united-states-america. The most recent data available from the US Bureau of Justice Statistics: 2,217,947 total, comprised of 744,592 in local jails and 1,473,355 in state or federal prisons. E. Ann Carson, "Prisoners in 2014" (Bureau of Justice Statistics, 2015), http://www.bjs.gov/index.cfm?ty=pbdetail&iid=5387.

24. "The Bureau of Prisons ended Fiscal Year 2016 with 13,553 fewer inmates than it had one year ago. This is the third consecutive year of decreases in the inmate population after 34 successive years of increases." "Federal Inmate Population Declines," Federal Bureau of Prisons, September 30, 2016, https://www.bop. gov/resources/news/20161004_pop_decline.jsp. The First Step Act, passed into law in December 2018, promises wide ranging criminal justice reform. The problem, however, is that it does not address sentencing reform, which is central to solving the disaster of mass incarceration.

25. Undaunted, in 2008, states figured out a way around having to get voter approval by calling prison bonds something else (Lease Revenue Bonds) and, through the marvels of creative accounting, did not even have to show that the prisons they would build, of course, do not generate revenue. Alex Anderson, "Hiding Out in Prison Bonds," *Forbes*, October 22, 2008.

26. Christian Henrichson and Ruth Delaney, *The Price of Prisons: What Incarceration Costs Taxpayers* (Washington, DC: Vera Institute of Justice, 2012), 1–6. https://www.vera.org/publications/price-of-prisons-what-incarceration-costs-taxpayers.

27. The push for deinstitutionalization was popularized by the movie *One Flew over the Cuckoo's Nest* (1975). In academia by far the most influential books were Erving Goffman, *Asylums: Essays on the Social Situation of Mental Patients and Other Inmates* (New York: Doubleday, 1961); Michel Foucault, *Madness and Civilization: A History of Insanity in the Age of Reason*, trans. Richard Howard (New York: Vintage, 1964). Both of these books were masterpieces, both responsible, in part, for the later societal neglect of the mentally ill in Western civilization in the

twentieth century. One significant cause of the increase in the prison population in the twentieth century was the horrible truth that, due to the campaign by psychologists and sociologists in the 1960s and 1970s against the institutionalization of the mentally ill (Thomas Szasz, *The Myth of Mental Illness: Foundations of a Theory of Personal Conduct* [New York: Harper/Collins, 2011]), coupled with the antipsychiatry movement, two things happened. First, mental asylums everywhere were emptied out and closed. The argument was that the mentally ill should be freed from asylums because they had the "right to be different" (Nicholas N. Kittrie, *The Right to Be Different: Deviance and Enforced Therapy* [New York: Pelican, 1973]). Second, the introduction of new drugs for the treatment of mental illness made some of this deinstitutionalization in theory justifiable, but there was no procedure or infrastructure in place to ensure that those released from institutions would continue to take their prescribed medicines. Many ended up on the streets of large cities begging and homeless, and many found their way into America's prisons. Studies have clearly established that the mentally ill account for around twenty percent of the prison and jail population. Easily the most comprehensive assessment of the evidence is E. Fuller Torrey et al., *More Mentally Ill Persons Are in Jails and Prisons Than Hospitals: A Survey of the States* (Arlington, VA: Treatment Advocacy Center, 2010), https://www.treatmentadvocacycenter.org/storage/documents/final_jails_v_hospitals_study.pdf. This is the civilized solution to mental illness that persists in the twenty-first century. Are the mentally ill more free in a prison than in a mental institution?

28. For example, Aeschylus borrowed the ideas for his Oresteian tragedy from the dim beginnings of Greek history, an unending cycle of vengeful killings, where even the gods could not agree on who was the criminal and who was the punisher. It is the lesser known tragedy that lies behind the story of the wooden horse, and how it was used to defeat the city of Troy. Known as the curse of Agamemnon, it is one of the earliest examples of revenge in Western civilization. The question of justice was too difficult for mortals to resolve: only the gods could decide. And that decision was an uneasy one, leaving a residue of vengeance within the idea of justice that remains until this very day. Aeschylus, *The Oresteian Trilogy*, trans. Philip Vellacott (London: Penguin, 1956).

29. The connection between modern myths of vengeance and ancient myths, as assumed here, is wonderfully demonstrated by Jacob Burckhardt in his 1858 classic *The Civilization of the Renaissance in Italy*, trans. S. G. C. Middlemore (New York: Penguin, 1990). Burckhardt describes the cultural process by which the Italians turned vengeance into an art at both the high levels of culture and the lower levels of peasantry: "Revenge was declared with perfect frankness to be a necessity of human nature" (277) and "Even among the peasantry, we read of Thyestean banquets and mutual assassination on the widest scale" (275).

30. This argument has been made in detail in Graeme R. Newman, *The Punishment Response*, 2nd ed. (New York: Routledge, 2017).

31. The psychological analysis is touched on by Sigmund Freud, *Civilization and Its Discontents*, trans. James Strachey (New York: W. W. Norton, 1961). Also, by Erich Fromm, *The Anatomy of Human Destructiveness* (New York: Holt, Rinehart and Winston, 1973), chs. 9–10. Kevin M. Carlsmith, John M. Darley, and Paul H. Robinson, in a survey—"Why Do We Punish? Deterrence and Just Deserts as Motives for Punishment," *Journal of Personality and Social Psychology* 83, no. 2 (2002): 284–99—found that the people strongly stated preferences for a deterrence-based criminal justice system, but, at the same time, favored a retributive rationale when considering individual sentencing decisions. Respondents felt the need to punish those who intentionally commit "wrong" actions because of "instantly available intuitions that supply their own definitive answers about this" (285), suggesting that an individual is "more likely to voluntarily comply with legal codes when he or she perceives that the system treats people fairly—that is, according to his or her intuitions about what is just" (285)—that is to say, punished retributively, deserving punishment.

32. A number of works have traced the role of the prison as part of the "treatment model" of penology. See, for example, Carl E. Schneider, "The Rise of Prisons and the Origins of the Rehabilitative Ideal," *Michigan Law Review* 77, no. 3 (1979): 707–46. Much of this writing occurred in the 1970s and 1980s. There is a noticeable lack of scholarly writing concerning the rehabilitative ideal in this century. For an exception and excellent overview of the rehabilitative ideal and its consideration by the Supreme Court, see Chad Flanders, "The Supreme Court and the Rehabilitative Ideal," Legal Studies Research Papers Series 2014-3, Saint Louis University School of Law, 2014.

33. Alan M. Dershowitz. *Fair and Certain Punishment*, Twentieth Century Fund, Task Force on Criminal Sentencing (New York: McGraw-Hill, 1976). It is possible that Dershowitz may have shifted his view to come closer to corporal punishment, given his recent argument for the legality of torture under controlled circumstances. See Alan M. Dershowitz, *Why Terrorism Works: Understanding the Threat, Responding to the Challenge* (New Haven, CT: Yale University Press, 2002); "Tortured Reasoning," in *Torture: A Collection*, ed. Sanford Levinson (New York: Oxford University Press, 2004), 257–80. His detractors are many. See, for example, Alfred W. McCoy, *Torture and Impunity: The U.S. Doctrine of Coercive Interrogation* (Madison: University of Wisconsin Press, 2012), 161–67, though this is an obviously ideologically biased book. Much of the argument concerning torture revolves around the issue of whether there is ever any situation in which torture is morally justifiable. Uwe Streinhoff, *On the Ethics of Torture* (Albany: State University of New York Press, 2013), calls those who answer "no" to this question the "absolutists." He recounts many (imaginary) situations in which torture is obviously justifiable, but many of these situations are constructed on the basis of his very broad definition of torture.

34. This is most apparent in the use of different forms of the death penalty. See Newman, *The Punishment Response*, ch. 2.

35. In colonial America, garrulous women who nagged at their husbands too much were, appropriately, gagged by the punishment of a metal bridle (called the "scold's bridle") that was placed over their heads and clamped on their mouths, a painful contraption that responded directly to the offense (also a punishment of incapacitation, as we will discuss further in chapter 5). Another reflection of the quality of the crime in the punishment was to punish a criminal on the very spot where the offense occurred, a practice in English criminal law up until the eighteenth century. Or certain parts of the body were identified as the seat of the crime: to cut out the heart of a traitor, remove the kidneys of a thief, remove the genitals of a rapist or adulterer (also punishments of incapacitation). William Andrews, *Bygone Punishments* (London: William Andrews. 1899).

36. Dante Alighieri, *Hell*, trans. Dorothy L. Sayers (London: Penguin, 1955). For an excellent analysis of Dante's unique theory of punishment applied to modern criminal justice, see Robert A. Ferguson, *Inferno: An Anatomy of American Punishment* (Cambridge, MA: Harvard University Press, 2014). And, for its relationship to vengeance, see Pietro Marongiu and Graeme Newman, *Vengeance: The Fight against Injustice* (Totowa, NJ: Rowman and Littlefield, 1987), ch. 4.

37. The application of "day fines" in Finland and other Scandinavian countries attempts to get around this problem. The fine is made proportional to traffic offenders' incomes. It is an example of the "redistribution of punishment." See Suzanne Daley, "Speeding in Finland Can Cost a Fortune, If You Already Have One," *New York Times*, April 25, 2015.

38. In fact, there are some crimes for which fines appear to punish indirectly the victim as much or more than the offender. It has become the practice, for example, to fine husbands for assaulting their wives, a punishment that seems to encourage the "overflow" of the punishment on to the wife.

39. We also know that forced labor is the least productive. It would become a very expensive way to "repay" the crime. In fact, the state would end up paying for it just as it did in the so-called prison factories that were supposed to pay for themselves at the beginning of the twentieth century. Instead, they were a dismal failure. Chief Justice Burger's call in 1985 for the reintroduction of prison factories is yet another cry of the conservative's paradox. He wants severe punishment; prisons are the only currently available severe punishment; but they cost far too much. Any penologist knows that prison factories have not, and cannot, work. See, for example, John A. Conley, "Prisons, Production, and Profit: Reconsidering the Importance of Prison Industries," *Journal of Social History* 14, no. 2 (1980): 257–75.

40. For a positive look at the prison industry see UNICOR's report that, as of 2017, there were 17,041 inmates participating in the federal prison industries program. UNICOR, *Federal Prison Industries, Inc.: Annual Management Report, Fiscal Year 2018*, https://www.unicor.gov/publications/reports/FY2018_AnnualMgmtReport. pdf. A recent study by the National Institute of Justice reported that there was no significant difference in recidivism rates, after three years, between those who were

in work release programs and those who were not. Cindy J. Smith et al., "Correctional Industries Preparing Inmates for Re-entry: Recidivism and Post-release Employment," research report submitted to the US Department of Justice, May 2006, https://www.ncjrs.gov/pdffiles1/nij/grants/214608.pdf.

41. Eliana Rae Eitches, "Coerced Prison Labor without Union Protection: The Exploitation of the Prison Industrial Complex" (Academic Commons, Columbia University Libraries, 2010), doi:10.7916/D8VX0QZB.

42. The argument is made most strongly by Morris and Tonry, *Between Prison and Probation*. They also presume that the lower prison rates of European countries are somehow due to their use of fines. This ignores the cultural differences in attitude towards punishment, not to mention that the prison rates are driven by many factors, the crime rate being an obvious, but not the only, one.

43. There are probably over one thousand books and articles condemning the use of mass incarceration. Jonathan Simon, "Mass Incarceration on Trial," *Punishment and Society* 13, no. 3 (2011): 251–55, provides a careful analysis of the implications of the Supreme Court decision of *Brown v. Plata* for the future of mass incarceration in America; Ernest Drucker, *A Plague of Prisons: The Epidemiology of Mass Incarceration in America* (New York: New Press, 2013); Mary D. Looman and John D. Carl, *A Country Called Prison: Mass Incarceration and the Making of a New Nation* (New York: Oxford University Press, 2015).

Chapter Five

1. While there are many methodological issues involved, the majority of research does not show that prison terms and other types of criminal justice interventions reduce crime rates. Daniel S. Nagin, "Deterrence in the Twenty-First Century," *Crime and Justice* 42, no. 1 (2013): 199–263.

2. Anthony A. Braga and David L. Weisburd, "The Effects of Focused Deterrence Strategies on Crime: A Systematic Review and Meta-analysis of the Empirical Evidence," *Journal of Research in Crime and Delinquency* 49, no. 3 (2011): 323–58. See also Ross Homel, "Drivers Who Drink and Rational Choice: Random Breath Testing and the Process of Deterrence," in *Routine Activity and Rational Choice*, ed. Ronald V. Clarke and Marcus Felson, Advances in Criminological Theory 5 (New Brunswick, NJ: Transaction, 1993), 59–84; Beau Kilmer et al., "Efficacy of Frequent Monitoring with Swift, Certain, and Modest Sanctions for Violations: Insights from South Dakota's 24/7 Sobriety Project," *American Journal of Public Health* 103, no. 1 (2013): e37–e43. For a critical appraisal of the ineffectiveness of deterrence from a legal point of view, see Kevin C. Kennedy, "A Critical Appraisal of Criminal Deterrence Theory," *Dickinson Law Review* 88, no. 1 (1983): 1–13.

3. A rare study of the deterrent effects of corporal punishment on children in the classroom avoids some of the complexities of the criminal justice system. See

Harold A. Hoff, *Corporal Punishment: Is It Effective? An Empirical Study of School Punishment Records* (n.p.: Create Space Independent Publishing, 2014).Though this study has its own methodological problems, the conclusions of this study were that (1) corporal punishment reduced recidivism of children younger than fifteen and (2) drastically increasing the intensity of corporal punishment did not increase its deterrent effect. Though methodologically questionable, the author claimed that the effectiveness of corporal punishment in the schools studied (Canada, Australia, and England) was more effective than the deterrent effect of prisons in the United States.

4. See, for example, the rancorous debate in the section titled "Directions in Deterrence Theory and Policy" in *Criminology and Public Policy* 15, no. 3 (2016): 721–836.

5. Little new research on the effectiveness of punishment in general has been conducted since that time, and practically none on corporal punishment itself. Most reviews of the research affirm the considerable effectiveness of punishment, including corporal punishment, in controlling behavior, although all add that there may be negative side effects. See Jeanne Ellis Ormrod, "Applications of Instrumental Conditioning," in *Human Learning*, 6th ed. (New York: Pearson, 2012), 113–25. Research on humans continues, particularly on individuals with various kinds of disabilities who are unable to function unless the unwanted behaviors or body movements can be suppressed. Negative stimuli such as nasty tasting substance, loud noise, and nausea-inducing drugs are used to treat some disorders such as alcoholism or smoking. In the 1960s and 1970s the approach was used to treat homosexuality (then considered an illness), resulting in serious complications. The APA (American Psychological Association) has banned its use in this case. Research suggests that negative stimuli may suppress unwanted behaviors but that its effectiveness for the long term has not been established. W. Stewart Agras, "Behavior Therapy in the Management of Chronic Schizophrenia," *American Journal of Psychiatry* 124, no. 2 (1967): 240–43; Ricks Warren and Robert T. Kurlychek, "Treatment of Maladaptive Anger and Aggression: Catharsis vs. Behavior Therapy," *Corrective and Social Psychiatry and Journal of Behavior Technology, Methods and Therapy* 27, no. 3 (1981): 35–139; Sandra L. Harris and Robin Ersner-Hershfield, "Behavioral Suppression of Seriously Disruptive Behavior in Psychotic and Retarded Patients: A Review of Punishment and Its Alternatives," *Psychological Bulletin* 85, no. 6 (1978): 1352–75; Saul Axelrod and Jack Apasche, eds., *The Effects of Punishment on Human Behavior* (Cambridge, MA: Academic Press, 2013). Electronic dog collars are widely available on the market. It is also important to understand that most aversive therapy (that is, painful therapy) uses a "classical conditioning" model requiring that the pain be applied contiguous with the behavior to be suppressed. Of course, in the criminal justice system, this is impossible. The punishment always comes *after*, often *well after*, the forbidden behavior. Even in other settings, such as home or school, the punishment almost always comes after the infraction, not at the same time. A recent study of what I would call "virtual punishment" (human subjects, usually

university students, are provided with scenarios, and they answer questions about them) tested the celerity and certainty of punishment in criminal justice settings. They discovered a U curve of deterrence where certainty was extremely effective, as was uncertainty when celerity was not. Johannes Buckenmaier, Eugen Dimant, Ann-Christin Posten, and Ulrich Schmidt, *On Punishment Institutions and Effective Deterrence of Illicit Behavior* (Kiel Working Paper 2090, Kiel Institute for the World Economy and University of Johannesburg, 2017).

6. Robert Martinson, "What Works? Questions and Answers about Prison Reform," *Public Interest* 35 (Spring 1974): 22–54. There have been some attempts to resurrect the finding of Martinson and many attempts to soften his dictum. See, for example, Rick Sarre, "Beyond 'What Works?' A 25 Year Jubilee Retrospective of Robert Martinson's Famous Article," *Australian and New Zealand Journal of Criminology* 34 (2001): 38–46; Paul Gendreau and Robert R. Ross, "Revivification of Rehabilitation: Evidence from the 1980s," *Justice Quarterly* 4, no. 3 (1987): 349–407. The nothing works thesis was again affirmed by David Farabee, *Rethinking Rehabilitation* (Washington, DC: AEI Press, 2005); followed by another attempt to neutralize his thesis by Francis T. Cullen, Paula Smith, Christopher T. Lowenkamp, and Edward J. Latessa, "Nothing Works Revisited: Deconstructing Farabee's *Rethinking Rehabilitation*," *Victims and Offenders* 4, no. 2 (2009): 101–23.

7. Of course, much psychological research on punishment has also investigated the effects of rewards on changing behavior. See Laetitia B. Mulder, "The Difference between Punishments and Rewards in Fostering Moral Concerns in Social Decision Making," *Journal of Experimental Social Psychology* 44, no. 6 (2008): 1436–43. Clearly, this presents a problem in criminal justice where it is inconceivable that criminals would be rewarded for their crimes rather than punished. Yet the novel by famed learning psychologist B. F. Skinner, *Walden II*, imagined such a society.

8. Robert Graham Caldwell, *Red Hannah: Delaware's Whipping Post* (Philadelphia: University of Pennsylvania Press, 1947). Caldwell's views against whipping were vigorously advanced, which probably affected his objectivity. For a more detailed analysis and discussion of bias in the research, see Graeme R. Newman, *Just and Painful: A Case for the Corporal Punishment of Criminals* (New York: Macmillan, 1983), ch. 13.

9. For a more detailed discussion of the committee's bias, see Newman, *Just and Painful*, ch. 13.

10. The Home Office Committee did locate two cases in which whipping alone was the punishment, and actually found that whipping had a decided deterrent effect. Of course, because of the small sample, we cannot draw any definite conclusions from such observations.

11. Departmental Committee on Corporal Punishment, *Command Paper*, No. 5684, Honourable Edward Cardogan, chairman (London: HMSO, 1938).

12. The committee was confronted with some good arguments. For example, some witnesses complained that merely to give a juvenile probation for an offense

that might have included very substantial damage to property and even to life and limb did not seem just, or at least failed to fit the punishment to the crime (retribution). Yet the committee dismissed this evidence on the grounds that it could not allow criminal justice to be "dominated by these few exceptions," and that it was by its deterrent value that corporal punishment should be judged. The committee had set as its task to discover whether corporal punishment had deterred crime in England and Wales, and its conclusion was, predictably, that it could not be shown to have done so, and therefore should be abolished.

13. Committee on Corporal Punishment, *Command Paper*.

14. The committee never considered seriously the possibility of using corporal punishment in and of itself without prison, except in the case of juveniles, for whom it was also rejected because it was not in line with the treatment philosophy. All of the data on which it based its conclusions were data in which corporal punishment had been administered in addition to a prison term (as in the Caldwell study), so that it was never possible to separate the effects of the two. For a more extensive analysis of the research and bias in both the Caldwell and British Home Office studies, see Newman, *Just and Painful*.

15. Whether or not it is a justified criticism itself remains an open question, since some argue that the reason there are disproportionately more minorities in prison is that they commit a disproportionate amount of crime. Heather MacDonald, "Obama's Tragic Let 'Em Out Fantasy," *Wall Street Journal*, October 23, 2015.

16. We have seen that there are some situations in which individual (not general) deterrent techniques were not too different from the position advanced by the defenders of classic retribution, in which the aim was to punish only a specific piece of behavior, leaving the individual untouched. To repeat, punish the act, not the actor. This would mean, among other things that punishing an individual for a second or subsequent offense, as occurs with "three strikes" laws advocated by utilitarians of various stripes is morally offensive to retribution, especially if the severity of the punishment was increased in conjunction with each repeated offense. The classic exposition of this view of retribution is J. D. Mabbott, "Punishment," *Mind* 48, no. 190 (1939): 152–67.

Chapter Six

1. Michel Foucault, *Madness and Civilization: A History of Insanity in the Age of Reason*, trans. Richard Howard (New York: Vintage, 1964).

2. Michel Foucault, *Discipline and Punish: The Birth of the Prison*, trans. Alan Sheridan (New York: Pantheon, 1977).

3. Cyndi Banks, *Prisons in the United States: A Reference Handbook* (Santa Barbara, CA: ABC-CLIO, 2017).

4. For example, replacing the dreadful Rikers Island jail with a series of county jails. See Fred Cohen, "A Friendly Exchange: From Rikers Island Jail to a Progressive Prison," *Correctional Law Reporter*, June/July 2017.

5. Jess Maghan, "Long-Term and Dangerous Inmates: Maximum Security Incarceration in the United States" (working paper, Great Cities Institute, College of Urban Planning and Public Affairs, University of Illinois at Chicago, 1996).

6. One can do it within maximum security institutions, but predicting violence outside of those institutions is unreliable. See Henrik Belfrage, Ran Fransson, and Susanne Strand, "Prediction of Violence Using the HCR-20: A Prospective Study in Two Maximum-Security Correctional Institutions," *Journal of Forensic Psychiatry* 11, no. 1 (2000): 167–75. What appears to be a possible exception is the work by Richard Berk using massive quantities of data to develop algorithms to predict future offending. Claims of over 90 percent accuracy of predicting who will commit are certainly striking. See Trey Popp, "Black Box Justice," *Pennsylvania Gazette*, September/October 2017; Richard Berk and Justin Bleich, "Statistical Procedures for Forecasting Criminal Behavior: A Comparative Assessment," *Criminology and Public Policy* 12, no. 3 (2013): 513–44. There are considerable moral, ethical and legal problems that lie in the way of these robotic solutions. See Alexandra Chouldechova and Max G'Sell, "Fairer and More Accurate, but for Whom?," June 30, 2017, arXiv:1707.00046. Further, Rhys Hester and Todd Hartman, "Conditional Race Disparities in Criminal Sentencing: A Test of the Liberation Hypothesis from a Non-guidelines State," *Journal of Quantitative Criminology* 33, no. 1 (2017): 77–100; Rhys Hester and Eric L. Sevigny, "Court Communities in Local Context: A Multilevel Analysis of Felony Sentencing in South Carolina," *Journal of Crime and Justice* 39, no. 1 (2016): 55–74.

7. Bernard E. Harcourt, *Against Prediction: Profiling, Policing, and Punishing in an Actuarial Age* (Chicago: University of Chicago Press, 2008).

8. Daniel P. Mears, *Evaluating the Effectiveness of Supermax Prisons* (Washington, DC: Urban Institute, 2006), https://www.urban.org/research/publication/evaluating-effectiveness-supermax-prisons.

9. Computed from the incomplete list on *Wikipedia*, "List of Serial Killers in the United States," https://en.wikipedia.org/wiki/List_of_serial_killers_in_the_United_States.

10. John D. Finn, "Brutal 'Oregon Boot' Made Our State Prison Famous," *Offbeat Oregon*, March 9, 2014, http://offbeatoregon.com/1403b.oregon-boot-cruel-unusual-punishment.html.

11. This partial list is taken in part from Penal Reform International, *Instruments of Restraint. Addressing Risk Factors to Prevent Torture and Ill-Treatment*, Factsheet (London: Penal Reform International, 2013), https://cdn.penalreform.org/wp-content/uploads/2016/01/factsheet-5-restraints-2nd-ed-v5.pdf.

12. Valid data are particularly difficult to find. Generally, at any one time there are probably about eighty to a hundred thousand criminals in solitary confinement.

"Supermax" prisons are commonly a repository for extended solitary confinement, some inmates spending years or even decades in solitary. See Solitary Watch for a useful collection of facts and figures, http://solitarywatch.com/facts/faq/. The movement for abolition of solitary confinement is growing. See, for example, Amy Fettig, "What Is Driving Solitary Confinement Reform?," *Correctional Law Reporter*, October/November 2016.

13. One is reminded of *Murderers among Us*, the title of Simon Wiesenthal's book in which he recounted his pursuit of Nazi war criminals. Many such individuals lived among ordinary people who had no idea of their previous crimes. Simon Wiesenthal, *Murderers among Us* (New York: McGraw-Hill, 1967).

14. The pivotal Supreme Court case was Smith v. Doe, 538 U.S. 84, 89 (2003), where it found that sex offender registries were administrative, not punitive, and therefore were not unconstitutional according to the Eighth Amendment. Recent cases have argued that they violate the due process clause of the Fourth Amendment. Of course, if we applied this argument to prison, the same would apply. For an exhaustive review, see Catherine L. Carpenter and Amy E. Beverlin, "The Evolution of Unconstitutionality in Sex Offender Registration Laws," *Hastings Law Journal* 63, no. 4 (2012): 1071–1133.

15. See, for example, Joan Petersilia, *House Arrest* (Washington, DC: US Department of Justice, National Institute of Justice, 1988); US Probation and Pretrial Services, *Home Confinement*, Court and Community (n.p.: author, 2000), http://www.nhp.uscourts.gov/sites/default/files/pdf/cchome.pdf; Paul J. Hofer and Barbara S. Meierhoefer, *Home Confinement: An Evolving Sanction in the Federal Criminal Justice System* (Washington, DC: Federal Judicial Center, 1987).

16. There are also different degrees of severity of home confinement that range from total confinement to the home, physically, to allowance of visitors, allowance to visit a doctor or go shopping, and so on. Many uses of these options are commonly applied to probation or parole, but they threaten incarceration if the rules are broken.

17. See, for example, Erving Goffman, *Asylums: Essays on the Social Situation of Mental Patients and Other Inmates* (New York: Doubleday, 1961), probably the most influential book that spawned the deinstiutionalization movement. See also note 27 in chapter 4.

18. Christian Haasen et al., "Heroin-Assisted Treatment for Opioid Dependence: Randomised Controlled Trial," *British Journal of Psychiatry* 191, no. 1 (2007): 55–62.

19. The cost estimates differ widely, depending on whether they are assessed by advocates for or against the death penalty. However, both prison without parole and the death penalty cost roughly the same, that is, very expensive. It costs about $150 thousand a year to maintain an inmate on death row, plus over a million dollars to kill him. Life in prison without parole comes to around $5 million for a life term of fifty years.

20. Low-level life support currently costs about $2 thousand a day in an intensive care unit. However, this cost would be driven down given that the inmate in induced coma is healthy at the start of the coma, and needs only low-level life support to keep him alive.

21. Graeme R. Newman, *The Punishment Response*, 2nd ed. (New York: Routledge, 2017), 7.

22. Arye Rattner, "Convicted but Innocent: Wrongful Conviction and the Criminal Justice System," *Law and Human Behavior* 12, no. 3 (1988): 283–93.

23. D. Michael Risinger, "Innocents Convicted: An Empirical Justified Factual Wrongful Conviction Rate," *Journal of Criminal Law and Criminology* 97, no. 3 (2007): 761–806.

24. We are unable to selectively forget. Only God can do that: " 'They will all know Me, from the least of them to the greatest of them,' declares the Lord, 'for I will forgive their iniquity, and their sin I will remember no more.' " Jeremiah 31:34 (ESV).

25. David J. Rothman, *Discovery of the Asylum: Social Order and Disorder in the New Republic*, rev. ed. (New Brunswick, NJ: Aldine Transaction, 2002).

26. Graeme R. Newman, "A Theory of Deviance Removal," *British Journal of Sociology* 26, no. 2 (1975): 203–17; "Theories of Punishment Reconsidered: Rationalizations for Removal," *International Journal of Criminology and Penology* 3, no. 2 (1975): 163–82.

27. See Newman, *The Punishment Response*, for a review of these criticisms.

28. For an examination of the norm of reciprocity in relation to punishment, see Newman, *The Punishment Response*.

29. I have made this point several times throughout the book. See Digby Anderson, ed., *This Will Hurt: The Restoration of Virtue and Civic Order* (New York: National Review Books, 1995), for a collection of essays reaffirming the connection between punishment, guilt, and morality.

30. Dante Aleghieri, *Hell* and *Purgatory*, trans. Dorothy L. Sayers (London: Penguin, 1955).

31. While vengeance does play an important part in Dante, it is more an expression of Dante's anger against his own particular political enemies. See Pietro Marongiu and Graeme R. Newman, *Vengeance: The Fight against Injustice* (Totowa, NJ: Littlefield Adams, 1986).

32. See, for example, Ernest van den Haag, *Punishing Criminals: Concerning a Very Old and Painful Question* (New York: Basic Books, 1975); Richard Dagger, "Restitution, Punishment, and Debts to Society," in *Victims, Offenders, and Alternative Sanctions*, ed. Joe Hudson and Burt Galaway (Lexington, MA: D. C. Heath, 1980), 3–13.

33. Barnett takes the most extreme position on this point. See Randy E. Barnett, "Restitution: A New Paradigm of Criminal Justice," *Ethics* 87, no. 4 (1977): 279–301.

34. van den Haag, *Punishing Criminals*.

35. Nils Christie, *The Limits to Pain* (London: Robertson, 1981). See also Harold E. Pepinsky, "This Can't Be Peace: A Pessimist Looks at Punishment," in *Punishment and Privilege*, ed. Graeme R. Newman, 2nd ed. (New York: Harrow and Heston, 2018), 120–32; Hadar Dancig-Rosenberg and Tali Galt, "Restorative Criminal Justice," *Cardozo Law Review* 34, no. 6 (2013): 2313–46.

36. This observation is surely no great surprise: it is why, in feuding societies, the reaping of revenge on the offender *or* his family or other members of his clan has been seen as entirely appropriate. Marongiu and Newman, *Vengeance*. Exactly the same model applies to juvenile gang "warfare": Sanyika Shakur, *Monster: The Autobiography of an L.A. Gang Member* (New York: Penguin, 1994).

37. Newman, *The Punishment Response*. The "good" that was served by these debt payments is generally considered by scholars of the Middle Ages to have been considerable: it averted the interminable and extremely violent process of feuding. See also Donald Black, "Crime as Social Control," *American Sociological Review* 48, no. 1 (1983): 34–45.

38. Indeed, this view of evil has even made its way into the writings of some criminologists. See, for example, Nigel Walker, *The Aims of the Penal System* (Edinburgh: Edinburgh University Press, 1966).

39. Newman, *The Punishment Response*.

40. Barnett, "Restitution."

41. See Dagger, "Restitution, Punishment, and Debts," for an extensive and convincing critique.

42. Dagger, "Restitution, Punishment, and Debts," 363.

43. Stephen Schafer, *Compensation and Restitution to Victims of Crime*, 2nd ed. (Montclair, NJ: Patterson Smith, 1970).

44. Others have argued that restitution is quite compatible with other aims of punishment, such as deterrence or the "expressive" function of punishment. Dagger, "Restitution, Punishment, and Debts."

45. There has always been a critical shortage of donor organs. See Graeme R. Newman, *Just and Painful: A Case for the Corporal Punishment of Criminals*, 2nd ed. (New York: Harrow and Heston, 1995), ch. 15, for a review. Recent statistics show that the shortage is much worse. See T. Randolph Beard, David L. Kaserman, and Rigmar Osterkamp, *The Global Organ Shortage: Economic Causes, Human Consequences, Policy Responses* (Redwood City, CA: Stanford University Press, 2013).

46. "Organ Donation and Transplantation Can Save Lives," on index page of Organ Procurement and Transplantation Network, US Department of Health and Human Services, https://optn.transplant.hrsa.gov.

47. Donate Life America, "Deaths Equivalent to 22 Jumbo Jets Crashing Every Year Due to Organ Donor Shortage," press release, June 17, 2014, https://www.donatelife.net/news/deaths-equivalent-to-22-jumbo-jets-crashing-every-year-due-to-organ-donor-shortage-press-release/.

48. See Alex Tabarrok, "The Meat Market," *Wall Street Journal*, January 8, 2010, https://www.wsj.com/articles/SB10001424052748703481004574646233272990474.

49. In 1990, *Time Magazine* reported that Turkish peasants were selling their kidneys for $4.4 thousand each in Britain.

50. See, for example, C. S. Lewis, "The Humanitarian Theory of Punishment," in *Contemporary Punishment*, ed. Rudolph J. Gerber and Patrick D. McAnany (Notre Dame, IN: University of Notre Dame Press, 1972).

51. Of course, there are many legal, moral, and political issues involved. See, for example, the *Wikipedia* entry on the topic, "Organ Donation in the United States Prison Population," https://en.wikipedia.org/wiki/Organ_donation_in_the_United_States_prison_population.

52. David J. Rothman and Sheila M. Rothman, "The Organ Market," *New York Review of Books*, October 23, 2003, https://www.nybooks.com/articles/2003/10/23/the-organ-market/

53. See Newman, *The Punishment Response*, for a history of dissection as a punishment in the early eighteenth century, and its relationship to the early growth of medical sciences.

54. Quoted in Shu S. Lin et al., "Prisoners on Death Row Should Be Accepted as Organ Donors," *Annals of Thoracic Surgery* 93, no. 6 (2012): 773–79.

55. He reported that the corrections department denied his request on the grounds that "the interests of the public and condemned inmates are best served by denying the petition." Lin et al., "Prisoners," 774.

Chapter Seven

1. James E. Mazur, *Learning and Behavior*, 3rd ed. (Englewood Cliffs, NJ: Prentice Hall, 1994), 165–66.

2. Mazur, *Learning and Behavior*, 169–70.

3. Norval Morris and Michael Tonry, *Between Prison and Probation: Intermediate Punishments in a Rational Sentencing System* (New York: Oxford University Press, 1991).

4. Robin McKie, "Shamed Nobel Laureate Tim Hunt 'Ruined by Rush to Judgment after stupid remarks.'" *Guardian*, June 13, 2015, https://www.theguardian.com/science/2015/jun/13/tim-hunt-forced-to-resign.

5. Given a clearer penal philosophy oriented to control, however, it is possible that prison could be turned into a punishment that provides much more control and specificity than is currently possible. See Charles H. Logan, *Criminal Justice Performance Measures for Prisons* (Washington, DC: National Institute of Justice, 1993).

6. Cathy S. Widom, "Does Violence Beget Violence? A Critical Examination of the Literature," *Psychological Bulletin* 106, no. 1 (1989): 3–28; see also Emily M. Wright and Abigail A. Fagan, "The Cycle of Violence in Context: Exploring the

Moderating Roles of Neighborhood Disadvantage and Cultural Norms," *Criminology* 51, no. 2 (2013): 217–49.

7. In the studies that surveyed random samples of the adult population, the questions asked the respondents were not in fact about corporal punishment, but about violence. Straus equates violence with corporal punishment without taking into account the context in which corporal punishment occurs—not necessarily one of abuse, as he automatically assumes, but more often one of discipline. Murray A. Straus, *Beating the Devil Out of Them: Corporal Punishment in American Families* (New York: Lexington, 1994). In fact electric shock has been found to curtail aggressive behavior.

8. Kenneth L. Lichstein and Laura Schreibman, "Employing Electric Shock with Autistic Children: A Review of the Side Effects," *Journal of Autism and Childhood Schizophrenia* 6, no. 2 (1976): 163–73; John Crosbie, "Negative Reinforcement and Punishment," in *Handbook of Research Methods in Human Operant Behavior*, ed. Kennon A. Lattal and Michael Perone (New York: Plenum Press,1998), 163–89; Johnny L. Matson and Marie E. Taras, "A 20 Year Review of Punishment and Alternative Methods to Treat Problem Behaviors in Developmentally Delayed Persons," *Research in Developmental Disabilities* 10, no. 1 (1989): 85–104; Johnny L. Matson and Thomas M. DiLorenzo, *Punishment and Its Alternatives: A New Perspective for Behavior Modification* (New York: Springer, 1984); Dorothea C. Lerman and Christina M. Vorndran, "On the Status of Knowledge for Using Punishment: Implications for Treating Behavior Disorders," *Journal of Applied Behavior Analysis* 35, no. 4 (2002): 431–64; Deborah Gorman-Smith and Johnny L. Matson, "A Review of Treatment Research for Self-injurious and Stereotyped Responding," *Journal of Mental Deficiency Research* 29, no. 4 (1985): 295–308; Sandra L. Harris and Robin Ersner-Hershfield, "Behavioral Suppression of Seriously Disruptive Behavior in Psychotic and Retarded Patients: A Review of Punishment and Its Alternatives," *Psychological Bulletin* 85, no. 6 (1978): 1352–75; Farzana Shehla, "Behavior Modification through Punishment: Does It Work?," *Excellence* 2, no. 1 (2014): 42–51; Rachel H. Thompson et al., "Effects of Reinforcement for Alternative Behavior during Punishment of Selfinjury," *Journal of Applied Behavior Analysis* 32, no. 3 (1999): 317–28.

9. Doris L. MacKenzie and Gaylene S. Armstrong, eds., *Correctional Boot Camps: Military Basic Training or a Model for Corrections?* (Thousand Oaks, CA: Sage, 2004). And parallel to "shock incarceration" are the camps and other institutions run by the "troubled teen industry." Jesse Hyde, "Life and Death in a Troubled Teen Boot Camp," *Rolling Stone*, November 12, 2015, http://www.rollingstone.com/culture/news/life-and-death-in-a-troubled-teen-boot-camp-20151112.

10. There is a complicated relationship between repression (deterrence) and its unintended side effects, retaliation and resentment. See, for example, Gary Lafree, Laura Dugan, and Raven Korte, "The Impact of British Counterterrorist Strategies on Political Violence in Northern Ireland: Comparing Deterrence and Backlash Models," *Criminology* 47, no. 1 (2009): 17–45; Keren Sharvit et al., "The Effects

of Israeli Use of Coercive and Conciliatory Tactics on Palestinian's Use of Terrorist Tactics: 2000–2006," *Dynamics of Asymmetric Conflict* 6, nos. 1–3 (2013): 22–44.

11. Merry Morash and Lila Rucker, "A Critical Look at the Idea of Boot Camp as a Correctional Reform," *Crime and Delinquency* 36, no. 2 (1990): 204–22; see also Tiffany Bergin, *The Evidence Enigma: Correctional Boot Camps and Other Failures in Evidence-Based Policymaking* (London: Routledge, 2013), ch. 2.

12. See Mark Pizzato, *Theatres of Human Sacrifice: From Ancient Ritual to Screen Violence*, Psychoanalysis and Culture (New York: State University of New York Press, 2004), who reviews the various theories of why violence is so spectacular and how it functions in movies and theater. Also Thomas Scheff, *Catharsis in Healing, Ritual and Drama* (Los Angeles: University of California Press, 2014).

13. An overview of alternatives to incarceration cites mixed recidivism results in New York City when comparing alternative incarceration participants to incarcerated counterparts but still (persuasively) argues for their retention: "Even where recidivism rates are comparable, alternative incarceration sentences avoid the financial costs of incarceration, the disruption of employment, and the human costs of frayed family relations and depleted communities." Marsha Weissman, "Aspiring to the Impracticable: Alternatives to Incarceration in the Era of Mass Incarceration," *New York University Review of Law and Social Change* 33 (2009): 244. For arguments in favor of community alternatives, see website of Center for Community Alternatives, http://www.communityalternatives.org/.

14. For examples, see Calvert R. Dodge, *A World without Prisons: Alternatives to Incarceration throughout the World* (Lexington, MA: D. C. Heath, 1979); also, D. Biles, "Imprisonment and Its Alternatives," *Australian Law Journal* 55, no. 3 (1981): 126–34, who suggests that the effectiveness of alternatives should be measured by the public acceptance of them as punishments. See also Christopher Hartney and Susan Marchionna, *Attitudes of US Voters toward Non-serious Offenders and Alternatives to Incarceration* (Oakland, CA: National Council on Crime and Delinquency, 2009), http://www.nccdglobal.org/sites/default/files/publication_pdf/focus-voter-attitudes.pdf. This survey found that a majority of respondents favored community alternatives to prison for nonserious crimes. Buried in a footnote and in small print is the definition of nonserious crime: "For the purposes of the poll and this Focus, we define 'nonviolent, non-serious offenders' as those convicted of nonviolent, nonsexual crimes in which the value of lost property did not exceed $400." This definition of a nonserious crime of course biased the responses. These crimes are not the problem. It is crimes that are more serious than this, including some drug and violent crimes for which alternatives to incarceration are needed.

15. One of many instances: "Man Arrested in Sex Sting Operation Commits Suicide," WDEZ, September 25, 2013, http://wdez.com/news/articles/2013/sep/25/man-arrested-in-sex-sting-operation-commits-suicide/.

16. There is a vast amount of research demonstrating this fact: Amy E. Hirsch et al., *Every Door Closed: Barriers Facing Parents with Criminal Records* (Philadelphia:

Community Legal Services, 2002), http://www.clasp.org/resources-and-publications/files/every_door_closed.pdf; Megan Comfort, "Punishment Beyond the Legal Offender," *Annual Review of Law and Social Science* 3 (2007): 271–96. Comfort argues that not only are suspects' or inmates' networks of relationships negatively affected by potential loss of finances and stigma, but also typically do not reap the "benefits" that prisoners do, such as getting a GED in prison, job training, or alcoholic rehabilitation. Meredith Martin Rountree, "Law and Loss: Notes on the Legal Construction of Pain," *American Journal of Criminal Law* 41, no. 2 (2014): 4–17. Rountree catalogs the racial disparities in mass incarceration throughout the 1990s and early 2000s. She notes, "The health of the families of those incarcerated may deteriorate, and incarceration can compound family instability. Over half of all prisoners have children under the age of eighteen, and about 45 percent of those parents were living with their children at the time they were sent to prison. As of 2008, 1.75 percent of white children, 3.5 percent of Latino children, and 11 percent of black children—about 1.2 million—had a parent in prison" (5). See also Christopher Muller and Christopher Wildeman, "Punishment and Inequality," in *Handbook of Punishment and Society*, ed. Jonathan Simon and Richard Sparks (Thousand Oaks, CA: Sage, 2012), 169–85; Paddy Hillyard and Steve Tombs, "From 'Crime' to Social Harm?," *Crime, Law and Social Change* 48, nos. 1–2 (2007): 9–25; Paddy Hillyard, Christina Pantazis, Steve Tombs, and Dave Gordon, " 'Social Harm' and Its Limits?," in *Criminal Obsessions: Why Harm Matters More Than Crime*, ed. Paddy Hillyard, Christina Pantazis, Steve Tombs, Dave Gordon, and Danny Dorling (London: Crime and Society Foundation, 2005), 59–73; Christopher Wildeman, Kristin Turney, and Youngmin Yi, "Paternal Incarceration and Family Functioning: Variation across Federal, State, and Local Facilities," *Annals of the American Academy of Political and Social Science* 665, no. 1 (2016): 80–97; Sarah Halpern-Meekin and Kristin Turney, "Relationship Churning and Parenting Stress among Mothers and Fathers," *Journal of Marriage and Family* 78, no. 3 (2016): 715–29; Kristin Turney, "Beyond Average Effects: Incorporating Heterogeneous Treatment Effects into Family Research," *Journal of Family Theory and Review* 7, no. 4 (2015): 468–81; Kristin Turney, "Liminal Men: Incarceration and Relationship Dissolution," *Social Problems* 62, no. 4 (2015): 499–528.

17. Jill Levenson and Richard Tewksbury, "Collateral Damage: Family Members of Registered Sex Offenders," *American Journal of Criminal Justice* 34, nos. 1–2 (2009): 54–68.

18. Each case where the death penalty is sought costs around $2 million. Maintaining an offender on death row costs $90 thousand a year according to the Death Penalty Information Center website at https://files.deathpenaltyinfo.org/documents/pdf/FactSheet.f1564498881.pdf. One study found that seeking the death penalty in federal murder cases is eight times more expensive than prosecuting for prison sentences. See Subcommittee on Federal Death Penalty Cases, Committee on Defender Services, Judicial Conference of the United States, *Federal Death Penalty*

Cases: Recommendations concerning the Cost and Quality of Defense Representation (1998), https://www.uscourts.gov/sites/default/files/original_spencer_report.pdf. The cost also carries over into the cost of incarcerating such inmates. See Katherine Baicker, "The Budgetary Repercussions of Capital Convictions" (Working Paper 8382, National Bureau of Economic Research, Cambridge, MA, 2001), http://www.nber.org/papers/w8382.pdf. Also, Vera Institute of Justice, *Recalibrating Justice: A Review of 2013 State Sentencing and Corrections Trends*, 2013, https://www.vera.org/newsroom/press-releases/thirty-five-states-enacted-reforms-to-reduce-prison-populations-lower-costs-and-improve-public-safety-in-2013-new-review-says.

19. The Vera Institute study of 2012 estimated that the cost per inmate was over $30 thousand, in some states much more. The combined cost for the 40 states surveyed was close to $40 billion. Christian Henrichson and Ruth Delaney, *The Price of Prisons: What Incarceration Costs Taxpayers* (Washington, DC: Vera Institute of Justice, 2012). The increasing age of those incarcerated is also contributing to increased cost. See Lauren Kirchner, "The Elderly Prison Population Is Soaring and So Are Its Costs," *Pacific Standard*, April 2, 2015, https://psmag.com/the-elderly-prisoner-population-is-soaring-and-so-are-its-costs-24ddd8d28877#.fodtiaa4y.

20. In general, probation is cheaper than prison (it ought to be!), especially for drug offenders. See Doug McVay, Vincent Schiraldi, and Jason Ziedenberg, *Treatment or Incarceration? National and State Findings on the Efficacy and Cost Savings of Drug Treatment versus Imprisonment* (Washington, DC: Justice Policy Institute, 2004), http://www.justicepolicy.org/uploads/justicepolicy/documents/04-01_rep_md treatmentorincarceration_ac-dp.pdf. With the exception of electronic monitoring, there appears to be no definitive evidence that probation reduces recidivism. See National Institute of Justice, *Electronic Monitoring Reduces Recidivism* (Washington, DC: US Department of Justice, Office of Justice Programs, 2011), https://www.ncjrs.gov/pdffiles1/nij/234460.pdf.

21. *Times Union*, September 17, 1995, 1, cited in Graeme R. Newman, *Just and Painful: A Case for the Corporal Punishment of Criminals*, 2nd ed. (New York: Harrow and Heston, 1995), 99. Also, Mark Scolforo, "States Begin to Go After Restitution Owed by Criminals," *Times Union*, December 22, 2007, http://www.timesunion.com/news/nation-world/article/States-begin-to-go-after-restitution-owed-by-1837869.php.

22. Campbell Robertson, "For Offenders Who Can't Pay, It's a Pint of Blood or Jail Time," *New York Times*, October 19, 2015. Said Judge Wiggins of Marion, Alabama, "If you don't have any money, go out there and give blood and bring in a receipt indicating you gave blood."

23. Dante was an expert at this art. See especially his volume *Purgatory*, trans. Dorothy L. Sayers (London: Penguin, 1955).

24. Surveys showed that the majority of victims and their families felt that the truth and reconciliation commission was basically used for political expediency. Brandon Hamber et al. "Survivors' Perceptions of the Truth and Reconciliation

Commission and Suggestions for the Final Report," Centre for the Study of Violence and Reconciliation and the Khulumani Support Group, February 1998, https://www.csvr.org.za/index.php/publications/1705-submission-to-the-truth-and-reconciliation-commission-survivors-perceptions-of-the-truth-and-reconciliation-commission-and-suggestions-for-the-final-report.html.

25. "Therein lies the central irony of the Commission. As people give more and more evidence of the things they have done they get closer and closer to amnesty and it gets more and more intolerable that these people should be given amnesty." William Kentridge, "Director's Note," in *Ubu and the Truth Commission*, by Jane Taylor (Cape Town: University of Cape Town Press, 2007), xi.

26. An interesting exception to this observation is Justice Action, "Cost-Effectiveness of Prisons," http://www.justiceaction.org.au/index.php?option=com_content&view=article&id=801:cost-effectiveness-of-prisons&catid=204&Itemid=1022. This study of New South Wales (Australia) criminal punishments compared the cost of long and short terms of imprisonment, drug court, periodic detention, home detention, probation, and parole. The cheapest were probation and parole, around $5 a day. The most expensive, of course, prison, on average $160 a day. The cost of prison was defined as "both tangible (including the costs of building, maintaining and running prisons) and hidden costs (including psychological trauma, the impact on family members and the impact on employment and housing opportunities)."

27. See McVay, Schiraldi, and Ziedenberg, *Treatment or Incarceration?* This study found that drug treatment instead of a prison term was cost effective.

28. The treatise was first published in 1764. Beccaria's grandson, the great Italian novelist Allesandro Manzoni, noted wryly that although Beccaria's treatise seemed to have spawned the movement against torture in Europe, the work was badly misinformed as to the criminal justice practices of the day. See also Graeme R. Newman and Pietro Marongiu, "Penological Reform and the Myth of Beccaria," *Criminology* 28, no. 2 (1990): 325–46. A new annotated translation of the treatise by the same authors extends this critique and offers insights into many of the more obscure passages of the treatise: Cesare Beccaria, *On Crimes and Punishments*, trans. Graeme R. Newman and Pietro Marongiu (New Brunswick, NJ: Transaction, 2009).

29. The first strong statement against discretion was by Marvin E. Frankel, *Criminal Sentences: Law without Order* (New York: Hill and Wang, 1972). For an assessment of their effectiveness in federal courts, Kate Smith and José A. Cabranes, *Fear of Judging: Sentencing Guidelines in the Federal Courts* (Chicago: University of Chicago Press, 1998). For a review of the main issues, see Loraine Gelsthorpe and Nicola Padfield, eds., *Exercising Discretion: Decision Making in the Criminal Justice System and Beyond* (London: Willan, 2003); Cassia Spohn, *How Do Judges Decide? The Search for Fairness and Justice in Punishment*, 2nd ed. (Thousand Oaks, CA: Sage, 2009).

30. It is not so much the types of punishments offered in Shari'a law that are a problem, but rather a disagreement between Western law and Shari'a as to the matching of the seriousness of the punishment to the seriousness of the crime.

31. This philosophy was expressed by Judge Russell Leggett who was interviewed on the ABC network *Nightline* concerning his deliberations as to the sentencing of Jean Harris for the murder of the famous diet doctor in 1980: "Each case is unique," he said, "the judge must weigh up the circumstances for each case." We may interpret such pronouncements as the judge's attempt to reassert his right of discretion. Jean Harris was sentenced to fifteen years in prison for the murder of her lover, Herman Tarnower, in 1980, Scarsdale, New York.

32. For a critical review of how judges make decisions, see Spohn, *How Do Judges Decide?*

33. Morris and Tonry, *Between Prison and Probation*, criticized the guidelines movement for paying too much attention to the in-or-out decision of prison. They argued that this focus detracted from the consideration of other types of punishments, and they were right. But what other types of punishments for serious crimes were there then or are available now? There are still no credibly painful alternative punishments to prison for serious offenders, or any persons sentenced to prison for that matter.

34. See, for example, Alleyne v. United States, 570 U.S. 99 (2013).

35. See Michael Tonry, "Structured Sentencing," *Crime and Justice* 10 (1988): 267–337.

36. The interested reader may wish to refer to Jack M. Kress, *Prescription for Justice: The Theory and Practice of Sentencing Guidelines* (Boston, MA: Ballinger, 1980), still the seminal work in this field, for a more detailed account of the origin, research, and practice of sentencing guidelines.

37. In twenty-first-century language, these variables are what make up sentencing "algorithms." See Adam Liptak, "Sent to Prison by a Software Program's Secret Algorithms," *New York Times*, May 1, 2017: Chief Justice Roberts noted in an address at RPI, May 2017, that "the day of using artificial intelligence in courtrooms is already here."

38. A number of systems even have a provision by which, if the judge feels that she must go outside these guidelines (either to give greater or lesser punishment), she must give an explanation for doing so. Some interpret this practice as providing a constraint upon the judge by requiring her to justify departure from the usual practice, thus limiting the chances of excessive punishments. In addition, by requiring an explanation as to the reasons for departure, it is possible to review all the exceptions after a given time, and, if it becomes apparent that there are more exceptions than the rule, the guidelines may be changed to bring them into line with the general sentencing practices of judges. Finally, the proponents say, by being allowed to depart in particular cases, recognition is given to the possibility that there may be something to the argument that each case is unique. However, it is very clear from the constructors of the sentencing guidelines that judges do not see each case as unique, that they do in fact see most cases as being rather similar, with only very few requiring exceptional treatment. For a review of the sentencing guidelines literature, see Tonry, "Structured Sentencing."

39. In the past decade there has been a lot of literature about artificial intelligence/algorithms replacing judges. See Nikolaos Aletras et al., "Predicting Judicial Decisions of the European Court of Human Rights: A Natural Language Processing Perspective," *PeerJ Computer Science* 2, e93 (2016), doi:10.7717/peerj-cs.93; Monidipa Fouzder, "Artificial Intelligence Mimics Judicial Reasoning," *Law Society Gazette*, June 22, 2016, https://www.lawgazette.co.uk/law/artificial-intelligence-mimics-judicial-reasoning/5056017.article; Mark W. Klingensmith, "Computers Laying Down the Law: Will Judges Become Obsolete?," *Florida Bar Journal* 90, no. 1 (2016), https://www.floridabar.org/divcom/jn/jnjournal01.nsf/8c9f13012b96736985256aa900624829/b31e0be4da96963485257f29005a0048!OpenDocument.

40. Jeffrey T. Ulmer and Julia Laskorunsky. "Sentencing Disparities," in *Advancing Criminology and Criminal Justice Policy*, ed. Thomas G. Blomberg, Julie Mestre Brancale, Kevin M. Beaver, and William D. Bales (London: Routledge, 2016), 170–86.

41. However, sentencing guidelines offers much more than the popular solution proposed by the 1976 Committee on Incarceration, which was mandatory sentences to be decided on by the legislature. That solution simply removed discretion away from the judge and on to the legislative and prosecutorial level. The apparent cyclical movement of discretion from judges to legislatures and back again is described in Alan M. Dershowitz, "Criminal Sentencing in the United States: An Historical and Conceptual Overview," *Annals of the American Academy of Political and Social Science* 423, no. 1 (1976): 117–32. For a recent review, see Andrew von Hirsch, *Deserved Criminal Sentences: An Overview* (Oxford: Hart, 2017).

42. An eloquently stated plea for this state of affairs is by Simon Dinitz, "Are Safe and Humane Prisons Possible?," *Australian and New Zealand Journal of Criminology* 14, no. 1 (1981): 3–19.

43. The perceptive reader may see that this proposition appears to violate the retributive position, which in its original construction assumes that offenders are free agents who choose to break the law. That is to say, intent becomes a major focus of criminal law. New retribution, however, advocates attending to the act, not the actor, leaving the question of choice or intent aside. In other words, "strict liability." See Graeme R. Newman, *Just and Painful: A Case for the Corporal Punishment of Criminals* (New York: Macmillan, 1983).

44. Jeffrey Reiman, *The Rich Get Richer and the Poor Get Prison: Ideology, Class, and Criminal Justice*, 8th ed. (Boston: Allyn and Bacon, 2006), 201. Conservatively, Reiman limits this dictum to "intentional harm-producing acts" (201).

45. The current shift in emphasis to regulation as a means of social control, where strict liability is a common legal concept, hints at this possibility, a prime example being the decriminalization of marijuana possession and sale. See Joshua D. Freilich and Graeme R. Newman, "Transforming Piecemeal Social Engineering into 'Grand' Crime Prevention Policy," *Journal of Criminal Law and Criminology* 105, no. 1 (2015): 203–32; Richard H. Thaler and Cass R. Sunstein, *Nudge:*

Improving Decisions about Health, Wealth, and Happiness (New Haven, CT: Yale University Press, 2008).

46. Although there is a clear movement towards making crime a problem of regulation that would make finding of guilt easier, and, perhaps, broaden the range of possible punishments available. See Joshua D. Freilich and Graeme R. Newman, "The New Criminology of Crime Control," *Annals of the American Academy of Political and Social Science* 679, no. 1 (2018): 8–18.

47. Beccaria, *On Crimes and Punishments*, 69.

48. Graeme R. Newman, *The Punishment Response*, 2nd ed. (New York: Routledge, 2017), chs. 1, 3.

49. Graeme R. Newman, "Khomeini and Criminal Justice: Notes on Crime and Culture," *Journal of Criminal Law and Criminology* 73, no. 2 (1982): 561–81. See further chapter 9.

50. Patrick Roth, "Va. Man Sentenced to 132 Years in Prison for Stealing Tires," *Washington's Top News*, July 18, 2017, http://wtop.com/loudoun-county/2017/07/loudoun-county-tire-thief-gets-137-years-prison/.

Chapter Eight

1. When the robots became more human, they became much more violent, driven by revenge.

2. Geoffrey Scarre, "Corporal Punishment," *Ethical Theory and Moral Practice* 6, no. 3 (2003): 295–316; Kevin J. Murtagh, "Is Corporally Punishing Criminals Degrading?," *Journal of Political Philosophy* 20, no. 4 (2012): 481–98; *Corporal Punishment: A Humane Alternative to Incarceration* (Cambridge, MA: LFB Scholarly, 2012).

3. Similar devices used for stunning obstreperous offenders in the courtroom are already available and could be adapted for universal use. See, for example, the device BAND-IT (http://www.stuntronics.com), which can deliver some 50,000 volts. However, these are used to stun or restrain. We here are talking about simple quick and easy punishment that does not need to stun the individual, just hurt him.

4. Richard A. Sternback, *Pain: A Psychophysiological Analysis* (New York: Academic Press, 1968). See also Douglas F. Zatzick and Joel E. Dimsdale, "Cultural Variations in Response to Pain Stimuli," *Psychosomatic Medicine* 52 (1990): 544–57.

5. Hans W. Kosterlitz and Lars Y. Terenius, eds., *Pain and Society* (Berlin: Verlag Chemie, 1980).

6. Most research in the use of electric shock on humans has been on seriously disruptive behavior among intellectually handicapped individuals. None of this research has been shown to have serious negative side effects. Most of it has shown that electric shock is an effective punishment in controlling specific undesirable behaviors. The ethics of using shock against such individuals is of course another matter.

7. See, for example, Jacobo Timerman, *Prisoner without a Name, Cell without a Number* (Madison: University of Wisconsin Press, 2002); Frank Graziano, *Divine Violence: Spectacle, Psychosexuality and Radical Christianity in the Argentine "Dirty War"* (Boulder, CO: Westview Press, 1992); Frantz Fanon, *The Wretched of the Earth* (New York: Grove, 1968).

8. Mark Zborowski, *People in Pain* (San Francisco: Josey Bass, 1969).

9. B. Berthold Wolff and Sarah Langley, "Cultural Factors and Response to Pain: A Review," *American Anthropologist* 70, no. 3 (1968): 495–501; Mary-Jo DelVecchio Good et al., eds., *Pain as Human Experience: An Anthropological Perspective* (Berkeley: University of California Press, 1992); Claudia M. Campbell and Robert R. Edwards, "Ethnic Differences in Pain and Pain Management," *Pain Management* 2, no. 3 (2012): 219–30.

10. Zatzick and Dimsdale, "Cultural Variations." See also John J. Bonica and Denise G. Albe-Fessard, eds., *Proceedings of the First World Congress on Pain* (New York: Raven Press, 1976). The sensation of pain is universal, but the tolerance of pain varies considerably: Mary Moore Free, "Cross-cultural Conceptions of Pain and Pain Control," *Baylor University Medical Center Proceedings* 15, no. 2 (2002): 143–45.

11. Quoted in John Braithwaite, *Prisons, Education, and Work: Towards a National Employment Strategy for Prisoners* (Brisbane: University of Queensland Press, 1980), 14.

12. Christopher J. Mumola, *Suicide and Homicide in State Prisons and Local Jails*, Bureau of Justice Statistics Special Report (Washington, DC: US Department of Justice, Office of Justice Programs, 2005). Considerable variation also has been found in respect to self-injury in prison, but these are not conclusive. See Hayden P. Smith and Robert J. Kaminski, "Self-Injurious Behaviors in State Prisons: Findings from a National Survey," *Criminal Justice and Behavior* 38, no. 1 (2011): 26–41.

13. See, in this regard, Asenath Petrie, *Individuality in Pain and Suffering* (Chicago: University of Chicago Press, 1967), who has identified "augmenters" and "reducers" in the perception of pain and suffering. This differentiation, though not yet shown to be related to any class or ethnic background, may nevertheless tell us that the way in which prison is perceived is unquestionably different according to each individual. The augmenters are those whose perceptual processes must increase the intensity with which they feel a stimulus. The reducers are those whose perceptual processes do the opposite, and so reduce the amount of intensity of the stimulus. The augmenters are those who are most likely to suffer from being isolated in prison, since they must constantly augment or add to their stimulation. They are the ones who suffer severely from boredom, and for whom lack of stimulation of any kind is a severe form of punishment. On the other hand the reducers find even the minimal amount of stimulation enough, and so are less likely to suffer from the isolation of prison—provided, of course, they are able to live out their time in a prison that fosters individual isolation. In today's overcrowded conditions, this is doubtful.

14. Michael C. Campbell and Matt Vogel, "The Demographic Divide: Population Dynamics, Race and the Rise of Mass Incarceration in the United States," *Punishment and Society* 21, no. 1 (2019): 47–69. See also Todd R. Clear, and Natasha A. Frost. *The Punishment Imperative: The Rise and Failure of Mass Incarceration in America* (New York: New York University Press, 2015).

15. Michael Schwirtz, Michael Winerip, and Robert Gebeloff, "The Scourge of Racial Bias in New York State's Prisons," *New York Times*, December 3, 2016; Andrea C. Armstrong, "Race, Prison Discipline, and the Law," *UC Irvine Law Review* 5, no. 4 (2015): 759–82.

16. Prison riots are as old as prisons themselves. See Thyra Kabealo and Simon Dinitz, "Prison Riots and Revolts in the U. S., 1951–1971," *Quaderni di criminologia clinica* 15 (1973): 305–28; D. Asiz, "Historical Review of Prison Disturbances, 1970–1980" (unpublished report to the New York State Department of Corrections, 1981). See, for an account of the quintessential prison revolt, Tom Wicker, *A Time to Die: The Attica Prison Revolt* (New York: Haymarket, 2011).

17. It is a serious matter of public health. See Michael Massoglia and William Alex Pridemore, "Incarceration and Health," *Annual Review of Sociology* 41 (2015): 291–310.

18. William Gutiérrez Lombana and Sergio Esteban Gutiérrez Vidál, "Pain and Gender Differences: A Clinical Approach," *Revista colombiana de anestesiología* 40, no. 3 (2012): 207–12; A.-K. Schmitz, M. Vierhaus, and A. Lohaus, "Pain Tolerance in Children and Adolescents: Sex Differences and Psychosocial Influences on Pain Threshold and Endurance," *European Journal of Pain* 17, no. 1 (2013): 124–31.

19. Stefan Lautenbacher et al., "Age Effects on Pain Thresholds, Temporal Summation and Spatial Summation of Heat and Pressure Pain," *Pain* 115, no. 3 (2005): 410–18.

20. Laura D. Wandner et al., The Perception of Pain in Others: How Gender, Race, and Age Influence Pain Expectations," *Journal of Pain* 13, no. 3 (2012): 220–27.

21. See, for example, Thomas W. Foster, "Make-Believe Families: A Response of Women and Girls to the Deprivations of Imprisonment," *International Journal of Criminology and Penology* 3, no. 1 (1975): 71–78; Nancy G. La Vigne, Elizabeth Davies, and Diana Brazzell, *Broken Bonds: Understanding and Addressing the Needs of Children with Incarcerated Parents* (Washington, DC: Urban Institute, 2008), http://www.urban.org/research/publication/broken-bonds-understanding-and-addressing-needs-children-incarcerated-parents.

22. John Irwin, *Prisons in Turmoil* (Boston: Little, Brown, 1980); Anna Aizer and Joseph J. Doyle Jr., "Juvenile Incarceration, Human Capital and Future Crime: Evidence from Randomly-Assigned Judges" (NBER Working Paper No. 19102, National Bureau of Economic Research, 2013), http://nber.org/papers/w19102.

23. Murray A. Straus, *Beating the Devil Out of Them: Corporal Punishment in American Families* (New York: Lexington, 1994).

24. Matthew Pate and Laurie A. Gould, *Corporal Punishment around the World* (Santa Barbara, CA: Praeger, 2012), 78–79.

25. This case and the relevant polls were widely reported in both national and local media. Polls conducted by the media reported roughly similar findings: 49 percent of Americans approved of the sentence, although only 36 percent said they would approve of such a punishment being introduced into American criminal justice. Ronald Brownstein, "Singapore's Caning Sentence Divides Americans, Poll Finds," *Los Angeles Times*, April 21, 1994, https://www.latimes.com/archives/la-xpm-1994-04-21-mn-48524-story.html. Polls conducted by other national media reported similar findings. For a review, see Daniel Hall, "When Caning Meets the Eighth Amendment: Whipping Offenders in the United States," *Widener Journal of Public Law* 4, no. 2 (1995): 403–60.

26. In fact, this is why corporal punishment is often identified in research on child abuse as the beginning of a slippery slope of violence against children by their parents. This is well documented by Straus, *Beating the Devil Out of Them.*

27. Irwin, *Prisons in Turmoil.*

28. Solitary confinement is another example of the tendency to excess in punishment, particularly the rise in long term solitary confinement. See, for an overview of this abuse of prison as punishment, *Correctional Law Reporter*, October/November 2016.

29. See, for example, United States Bureau of Justice Statistics, *Performance Measures for the Criminal Justice System: Discussion Papers from the BJS-Princeton Project* (Washington, DC: GPO, 1993); Charles H. Logan, *Criminal Justice Performance Measures for Prisons* (Washington, DC; National Institute of Justice, 1993). While these papers focus on the performance of prisons in terms of fulfilling their basic mission of providing a secure environment for inmates, they do begin to show how the varying conditions of prison may be systematically identified and measured. More recent work has focused on comparisons between public and private prisons. See Alexander Volokh, "Prison Accountability and Performance Measures," 63 *Emory Law Journal* 63, no. 2 (2013): 339–416.

30. Elizabeth L. Jeglic, Holly A. Vanderhoff, and Peter J. Donovick, "The Function of Self-harm Behavior in a Forensic Population," *International Journal of Offender Therapy and Comparative Criminology* 49, no. 2 (2005): 131–42; Fatos Kaba et al., "Solitary Confinement and Risk of Self-Harm among Jail Inmates," *American Journal of Public Health* 104, no. 3 (2014): 442–47.

31. David Levy, *Love and Sex with Robots: The Evolution of Human-Robot Relations* (New York: Harper-Collins, 2009).

32. Jeremy Bentham, *The Rationale of Punishment* (London: Robert Heward, 1830), 82.

33. C. Farrell, "The Spanking Machine: A Resilient Myth in Popular Culture," http://corpun.com/machine.htm.

34. DeMoulin Bros., *The 1930 DeMoulin Bros. and Co. Fraternal Supply Catalog No. 439*, http://www.phoenixmasonry.org/masonicmuseum/demoulin/index. htm. "Burlesque and Side Degree Specialties; Paraphenalia and Costumes. Stunt Props, Tricks, Pranks, Practical Jokes, Humor, Magic, Goat Riding Carts, Paddling Machines, Electric Carpets and much, much, more!!!" It is not clear whether the items described in this catalog were actually built, though they are presented as for sale along with respective prices.

35. Farrell, "The Spanking Machine."

36. Jeremy Bentham, *The Rationale of Punishment*, 81.

37. In fact, some have suggested that judges could also be replaced by robots. See, for example, Josh Kendrick, "The Future of Sentencing Is Here: Robot Judges," *Mimesis Law*, July 18, 2016, http://mimesislaw.com/fault-lines/the-future-of-sentencing-is-here-robot-judges/11422.

38. That such algorithms may be developed in the very near future is assured. See Richard Berk, "Algorithmic Criminology," *Security Informatics* 2, no. 5 (2013).

39. I am not suggesting that slavery created the wealth to finance the industrial revolution, which is a different question and an ongoing debate. See, for example, Eric Williams, *Capitalism and Slavery* (Chapel Hill: University of North Carolina Press, 1994); Edward E. Baptist, *The Half Has Never Been Told: Slavery and the Making of American Capitalism* (New York: Basic Books, 2016); Robin Blackburn, *The Making of New World Slavery: From the Baroque to the Modern, 1492–1800* (New York: Verso, 1997). However, a persuasive argument could be made that the lives of the workers at the height of the Industrial Revolution were not that far from slavery. See the classic Friedrich Engels, *The Condition of the Working-Class in England in 1844; with a Preface written in 1892*, trans. Florence Kelley Wischnewetzky (n.p.: Createspace, 2016). And, more recently, Steven Marcus, *Engels, Manchester, and the Working Class* (Piscataway, NJ: Transaction, 2015).

40. Kevin Warwick, *March of the Machines: The Breakthrough in Artificial Intelligence* (Champaign: University of Illinois Press, 2004).

41. Tanya Lewis, "Don't Let Artificial Intelligence Take Over, Top Scientists Warn," *Live Science*, January 12, 2015, https://www.livescience.com/49419-artificial-intelligence-dangers-letter.html. "Stephen Hawking, Elon Musk and dozens of other top scientists and technology leaders have signed a letter warning of the potential dangers of developing artificial intelligence (AI)."

42. Luke Muehlhauser and Louie Helm, "Intelligence Explosion and Machine Ethics," in *Singularity Hypotheses: A Scientific and Philosophical Assessment*, ed. Amnon Eden, Johnny Søraker, James H. Moor, and Eric Steinhart (Berlin: Springer, 2012).

43. Emile Durkheim, *The Elementary Forms of Religious Life* (New York: Free Press, 1965).

44. See David Garland, *Punishment and Modern Society* (Chicago: University of Chicago Press), for an excellent account and analysis of Durkeim's punishment theory.

45. For an analysis of how the social contract forms the basis of the United States Declaration of Independence and Constitution, see Newman and Marongiu's introduction in Beccaria, *On Crimes and Punishments.*

46. See Graziano, *Divine Violence*, for an excellent analysis of this process.

Chapter Nine

1. Mohamed A. Arafa and Jonathan G. Burns, "Judicial Corporal Punishment in the United States? Lessons from Islamic Criminal Law for Curing the Ills of Mass Incarceration," *Indiana International and Comparative Law Review* 25, no. 3 (2015): 385–420.

2. See, for example, Paul Copan, *Is God a Moral Monster? Making Sense of the Old Testament God* (Ada, MI: Baker Books, 2011).

3. Many, if not all, Islamic legal systems have been affected by "foreign" legal codes. See Enid Hill, "Comparative and Historical Study of Modern Middle Eastern Law," *American Journal of Comparative Law* 26, no. 2 (1978): 279–304. However, "disinfecting" Islamic codes from Western influence has been in process at least since the Iranian revolution under Ayotolla Khomeini, who argued that Iranian Islamic law is "decivilized," not "uncivilized." See Graeme R. Newman, "Khomeini and Criminal Justice: Notes on Crime and Culture," *Journal of Criminal Law and Criminology* 73, no. 2 (1982): 561–81.

4. Nawal H. Ammar, "Islam and Crime," in *Encyclopedia of Crime and Punishment*, ed. David Levinson (Thousand Oaks, CA: Sage, 2002), 931–37; "Islamic Perspectives on Crime, Punishment, and Prison," in *Muslims in US Prisons: People, Policy, Practice*, ed. Nawal H. Ammar (Boulder, CO: Lynne Rienner. 2015), 29–45.

5. The following account is generally based on an excellent review of Islamic law: Rudolph Peters, *Crime and Punishment in Islamic Law: Theory and Practice from the Sixteenth to the Twenty-First Century* (Cambridge: Cambridge University Press, 2005).

6. "Whosoever slayeth a believer of set purpose, his reward is Hell forever." Qur'an 4:93. Murder is also forbidden in Qur'an 4:29, 5:32, 6:152, and 17:33.

7. Qur'an 17:33.

8. Qur'an 5:38.

9. Strictly speaking, this is inaccurate, since the aim was not so much to deter others through the threat of punishment, but rather to demonstrate the inherent truth or goodness in the prohibition. See Graeme R. Newman, *The Punishment Response*, 2nd ed. (New York: Routledge, 2017), for a discussion of reflected punishments. They are the oldest form of retribution. See also Mustafa Abdulmegid Kara, "Philosophy of Punishment in Islamic Law" (PhD diss., State University of New York at Albany, 1977).

10. Qur'an 24:2. In my copy of the Qur'an, the word adultery is often referred to as "lewdness," which is forbidden in Qur'an 4:15, for which the punishment was house imprisonment (another reflected punishment) "until death take them." The similarity between this punishment and the burial alive in ancient Rome of the vestal virgins who broke their vows is quite remarkable. The Qur'an also forbids adultery in Qur'an 17:32, 24:2, and 33:30.

11. Some Islamic scholars have insisted that Islamic law is "pure" and untouched by Jewish law. See Gamal Moursi Badr, "Islamic Law: Its Relation to Other Legal Systems," *American Journal of Comparative Law* 26, no. 2 (1978): 187–98. These scholars tend to focus on law rather than forms of punishment.

12. Qur'an 24:4.

13. Peters, *Crime and Punishment*.

14. Peters, *Crime and Punishment*, ch. 5. According to Peters, the countries that reintroduced Shari'a law mostly grafted it on to the remnants of colonial western legal systems. The crucial difference between these Islamic legal systems and the traditional Shari'a law is that they are enacted by the state. True Shari'a law does not need a state. It is governed by Muhammad and the clerics who represent him and does not need a state apparatus to implement it. See further below on Iranian law.

15. For a map of the distribution of Islamic law countries and descriptions of the comparative legal systems of countries, see Graeme R. Newman and Mahesh K. Nalla, eds., *Crime and Punishment around the World*, vol. 1, *Africa and the Middle East* (Santa Barbara, CA: ABC-CLIO, 2010).

16. See Pietro Marongiu and Graeme R. Newman, *Vengeance: The Fight against Injustice* (Totowa, NJ: Littlefield Adams, 1986), ch. 6. Also M. J. L. Hardy, *Blood Feuds and the Payment of Blood Money in the Middle East* (Leiden: E. J. Brill, 1963).

17. See Marongiu and Newman, *Vengeance*. The barbaricino code adhered to by feuding vigilante groups in the remote mountains of Sardinia reflects an attempt to codify traditional crimes and punishments without reference to the state as the third party or arbiter. It is also possible that some ancient Arabic customs have influenced the origins of this code. See Pietro Marongiu, *Criminalità e banditismo in Sardegna: Fra tradizione e innovazione* (Rome: Carocci, 2004); Antonio Pigliaru, *Il codice della vendetta barbaricina* (Milan: Giuffrè, 1975).

18. Marongiu and Newman, *Vengeance*, 6–7. Also, Muhammad Abdel Haleem, Adel Omar Sherif, and Kate Daniels, *Criminal Justice in Islam* (London: I. B. Tauris, 2003), provide a detailed account of judicial procedure in Shari'a law.

19. The United Nations ostensibly collects crime and justice data from all member countries, but the amount or extent of such data provided by Islamic nations is very limited compared to those of Western and even non-Western countries, such as Japan. Nor are there data on the crimes and punishments carried out in countries where there are large Islamic minorities that operate their own Islamic courts. See, for example, Maureen Cofflard, "British 'Sharia Courts' under Scrutiny,"

AFP, November 13, 2016, https://www.yahoo.com/news/british-sharia-courts-under-scrutiny-075656056.html.

20. By "authorities" we mean the judge (usually a mullah, a recognized legal scholar or local community leader) for *hadd* crimes, and police or state officials for various kinds for *ta'zir* crimes. See Peters, *Crime and Punishment*. In Islamic countries there is a complicated relationship between "church and state," as we would call the problem in the West. Critics of modern Islam (or, more precisely, predatory or extreme Islam) argue that the design of Islam today is to take over the West and establish a world caliphate, where religion and state are one. See Center for Security Policy, *Shariah: The Threat to America, an Exercise in Competitive Analysis*, Report of Team B II (Washington, DC: Center for Security Policy, 2010), https://www.centerforsecuritypolicy.org/2010/09/13/shariah-the-threat-to-america/.

21. Peters, *Crime and Punishment*, 7.

22. See generally, Nawal H. Ammar, ed., *Muslims in US Prisons: People, Policy, Practice* (Boulder, CO: Lynne Rienner, 2015). Also, her "Restorative Justice in Islam: Theory and Practice," in *The Spiritual Roots of Restorative Justice*, ed. Michael L. Hadley (Albany: State University of New York Press, 2001), 161–80.

23. Peters, *Crime and Punishment*, 27. Its application differs. In the case of banditry, repentance must have begun before the bandit is caught.

24. Nanami Shiono, *Julius Caesar: To the Banks of the Rubicon*, vol. 4 of *The Story of the Roman People*, translated by Ronald Dore (n.p.: Shinchosha, 2014), Kindle edition. Shiono artfully explains the functions of Roman law in this and other volumes of the series.

25. Peters, *Crime and Punishment*, 33–38.

26. Nawal H. Ammar, "Women in Islam: The Paradox of Unity and Diversity," *Chicago Seminary Journal*, Summer 1992, 21–38.

27. See, for example, the many reports of "political Islam," such as those of Bill Warner, "Political Islam Has Subjugated Civilizations for 1,400 Years." https://www.politicalislam.com.

28. By transparency, here, we mean transparency to outside observers. Defenders of Islam would argue that it is all transparent to its believers and that the practices of Islamic courts are clearly observable to all believers because of their essentially local and public procedures in small communities.

29. Ruhollah Khomeini, *Sayings of the Ayatollah Khomeini*, trans. Harold J. Salemson (New York: Bantam, 1979), 30. See also Newman, "Khomeini and Criminal Justice."

30. Marongiu and Newman, *Vengeance*, 90–102.

31. The National Council for Resistance in Iran (NCRI) and the the People's Mojahedin Organization of Iran (PMOI) have long campaigned against the mullahs assuming too much power.

32. Beccaria, *On Crimes and Punishments*, 121.

33. Center for Security Policy, *Shariah*.

34. Associated Press, "Prosecutors Seek Caning for Gay Couple in Indonesia's Aceh," May 10, 2017.

35. Cited in Ghassem Ghassemi, "Criminal Punishment in Islamic Societies: Empirical Study of Attitudes to Criminal Sentencing in Iran," *European Journal on Criminal Policy and Research* 15, nos. 1–2 (2009): 176.

36. Ghassemi, "Criminal Punishment."

37. There appears to be considerable popular support among Muslim communities for Shari'a courts to preside over much civil law, particularly divorce. A survey of 3,000 Muslims in Britain found that four in ten respondents supported the proposition that some aspects of Shari'a law should replace British law. "Unsettled Belonging: Britain's Muslim Communities," Policy Exchange, *Sunday Express*, December 4, 2016.

38. State v. Cannon, 55 Del. 587, 596, 190 A.2d 514, 518–19 (1963), made this quite clear. However, this observation applies only to judicial corporal punishment not corporal punishment used for prison discipline, though, as noted later, the Supreme Court did muddle the waters in a dictum that some of its findings in the case of Jackson v. Bishop, 404 F.2d 571 (8th Cir. 1968) might be extended to cover judicial corporal punishment.

39. For a thorough and complete account of the constitutionality and judicial history of corporal punishment in the United States, see John Dewar Gleissner, "Prison Overcrowding Cure: Judicial Corporal Punishment of Adults," *Criminal Law Bulletin* 49, no. 4 (2013): 711–55.

40. Gleissner, "Prison Overcrowding."

41. Michael P. Matthews, "Caning and the Constitution: Why the Backlash against Crime Won't Result in the Back-Lashing of Criminals," *New York Law School Journal of Human Rights* 14 (1998): 571–614, argues that such corporal punishment would be unconstitutional, but confuses corporal punishment in prison with judicial corporal punishment. See also Sean Maddan and William Hallahan, "Corporal Punishment in the 21st Century: An Examination of Supreme Court Decisions in the 1990s to Predict the Reemergence of Flagellance," *Journal of Crime and Justice* 25, no. 2 (2002): 97–120.

42. Brown v. Plata, 563 U.S. 493 (2011).

43. Weems v. United States, 217 U.S. 349 (1910).

44. Anthony F. Granucci, " 'Nor Cruel and Unusual Punishments Inflicted': The Original Meaning," *California Law Review* 57, no. 4 (1969): 839–65. For a thorough review of the many reasons why the framers of the Constitution did not view corporal punishment as cruel and unusual, see Daniel E. Hall, "When Caning Meets the Eighth Amendment: Whipping Offenders in the United States," *Widener Journal of Public Law* 4, no. 2 (1995): 403–60.

45. Harmelin v. Michigan, 501 U.S. 957 (1991).

46. There is one minor exception to this observation, which is the question of proportionality of the death penalty for crimes other than murder. For example,

the Supreme Court has found that the death penalty is disproportionate for rape: Coker v. Georgia, 433 U.S. 584 (1977).

47. Deborah A. Schwartz and Jay Wishingrad, "The Eighth Amendment, Beccaria, and the Enlightenment: An Historical Justification for the Weems v. United States Excessive Punishment Doctrine," *Buffalo Law Review* 24, no. 3 (1975): 783–838. It should be noted as well that Beccaria did not advocate the abolition of corporal punishment; rather, he advocated the abolition of torture as a means of obtaining confessions. For a further discussion of Beccaria's influence on the US Constitution, see Newman and Marongiu's introduction to Beccaria, *On Crimes and Punishments*. For a broader view of Beccaria's influence, see John Bessler, *The Birth of American Law: An Italian Philosopher and the American Revolution* (Durham, NC: Carolina Academic Press, 2014).

48. Robinson v. California, 370 U.S. 660 (1962).

49. Ewing v. California, 538 U.S. 11 (2003). *Ewing v. California* uses the *Rummel v. Estelle* and *Harmelin v. Michigan* cases as legal precedents. However, the "companion" case to *Ewing v. California*—Lockyer v. Andrade, 538 U.S. 63 (2003)— did reverse the court's ruling, finding that "two consecutive terms of 25 years to life for stealing approximately $150 in videotapes" was in violation of the Eighth Amendment, where the punishment was grossly disproportionate to the offense.

50. Graham v. West Virginia, 224 U.S. 616 (1912). Graham was sentenced under the West Virginia recidivist statute that mandated life imprisonment for a third felony conviction.

51. People v. Mosley, 358 N.Y.S.2d 1004 (1974).

52. Miller v. Alabama, 567 U.S. 460 (2012), overturned sentences of life imprisonment without parole for two fourteen-year-olds convicted of murder on the ground of violating Eighth Amendment rights.

53. Bell v. Wolfish, 441 U.S. 520 (1979).

54. Rhodes v. Chapman,452 U.S. 337 (1981). See also Farmer v. Brennan, 511 U.S. 825 (1994), which ruled that the defendant's Eighth Amendment rights were violated by the "deliberate indifference" of the prison warden who placed the defendant—a feminine transsexual inmate—within the general male prison population and as a result was beaten and raped.

55. Ingraham v. Wright, 430 U.S. 651 (1977).

56. Or deliberate indifference? See Fred Cohen, "Deliberate Indifference: A Divided En Banc Seventh Circuit Speaks," *Correctional Law Reporter*, December/ January 2017, 1.

57. Take the case of Anders Breivik in 2016, a Norwegian case of human rights, occurring within an ostensibly "liberal" Scandinavian prison system, where the case was won on the basis that he received "more punishment" (greater periods of solitary confinement) than most other prisoners in the country. According to the BBC, the judge said, "His prison regime deviated so markedly from that enforced upon any other prisoner in Norway, regardless of the severity of their crimes, that it had to be considered an extra punishment." "Anders Behring Breivik,

Norway Murderer, Wins Human Rights Case," BBC, http://www.bbc.com/news/world-europe-36094575.

58. Adam J. Kolber, "The Subjective Experience of Punishment," *Colombia Law Review* 109, no. 1 (2009): 182–236.

59. Jackson v. Bishop, 404 F.2d 571 (8th Cir. 1968).

60. Jackson v. Bishop, 581.

61. Jackson v. Bishop, 581.

62. All quotes in this list are taken directly from pages 579 through 581 of the Jackson v. Bishop commentary.

63. See the recent thoroughly argued case that corporal punishment is not in and of itself degrading: Kevin J. Murtagh, *Corporal Punishment: A Humane Alternative to Incarceration* (Cambridge, MA: LFB Scholarly, 2012); "Is Corporally Punishing Criminals Degrading?," *Journal of Political Philosophy* 20, no. 4 (2012): 481–98.

64. Over 95 percent of parents favor the use of corporal punishment in the home: Murray A. Straus, *Beating the Devil Out of Them: Corporal Punishment in American Families* (New York: Lexington, 1994). According to the periodic University of Chicago General Social Survey, in the 1980s over 80 percent of individuals approved of spanking children, and this has remained at over 70 percent in 2014. African Americans favor spanking at considerably higher rates than do whites. Harry Enten, "Americans' Opinions on Spanking Vary by Party, Race, Region and Religion," *FiveThirtyEight*, September 15, 2014, http://fivethirtyeight.com/datalab/americans-opinions-on-spanking-vary-by-party-race-region-and-religion/.

65. If the public's support for the death penalty is any indication of its support for corporal punishment, it is clear that a majority would support it. Only rarely in the last one hundred years has the percentage of the population supporting capital punishment dropped below 50 percent. See Arthur L. Stinchcombe et al., *Crime and Punishment: Changing Attitudes in America* (San Francisco: Jossey-Bass, 1980). As of October 2015, Gallup reports that 61 percent favor the death penalty, down from 70 percent in 2003.

66. See, for an extensive listing of cases, Gleissner, "Prison Overcrowding," 720.

67. State v. Cannon, 55 Del. 587, 190 A.2d 514 (1963).

68. Gleissner, "Prison Overcrowding," 727. See also Michael Meranze, *Laboratories of Virtue: Punishment, Revolution, and Authority in Philadelphia, 1760–1835*, 2nd ed. (Chapel Hill: University of North Carolina Press, 1996).

69. Meranze, *Laboratories of Virtue*. See also Louis Hughes, *Thirty Years a Slave: From Bondage to Freedom* (n.p.: Bibliolife, 2009).

70. *Coker v. Georgia*.

71. Hall has clearly shown that corporal punishment would fit within these strictures of the court, and that retribution has been well recognized by the courts as a legitimate penal purpose. Hall, "Caning."

72. Alan Dershowitz makes a parallel argument in favor of legalizing carefully prescribed torture. He posits that under serious circumstances, such as the "ticking time bomb" scenario, low-level personnel are likely to break with a law that forbids

torture, if they are able to extract information from a suspect who knows the whereabouts of a "ticking time bomb." He argues that making torture legal under such circumstances shifts the responsibility higher up the enforcement chain and does not force low-level employees to make an impossible moral choice: Obey the law or allow many to be killed by the villain? Alan M. Dershowitz, "Tortured Reasoning," in *Torture: A Collection*, ed. Sanford Levinson (New York: Oxford University Press, 2004), 257–80. These arguments were anticipated by Michael Levin in his provocative essay "The Case for Torture," *Newsweek*, June 7, 1982, followed by his interview by *Penthouse Magazine*, October 1982.

73. See, for example, Rabindranath Tagore, "Civilization and Progress," a lecture delivered in China, 1924, Swaraj Foundation, http://www.swaraj.org/tagore-civilization.htm, where he argued that progress is not synonymous with civilization, that the latter is a self-serving invention of the West. He is probably right.

74. See, for example, A. P. Simester and Andreas von Hirsch, *Crimes, Harms, and Wrongs: On the Principles of Criminalisation* (London: Hart, 2014).

75. See, for example, Graeme R. Newman, *Comparative Deviance: Perception and Law in Six Cultures*, 2nd ed. (Patterson, NJ: Transaction, 2009); Donald S. Kenkel and Steven F. Koch, "Deterrence and Knowledge of the Law: The Case of Drunk Driving," *Applied Economics* 33, no. 7 (2010): 845–54. This study found that the public had little knowledge of the laws and their punishments concerning drunk driving. See also Paul H. Robinson and John M. Darley, "Does Criminal Law Deter? A Behavioural Science Investigation," *Oxford Journal of Legal Studies* 24, no. 2 (2004): 173–205.

76. Many polls have been conducted, and reported widely in the media. See, for example, "US Snapshots: Teens Wouldn't Spare the Rod," *USA Today*, April 11, 1995, which reports that 54.6 percent were in favor of corporal punishment for crimes.

77. Hall, "Caning."

78. Hall, "Caning." Hall provides an excellent and thorough assessment of the constitutionality of corporal punishment. His guidelines for legislation are much more extensive than shown here.

79. This argument is made convincingly by Jonathan Simon, *Mass Incarceration on Trial: A Remarkable Court Decision and the Future of Prisons in America* (New York: New Press, 2014). For an excellent review and commentary on his thesis, see James E. Robertson, review of *The Return of the Medical Model: Disease and the Meaning of Imprisonment from John Howard to Brown v. Plata*, by Jonathan Simon, *Correctional Law Reporter*, October/November, 2013.

80. Kim J. Masters, "Physical Restraint: A Historical Review and Current Practice," *Psychiatric Annals* 47, no. 1 (2017): 52–55.

81. "Establishment of Minimum Safety and Security Standards for Private Companies That Transport Violent Prisoners," 66 FR 64934, proposed rule by the Justice Department, December 17, 2001, https://www.federalregister.gov/

documents/2001/12/17/01-30937/establishment-of-minimum-safety-and-security-standards-for-private-companies-that-transport-violent.

82. James K. McAfee, Christopher Schwilk, and Megan Mitruski, "Public Policy on Physical Restraint of Children with Disabilities in Public Schools," *Education and Treatment of Children* 29, no. 4 (2006): 711–28.

83. Jackson v. California, 135 S. Ct. 677 (2014).

84. Much of the appeal argument revolves around whether the restraint device is visible or not. It is well established that visible shackles and other restraints may prejudice the jury against the defendant. For an overview of these cases, see Stephenson v. Wilson, 629 F.3d 732 (7th Cir. 2011). The Indiana Supreme Court has banned the use of stun belts. See Stephenson v. State, 864 N.E.2d 1022, 1033 (Ind. 2007). "The use of a stun belt, if perceived by the jury, produces all of the results that shackling does." Stephenson v. Wilson, 629 F.3d 732, 733 (7th Cir. 2011).

85. Ben Norton, "Scathing U.N. Report: 'Structural Racism' Endures in U.S., and the Government Has Failed to Protect African-Americans' Rights," *Salon*, October 7, 2016.

86. Peters, *Crime and Punishment*, ch. 5.

87. Commission on Human Rights, UN Commission on Human Rights, Resolution 2003/32, "Torture and Other Cruel, Inhuman or Degrading Treatment or Punishment," E/CN.4/RES/2003/32, April 23, 2003, https://www.refworld.org/docid/43f313310.html.

88. "Moratorium on the Use of the Death Penalty," United Nations General Assembly, Sixty-Seventh Session, December 20, 2012, https://undocs.org/en/A/RES/67/176, with 111 countries voting in favor, 41 against, and 34 abstentions (another 7 countries were absent at the time of the vote).

89. Peters, *Crime and Punishment*, ch. 5.

90. "France," *World Prison Brief*, http://www.prisonstudies.org/country/france.

91. For an outstanding legal and historical review of the tortured track to the *Plata* decision, see Jonathan Simon, "Return of the Medical Model: Disease and the Meaning of Imprisonment from John Howard to *Brown v. Plata*," *Harvard Civil Rights-Civil Liberties Law Review* 48, no. 1 (2013): 217–56.

92. This is a complicated issue, since research that has looked at this problem has difficulty separating out the selection problem (more psychopaths join the military) from the environmental effects such as PTSD resulting from active combat. In general, it seems that serious crime rates are lower for military personnel compared to ordinary citizens. See, for example, Daniel Engber, "Is There a Lot of Crime on Military Bases? Not as Much as You'd Think," *Slate*, November 5, 2009, http://www.slate.com/articles/news_and_politics/explainer/2009/11/is_there_a_lot_of_crime_on_military_bases.html. The crime rates for locals in Okinawa compared to the local US Military base are much higher than the military for all types of

crimes, including heinous crimes, according to Wikipedia: https://en.wikipedia.org/wiki/United_States_Forces_Japan#Crime. Overall, the prison rate of US veterans compared to nonveterans is lower: Jennifer E. Bronson et al., *Veterans in Prison and Jail, 2011–2012* (Washington, DC: Bureau of Justice Statistics, 2015).

Chapter Ten

1. Among those who underestimated the power of technology were Neil Postman, *Technopoly: The Surrender of Culture to Technology* (New York: Vintage, 1993); William G. Staples, *The Culture of Surveillance: Discipline and Social Control in the United States* (New York: St. Martin's, 1997); *Everyday Surveillance: Vigilance and Visibility in Postmodern Life* (New York: Rowman and Littlefield, 2000).

2. Opposition to punishment through surveillance and incapacitation without prison has already shown itself, calling it "e-carceration" and the "newest Jim Crow." This reveals the conflicted thinking of the liberal opposition to mass incarceration when faced with the (very unlikely) reduction in the use of prison as a punishment. It labels credible alternatives to prison as though they are as bad as or worse than prison, which, given the liberal opposition to mass incarceration and prison, is surely not possible. As we have seen throughout this book, any use of prison will lead to mass incarceration. See Michelle Alexander, "The Newest Jim Crow," *New York Times*, November 11, 2018; Fred Cohen, "E-carceration: A Comment," *Correctional Law Reporter*, February/March 2019.

3. Statistic Brain Research Institute, "Driving Citation Statistics," http://www.statisticbrain.com/driving-citation-statistics/.

4. Douglas Husak, *Overcriminalization: The Limits of the Criminal Law* (New York: Oxford University Press, 2009).

5. A student of corrections may recognize that I have just described a system for the individualization of punishment, an approach in early twentieth-century corrections once revered by judges, the belief that "each case is unique." It is, of course, ridiculous to imagine that such an individualized punishment could be achieved by a prison term of any length. Not so with MCP. Raymond Saleilles, *The Individualization of Punishment* (Boston: Little, Brown, 1911).

6. Insurance companies already offer insurance to potential victims of crime, such as, for example, coverage for identity theft. See Graeme R. Newman, *The Problem of Identity Theft*, guide no. 25 (Washington, DC: Center for Problem Oriented Policing. 2004).

7. Newman, Graeme R. "A Market Approach to Crime Prevention." In *Design against Crime: Crime Proofing Everyday Products*, edited by Paul Ekblom (Boulder, CO: Lynne Reinner, 2012), 87–106.

8. Thus, thinking of punishment as a commodity is much different from thinking of it as "social capital" of a society.

9. Jennifer Pak, "How Does China's Social Credit System Work?," *Marketplace*, February 13, 2018, https://www.marketplace.org/2018/02/13/world/qa-china-s-social-credit-system.

10. The move to reduce automobile accidents and death by improving their design has a long history. See Graeme R. Newman, "Car Safety and Car Security: An Historical Comparison," *Crime Prevention Studies* 17 (2004): 217–48.

11. Joshua D. Freilich and Graeme R. Newman, "The New Criminology of Crime Control," *Annals of the American Academy of Political and Social Science* 679 (2018): 8–18.

12. Can corporal punishment be administered in such a way as to minimize its violence? Most certainly. In fact the attempt by some to equate corporal punishment with violence is a cheap trick. See, once again, Murray A. Straus, *Beating the Devil Out of Them: Corporal Punishment in American Families* (New York: Lexington, 1994). Straus claims that even the slightest tap on the hand is violent. Yet he seems to exclude a sudden loud noise, even though one may argue that this stimulus can and does assault the body's senses more than would a "slap on the wrist." Similarly, while corporal punishment historically may have its origins in violence, so prison may have its origins in slavery. See J. Thorsten Sellin, *Slavery and the Penal System* (New York: Elsevier, 1976); Loïc Wacquant, "The New 'Peculiar Institution': On the Prison as Surrogate Ghetto," *Theoretical Criminology* 4, no. 3 (2000): 377–89.

Appendix A

1. See, for example, Tina Wan, "The Unnecessary Evil of Plea Bargaining: An Unconstitutional Conditions Problem and a Not-So-Least Restrictive Alternative," *Southern California Review of Law and Social Justice* 17, no. 1 (2007): 33–61.

2. *In re Medley*, 134 U.S. 160 (1890).

3. Approvingly quoted by Sigmund Freud in his classic *Civilization and its Discontents*, trans. James Strachey (New York: W. W. Norton, 1961), 57.

4. Shakespeare did not quite have it right. The oft quoted lines "The quality of mercy is not strained" and "It droppeth like the gentle rain from heaven" fail to acknowledge its selfish side: to make the (powerful) giver of mercy feel morally superior to the object of punishment when it is transformed into mercy.

5. Ellen Condliffe Lagemann, *Liberating Minds: The Case for College in Prison* (New York: New Press, 2016), 3.

Appendix B

1. The criminal prosecution of animals has a long history. See E. P. Evans, *The Criminal Prosecution and Capital Punishment of Animals* (London: Faber and Faber, 1987).

Works Cited

Aeschylus. *The Oresteian Trilogy*. Translated by Philip Vellacott. London: Penguin, 1956.

Agras, W. Stewart. "Behavior Therapy in the Management of Chronic Schizophrenia." *American Journal of Psychiatry* 124, no. 2 (1967): 240–43.

Aletras, Nikolaos, Dimitrios Tsarapatsanis, Daniel Preoţiuc–Pietro, and Vasileios Lampos. "Predicting Judicial Decisions of the European Court of Human Rights: A Natural Language Processing Perspective." *PeerJ Computer Science* 2, e93 (2016). doi:10.7717/peerj-cs.93.

Alexander, Michelle. "The Newest Jim Crow." *New York Times*, November 11, 2018.

Alleyne v. United States, 570 U.S. 99 (2013).

Ammar, Nawal H. "Islam and Crime." In *Encyclopedia of Crime and Punishment*, edited by David Levinson, 931–37. Thousand Oaks, CA: Sage, 2002.

———. "Islamic Perspectives on Crime, Punishment, and Prison." In *Muslims in US Prisons: People, Policy, Practice*, edited by Nawal H. Ammar, 29–45. Boulder, CO: Lynne Rienner, 2015.

———. "Restorative Justice in Islam: Theory and Practice." In *The Spiritual Roots of Restorative Justice*, edited by Michael L. Hadley, 161–80. Albany: State University of New York Press, 2001.

———. "Women in Islam: The Paradox of Unity and Diversity." *Chicago Seminary Journal*, Summer 1992, 21–38.

Amnesty International. *Report on Torture*. New York: Farrar, Straus and Giroux, 1975.

———. *Torture in 2014: 30 Years of Broken Promises*. London: Amnesty International, 2014. https://www.amnestyusa.org/sites/default/files/act400042014en.pdf.

Anderson, Alex. "Hiding Out in Prison Bonds." *Forbes*, October 22, 2008.

Anderson, Digby, ed. *This Will Hurt: The Restoration of Virtue and Civic Order*. New York: National Review Books, 1995.

Andrews, William. *Bygone Punishments*. London: William Andrews, 1899.

Apel, Robert, and Daniel S. Nagin. "Deterrence." In *Emerging Trends in the Social and Behavioral Sciences*, edited by Robert A. Scott and Stephen Michael Kosslyn, 1–10. New York: Wiley, 2015.

Arafa, Mohamed A., and Jonathan G. Burns. "Judicial Corporal Punishment in the United States? Lessons from Islamic Criminal Law for Curing the Ills of Mass Incarceration." *Indiana International and Comparative Law Review* 25, no. 3 (2015): 385–420.

Axelrod, Saul, and Jack Apasche, eds. *The Effects of Punishment on Human Behavior.* Cambridge, MA: Academic Press, 2013.

Badr, Gamal Moursi. "Islamic Law: Its Relation to Other Legal Systems." *American Journal of Comparative Law* 26, no. 2 (1978): 187–98.

Baicker, Katherine. "The Budgetary Repercussions of Capital Convictions." Working Paper 8382, National Bureau of Economic Research, Cambridge, MA, 2001. http://www.nber.org/papers/w8382.pdf.

Banks, Cyndi. *Prisons in the United States: A Reference Handbook.* Santa Barbara, CA: ABC-CLIO, 2017.

Baptist, Edward E. *The Half Has Never Been Told: Slavery and the Making of American Capitalism.* New York: Basic Books, 2016.

Barnes, Harry Elmer. *The Story of Punishment.* Boston: Stratford, 1930.

Barnett, Randy E. "Restitution: A New Paradigm of Criminal Justice." *Ethics* 87, no. 4 (1977): 279–301.

Beard, T. Randolph, David L. Kaserman, and Rigmar Osterkamp. *The Global Organ Shortage: Economic Causes, Human Consequences, Policy Responses.* Redwood City, CA: Stanford University Press, 2013.

Beccaria, Cesare. *On Crimes and Punishments.* Translated by Graeme R. Newman and Pietro Marongiu. New Brunswick, NJ: Transaction, 2009.

Belfrage, Henrik, Ran Fransson, and Susanne Strand. "Prediction of Violence Using the HCR-20: A Prospective Study in Two Maximum-Security Correctional Institutions." *Journal of Forensic Psychiatry* 11, no. 1 (2000): 167–75.

Bell v. Wolfish, 441 U. S. 520 (1979).

Bentham, Jeremy. *The Rationale of Punishment.* London: Heward, 1830.

Bergin, Tiffany. *The Evidence Enigma: Correctional Boot Camps and Other Failures in Evidence-Based Policymaking.* London: Routledge, 2013.

Berk, Richard. "Algorithmic Criminology." *Security Informatics* 2, no. 5 (2013).

Berk, Richard, and Justin Bleich. "Statistical Procedures for Forecasting Criminal Behavior: A Comparative Assessment." *Criminology and Public Policy* 12, no. 3 (2013): 513–44.

Bessler, John D. *The Birth of American Law: An Italian Philosopher and the American Revolution.* Durham, NC: Carolina Academic Press, 2014.

Biles, D. "Imprisonment and Its Alternatives." *Australian Law Journal* 55, no. 3 (1981): 126–34.

Bishop, George Victor. *Executions: The Legal Ways of Death.* Los Angeles: Sherbourne Press, 1965.

Black, Donald. "Crime as Social Control." *American Sociological Review* 48, no. 1 (1983): 34–45.

Blackburn, Robin. *The Making of New World Slavery: From the Baroque to the Modern, 1492–1800*. New York: Verso, 1997.

Bok, Sissela. *Lying: Moral Choice in Public and Private Life*. New York: Vintage, 1979.

Bowker, Lee H. *Prison Victimization*. New York: Elsevier, 1982.

Braga, Anthony A., and David L. Weisburd. "The Effects of Focused Deterrence Strategies on Crime: A Systematic Review and Meta-analysis of the Empirical Evidence." *Journal of Research in Crime and Delinquency* 49, no. 3 (2011): 323–58.

Braly, Malcolm. *False Starts*. London: Penguin, 1976.

Brand, C. E. *Roman Military Law*. Austin: University of Texas Press, 1968.

Braswell, Michael, Reid H. Montgomery, and Lucian X. Lombardo. *Prison Violence in America*. 2nd ed. Cincinnati: Anderson, 1994.

Brodsky, Stanley L., and Norman E. Eggleston, eds. *The Military Prison: Theory, Research, and Practice*. Carbondale: Southern Illinois University Press, 1970.

Bronson, Jennifer, E. Ann Carson, Margaret E. Noonan, and Marcus Berzofsky, *Veterans in Prison and Jail, 2011–2012*. Washington, DC: Bureau of Justice Statistics, 2015.

Brown, Norman O. *Life against Death*. Middletown, CT: Wesleyan University Press, 1959.

———. *Love's Body*. Berkeley: University of California Press, 1966.

Brown v. Plata, 563 US 493 (2011).

Brownstein, Ronald. "Singapore's Caning Sentence Divides Americans, Poll Finds." *Los Angeles Times*, April 21, 1994. https://www.latimes.com/archives/la-xpm-1994-04-21-mn-48524-story.html.

Buckenmaier, Johannes, Eugen Dimant, Ann-Christin Posten, and Ulrich Schmidt. "On Punishment Institutions and Effective Deterrence of Illicit Behavior." Kiel Working Paper 2090, Kiel Institute for the World Economy and University of Johannesburg, 2017.

Buckland, W. W. *A Text-Book of Roman Law: From Augustus to Justinian*. 3rd ed. London: Cambridge University Press, 2007.

Burckhardt, Jacob. *The Civilization of the Renaissance in Italy*. Translated by S. G. C. Middlemore. New York: Penguin, 1990.

Byrne, James M., Faye S. Taxman, and Donald Hummer. *The Culture of Prison Violence*. New York: Prentice Hall, 2007.

Caldwell, Robert Graham. *Red Hannah: Delaware's Whipping Post*. Philadelphia: University of Pennsylvania Press, 1947.

Campbell, Michael C. "Are All Politics Local? A Case Study of Local Conditions in a Period of 'Law and Order' Politics." *Annals of the American Academy of Political and Social Science* 664, no. 1 (2016): 43–61.

———. "Varieties of Mass Incarceration: What We Learn from State Histories." *Annual Review of Criminology* 1 (2018): 219–34.

Campbell, Michael C., and Matt Vogel. "The Demographic Divide: Population Dynamics, Race and the Rise of Mass Incarceration in the United States." *Punishment and Society* 21, no. 1 (2019): 47–69.

Campbell, Michael C., Matt Vogel, and Joshua Williams. "Historical Contingencies and the Evolving Importance of Race, Violent Crime, and Region in Explaining Mass Incarceration in the United States." *Criminology* 53, no. 2 (2015): 180–203.

Carlen, Pat, and Jacqueline Tombs. "Reconfigurations of Penality: The Ongoing Case of the Women's Imprisonment and Reintegration Industries." *Theoretical Criminology* 10, no. 3 (2006): 337–60.

Carlsmith, Kevin M., John M. Darley, and Paul H. Robinson "Why Do We Punish? Deterrence and Just Deserts as Motives for Punishment." *Journal of Personality and Social Psychology* 83, no. 2 (2002): 284–99.

Carpenter, Catherine L. and Amy E. Beverlin. "The Evolution of Unconstitutionality in Sex Offender Registration Laws." *Hastings Law Journal* 63, no. 4 (2012): 1071–1133.

Carson, E. Ann. *Bureau of Justice Statistics.* September 17, 2015, http://www.bjs.gov/index.cfm?ty=pbdetail&iid=5387.

Center for Security Policy. "Poll of U.S. Muslims Reveals Ominous Levels of Support for Islamic Supremacists' Doctrine of Shariah, Jihad." June 23, 2015. https://www.centerforsecuritypolicy.org/2015/06/23/nationwide-poll-of-us-muslims-shows-thousands-support-shariah-jihad/.

———. *Shariah: The Threat to America, an Exercise in Competitive Analysis.* Report of Team B II. Washington, DC: Center for Security Policy, 2010. https://www.centerforsecuritypolicy.org/2010/09/13/shariah-the-threat-to-america/.

Chester, Barbara. "Because Mercy Has a Human Heart: The Centers for Victims of Torture," In *Psychology and Torture*, edited by Peter Suedfeld, 165–84. New York: Taylor and Francis, 1990.

Chouldechova, Alexandra, and Max G'Sell. "Fairer and More Accurate, but for Whom?" June 30, 2017. arXiv:1707.00046.

Christie, Nils. *The Limits to Pain.* London: Robertson, 1981.

Cicero, Marcus Tullius. *The Political Works of Marcus Tullius Cicero: Comprising His Treatise on the Commonwealth; and His Treatise on the Laws.* Translated by Francis Barham. Vol. 1. London: Edmund Spettigue, 1841. http://oll.libertyfund.org/titles/546.

Claver, Scott. *Under the Lash: A History of Corporal Punishment in the British Armed Forces.* London: Torchstream Books, 1954.

Clear, Todd R., and Natasha A. Frost. *The Punishment Imperative: The Rise and Failure of Mass Incarceration in America.* New York: New York University Press, 2015.

Cofflard, Maureen, "British 'Sharia Courts' under Scrutiny." AFP, November 13, 2016. https://www.yahoo.com/news/british-sharia-courts-under-scrutiny-075656056.html.

Cohen, Fred. "Deliberate Indifference: A divided En Banc Seventh Circuit Speaks." *Correctional Law Reporter*, December/January 2017, 53–56.

———. "E-carceration: A Comment." *Correctional Law Reporter*, February/March 2019, 77.

———. "A Friendly Exchange: From Rikers Island Jail to a Progressive Prison." *Correctional Law Reporter*, June/July 2017, 5–6.

———. "U.S. Leads World in Women in Prison." *Correctional Law Reporter*, December/January 2017, 65.

Coker v. Georgia, 433 U.S. 584 (1977).

Comfort, Megan. "Punishment beyond the Legal Offender." *Annual Review of Law and Social Science* 3 (2007): 271–96.

Conley, John A. "Prisons, Production, and Profit: Reconsidering the Importance of Prison Industries." *Journal of Social History* 14, no. 2 (1980): 257–75.

Copan, Paul. *Is God a Moral Monster? Making Sense of the Old Testament God.* Ada, MI: Baker Books, 2011.

Crosbie, John. "Negative Reinforcement and Punishment." In *Handbook of Research Methods in Human Operant Behavior*, edited by Kennon A. Lattal and Michael Perone, 163–89. New York: Plenum Press, 1998.

Cullen, Francis T., Cheryl Lero Jonson, and Daniel S. Nagin. "Prisons Do Not Reduce Recidivism: The High Cost of Ignoring Science." *Prison Journal* 91, no. 3 (2011): 48s–65s.

Cullen, Francis T., Paula Smith, Christopher T. Lowenkamp, and Edward J. Latessa. "Nothing Works Revisited: Deconstructing Farabee's *Rethinking Rehabilitation*." *Victims and Offenders* 4, no. 2 (2009): 101–23.

Dagger, Richard. "Restitution, Punishment, and Debts to Society." In *Victims, Offenders and Alternative Sanctions*, edited by Joe Hudson and Burt Galaway, 3–13. Lexington, MA: D. C. Heath, 1980.

Daley, Suzanne. "Speeding in Finland Can Cost a Fortune, If You Already Have One." *New York Times*, April 25, 2015.

Dancig-Rosenberg, Hadar, and Tali Galt. "Restorative Criminal Justice." *Cardozo Law Review* 34, no. 6 (2013): 2313–46.

Dante Alighieri. *Purgatory.* Translated by Dorothy L. Sayers. London: Penguin, 1955.

———. *The Inferno.* Translated by Dorothy L. Sayers. London: Penguin, 1955.

Davis, Jennifer. "The London Garotting Panic of 1862: A Moral Panic and the Creation of a Criminal Class in Mid-Victorian England." In *Crime and the Law: The Social History of Crime in Western Europe since 1500*, edited by V. A. C. Gatrell, Bruce Lenman, and Geoffrey Parker, 190–213. London: Europa, 1980.

Death Penalty Information Center. "Arbitrariness: In the Leading Execution State, Many Receive Probation for Murder." November 19, 2007. http://www.deathpenaltyinfo.org/node/2217.

DeMoulin Bros. *The 1930 DeMoulin Bros. and Co. Fraternal Supply Catalog No. 439.* http://www.phoenixmasonry.org/masonicmuseum/demoulin/index.htm.

Departmental Committee on Corporal Punishment. *Command Paper*. No. 5684. Honourable Edward Cardogan, chairman. London: HMSO, 1938.

Dershowitz, Alan M. "Criminal Sentencing in the United States: An Historical and Conceptual Overview." *Annals of the American Academy of Political and Social Science* 423, no. 1 (1976): 117–32.

———. *Fair and Certain Punishment*. Twentieth Century Fund. Task Force on Criminal Sentencing. New York: McGraw-Hill, 1976.

———. "Tortured Reasoning." In *Torture: A Collection*, edited by Sanford Levinson, 257–80. New York: Oxford University Press, 2004.

———. *Why Terrorism Works: Understanding the Threat, Responding to the Challenge*. New Haven, CT: Yale University Press, 2002.

Dinitz, Simon. "Are Safe and Humane Prisons Possible?" *Australian and New Zealand Journal of Criminology* 14, no. 1 (1981): 3–19.

Dodge, Calvert R. *A World without Prisons: Alternatives to Incarceration throughout the World*. Lexington, MA: D. C. Heath, 1979.

Drucker, Ernest. *A Plague of Prisons: The Epidemiology of Mass Incarceration in America*. New York: New Press, 2013.

Durkheim, Emile. *The Elementary forms of Religious Life*. New York: Free Press, 1965.

Eitches, Eliana Rae. "Coerced Prison Labor without Union Protection: The Exploitation of the Prison Industrial Complex." Academic Commons, Columbia University Libraries, 2010. doi:10.7916/D8VX0QZB.

Elliott, Frank A. "A Neurological Perspective of Violent Behavior." In *The Science, Treatment, and Prevention of Antisocial Behaviors: Application to the Criminal Justice System*, edited by Diana H. Fishbein, ch. 19, 1–21. Kingston, NJ: Civic Research Institute, 2000.

Engber, Daniel, "Is There a Lot of Crime on Military Bases? Not as Much as You'd Think." *Slate*, November 5, 2009. http://www.slate.com/articles/news_and_politics/explainer/2009/11/is_there_a_lot_of_crime_on_military_bases.html.

Engels, Friedrich. *The Condition of the Working-Class in England in 1844; with a Preface written in 1892*. Translated by Florence Kelley Wischnewetzky. N.p.: Createspace, 2016.

Enten, Harry. "Americans' Opinions on Spanking Vary by Party, Race, Region and Religion." *FiveThirtyEight*, September 15, 2014. http://fivethirtyeight.com/datalab/americans-opinions-on-spanking-vary-by-party-race-region-and-religion/.

Evans, E. P. *The Criminal Prosecution and Capital Punishment of Animals*. London: Faber and Faber, 1987.

Ewing v. California, 538 U.S. 11 (2003).

Eysenck, H. J. *Crime and Personality*. 3rd. ed. London: Routledge and Kegan Paul, 1977.

Fabrega, Horacio, and Stephen Tyma. "Culture, Language and the Shaping of Illness: An Illustration Based on Pain." *Journal of Psychosomatic Research* 20, no. 4 (1976): 323–37.

Fair Sentencing Act of 2010, Pub. L. No. 111-220.

Fanon, Frantz. *The Wretched of the Earth*. New York: Grove, 1968.

Farabee, David. *Rethinking Rehabilitation*. Washington, DC: AEI Press, 2005.

Farmer v. Brennan, 511 U.S. 825 (1994).

Ferguson, Robert A. *Inferno: An Anatomy of American Punishment*. Cambridge, MA: Harvard University Press, 2014.

Fettig, Amy. "What Is Driving Solitary Confinement Reform?" *Correctional Law Reporter* 28, no. 3 (2016): 33–34.

Flanders, Chad. "The Supreme Court and the Rehabilitative Ideal." Legal Studies Research Papers Series 2014-3, Saint Louis University School of Law, 2014.

Foucault, Michel. *Discipline and Punish: The Birth of the Prison*. Translated by Alan Sheridan. New York: Pantheon, 1977.

———. *Madness and Civilization: A History of Insanity in the Age of Reason*. Translated by Richard Howard. New York: Vintage, 1964.

Fouzder, Monidipa. "Artificial Intelligence Mimics Judicial Reasoning." *Law Society Gazette*, June 22, 2016. https://www.lawgazette.co.uk/law/artificial-intelligence-mimics-judicial-reasoning/5056017.article.

Frankel, Marvin E. *Criminal Sentences: Law without Order*. New York: Hill and Wang, 1972.

Frase, Richard S. "Excessive Prison Sentences, Punishment Goals, and the Eighth Amendment: 'Proportionality' Relative to What?" *Minnesota Law Review* 89 (2005): 571–651.

Freilich, Joshua D., and Graeme R. Newman. "The New Criminology of Crime Control." *Annals of the American Academy of Political and Social Science* 679, no. 1 (2018): 8–18.

———. "Transforming Piecemeal Social Engineering into 'Grand' Crime Prevention Policy: Toward a New Criminology of Social Control." *Journal of Criminal Law and Criminology* 105, no. 1 (2015): 203–32.

Freud, Sigmund. *Civilization and Its Discontents*. Translated by James Strachey. New York: W. W. Norton, 1961.

———. *Totem and Taboo*. Translated by A. A. Brill. New York: Random House, 1946.

Fromm, Erich. *The Anatomy of Human Destructiveness*. New York: Holt, Rinehart and Winston, 1973.

Garland, David. *Punishment and Modern Society*. Chicago: University of Chicago Press, 1990.

Garn, Stanley M., ed. *Culture and the Direction of Human Evolution*. Detroit: Wayne State University Press, 1964.

Gaylin, Willard. *Partial Justice: A Study of Bias in Sentencing*. New York: Vintage, 1975.

Gaylin, Willard, Ira Glasser, Steven Marcus, and David J. Rothman. *Doing Good: The Limits of Benevolence*. New York: Pantheon, 1978.

Gelsthorpe, Loraine, and Nicola Padfield, eds. *Exercising Discretion: Decision Making in the Criminal Justice System and Beyond*. London: Willan, 2003.

Geltner, G. *Flogging Others: Corporal Punishment and Cultural Identity from Antiquity to the Present*. Amsterdam: Amsterdam University Press, 2014.

Gendreau, Paul, and Robert R. Ross. "Revivification of Rehabilitation: Evidence from the 1980s." *Justice Quarterly* 4, no. 3 (1987): 349–407.

Ghassemi, Ghassem. "Criminal Punishment in Islamic Societies: Empirical Study of Attitudes to Criminal Sentencing in Iran." *European Journal on Criminal Policy and Research* 15, nos. 1–2 (2009): 159–80.

Gleissner, John Dewar. "Prison Overcrowding Cure: Judicial Corporal Punishment of Adults." *Criminal Law Bulletin* 49, no. 4 (2013): 711–55.

Glenn, Myra C. *Campaigns against Corporal Punishment: Prisoners, Sailors, Women, and Children in Antebellum America.* Albany: State University of New York Press, 1984.

Goffman, Erving. *Asylums: Essays on the Social Situation of Mental Patients and Other Inmates.* New York: Doubleday, 1961.

Goldsworthy, Adrian. *Pax Romana: War, Peace, and Conquest in the Roman World.* New Haven: Yale University Press, 2017.

Gorman-Smith, Deborah, and Johnny L. Matson. "A Review of Treatment Research for Self-injurious and Stereotyped Responding." *Journal of Mental Deficiency Research* 29, no. 4 (1985): 295–308.

Gould, Laurie A., and Matthew Pate. "Discipline, Docility and Disparity: A Study of Inequality and Corporal Punishment." *British Journal of Criminology* 50, no. 2 (2010): 185–205.

Graham v. West Virginia, 224 U.S. 616 (1912).

Granucci, Anthony F. " 'Nor Cruel and Unusual Punishments Inflicted': The Original Meaning." *California Law Review* 57, no. 4 (1969): 839–65.

Graziano, Frank. *Divine Violence: Spectacle, Psychosexuality and Radical Christianity in the Argentine "Dirty War."* Boulder, CO: Westview Press, 1992.

Haag, Ernest van den. *Punishing Criminals: Concerning a Very Old and Painful Question.* New York: Basic Books, 1975.

Haasen, Christian, Uwe Verthein, Peter Degkwitz, Juergen Berger, Michael Krausz, and Dieter Naber. "Heroin-Assisted Treatment for Opioid Dependence: Randomised Controlled Trial." *British Journal of Psychiatry* 191, no. 1 (2007): 55–62.

Haleem, Muhammed Abdel, Adel Omar Sherif, and Kate Daniels. *Criminal Justice in Islam.* London: I. B. Tauris, 2003.

Hall, Daniel E. "When Caning Meets the Eighth Amendments: Whipping Offenders in the United States." *Widener Journal of Public Law* 4, no. 2 (1995): 403–60.

Halpern-Meekin, Sarah, and Kristin Turney. "Relationship Churning and Parenting Stress among Mothers and Fathers." *Journal of Marriage and Family* 78, no. 3 (2016): 715–29.

Hamber, Brandon, Traggy Maepa, Tlhoki Mofokeng, and Hugo van der Merwe. "Survivors' Perceptions of the Truth and Reconciliation Commission and Suggestions for the Final Report." Centre for the Study of Violence and Reconciliation and the Khulumani Support Group, February 1998. https://www.csvr.org.za/index.php/publications/1705-submission-to-the-truth-and-

reconciliation-commission-survivors-perceptions-of-the-truth-and-reconcilia-
tion-commission-and-suggestions-for-the-final-report.html.

Haney, Craig. *Reforming Punishment: Psychological Limits to the Pains of Imprisonment.*
Law and Public Policy. Washington, DC: American Psychological Association,
2005.

Harcourt, Bernard E. *Against Prediction: Profiling, Policing, and Punishing in an
Actuarial Age.* Chicago: University of Chicago Press, 2008.

Hardy, M. J. L. *Blood Feuds and the Payment of Blood Money in the Middle East.*
Leiden: E. J. Brill, 1963.

Harmelin v. Michigan, 501 U.S. 957 (1991).

Harris, Sandra L., and Robin Ersner-Hershfield. "Behavioral Suppression of Seriously
Disruptive Behavior in Psychotic and Retarded Patients: A Review of Punishment and Its Alternatives." *Psychological Bulletin* 85, no. 6 (1978): 1352–75.

Harrison, Brian W. "Torture and Corporal Punishment as a Problem in Catholic
Theology, Part II." *Roman Theological Forum* 119 (2005). http://www.rtforum.
org/lt/lt119.html.

Hartney, Christopher, and Susan Marchionna. *Attitudes of US Voters toward Nonserious
Offenders and Alternatives to Incarceration.* Oakland, CA: National Council on
Crime and Delinquency, 2009. http://www.nccdglobal.org/sites/default/files/
publication_pdf/focus-voter-attitudes.pdf.

Hay, Douglas, Peter Linebaugh, John G. Rule, E. P. Thompson, and Calvin Winslow.
Albion's Fatal Tree: Crime and Society in Eighteenth-Century England. New
York: Pantheon, 1975.

Henrichson, Christian, and Ruth Delaney. *The Price of Prisons: What Incarceration
Costs Taxpayers.* Washington, DC: Vera Institute of Justice. https://www.vera.
org/publications/price-of-prisons-what-incarceration-costs-taxpayers.

Hentig, Hans von. *Punishment: Its Origin, Purpose and Psychology.* Montclair, NJ:
Patterson Smith, 1973.

Hester, Rhys, and Todd K. Hartman. "Conditional Race Disparities in Criminal
Sentencing: A Test of the Liberation Hypothesis from a Non-guidelines State."
Journal of Quantitative Criminology 33, no. 1 (2017): 77–100.

Hester, Rhys, and Eric L. Sevigny. "Court Communities in Local Context: A Multilevel Analysis of Felony Sentencing in South Carolina." *Journal of Crime
and Justice* 39, no. 1 (2016): 55–74.

Hill, Enid. "Comparative and Historical Study of Modern Middle Eastern Law."
American Journal of Comparative Law 26, no. 2 (1978): 279–304.

Hillyard, Paddy, and Steve Tombs. "From 'Crime' to Social Harm?" *Crime, Law
and Social Change* 48, nos. 1–2 (2007): 9–25.

Hillyard, Paddy, Christina Pantazis, Steve Tombs, and Dave Gordon. " 'Social Harm'
and Its Limits?" In *Criminal Obsessions: Why Harm Matters More Than Crime,*
edited by Paddy Hillyard, Christina Pantazis, Steve Tombs, Dave Gordon,
and Danny Dorling, 59–73. London: Crime and Society Foundation, 2005.

Hirsch, Amy E., Sharon M. Dietrich, Rue Landau, Peter D. Schneider, Irv Ackelsberg, Judith Bernstein-Baker, and Joseph Hohenstein. *Every Door Closed: Barriers Facing Parents with Criminal Record*. Philadelphia: Community Legal Services, 2002. http://www.clasp.org/resources-and-publications/files/every_door_closed.pdf.

Hirsch, Andrew von. *Deserved Criminal Sentences: An Overview*. Oxford: Hart, 2017.

———. *Doing Justice: The Choice of Punishments*. Report of the Committee for the Study of Incarceration. Preface by Charles Goodell, chairman. New York: Hill and Wang, 1976.

Hofer, Paul J., and Barbara S. Meierhoefer. *Home Confinement: An Evolving Sanction in the Federal Criminal Justice System*. Washington, DC: Federal Judicial Center, 1987.

Hoff, Harold A. *Corporal Punishment: Is It Effective? An Empirical Study of School Punishment Records*. N.p.: Create Space Independent Publishing, 2014.

Homel, Ross. "Drivers Who Drink and Rational Choice: Random Breath Testing and the Process of Deterrence." In *Routine Activity and Rational Choice*, edited by Ronald V. Clarke and Marcus Felson, 59–84. Advances in Criminological Theory 5. New Brunswick, NJ: Transaction, 1993.

Howard, Gregory J., Graeme R. Newman, and William Pridemore. "Theory, Method and Data in Comparative Criminology." In *Criminal Justice 2000*, vol. 4, *Measurement and Analysis of Crime and Justice*, edited by National Institute of Justice. Washington, DC: National Institute of Justice, 2000.

Hughes, Louis. *Thirty Years a Slave: From Bondage to Freedom*. N.p.: Bibliolife, 2009.

Huntington, Samuel P. *The Clash of Civilizations and the Remaking of World Order*. New York: Simon and Schuster, 2011.

Husak, Douglas. *Overcriminalization: The Limits of the Criminal Law*. New York: Oxford University Press, 2009.

Hyde, Jesse. "Life and Death in a Troubled Teen Boot Camp." *Rolling Stone*, November 12, 2015. http://www.rollingstone.com/culture/news/life-and-death-in-a-troubled-teen-boot-camp-20151112.

Ignatieff, Michael. *A Just Measure of Pain: The Penitentiary in the industrial Revolution*. New York: Pantheon, 1978.

Ingraham v. Wright, 430 U.S. 651 (1977).

Irwin, John. *Prisons in Turmoil*. Boston: Little, Brown, 1980.

Irwin, John, and James Austin. *It's About Time: America's Imprisonment Binge*. Belmont, CA: Wadsworth, 1994.

Jackson v. Bishop, 404 F.2d 571 (8th Cir. 1968).

Jackson v. California, 135 S. Ct. 677 (2014).

Jeglic, Elizabeth L., Holly A. Vanderhoff, and Peter J. Donovick. "The Function of Self-harm Behavior in a Forensic Population." *International Journal of Offender Therapy and Comparative Criminology* 49, no. 2 (2005): 131–42.

Finn, John D. "Brutal 'Oregon Boot' Made Our State Prison Famous." *Offbeat Oregon*, March 9, 2014. http://offbeatoregon.com/1403b.oregon-boot-cruel-unusual-punishment.html.

Kaba, Fatos, Andrea Lewis, Sarah Glowa-Kollisch, James Hadler, David Lee, Howard Alper, Daniel Selling, et al. "Solitary Confinement and Risk of Self-Harm among Jail Inmates." *American Journal of Public Health* 104, no. 3 (2014): 442–47.

Kara, Mustafa Abdulmegid. "Philosophy of Punishment in Islamic Law." PhD diss., State University of New York at Albany, 1977.

Kendrick, Josh. "The Future Of Sentencing Is Here: Robot Judges." *Mimesis Law*, July 18, 2016. http://mimesislaw.com/fault-lines/the-future-of-sentencing-is-here-robot-judges/11422.

Kenkel, Donald S., and Steven F. Koch. "Deterrence and Knowledge of the Law: The Case of Drunk Driving." *Applied Economics* 33, no. 7 (2001): 845–54.

Kennedy, Kevin C. "A Critical Appraisal of Criminal Deterrence Theory." *Dickinson Law Review* 88, no. 1 (1983): 1–13.

Kentridge, William. "Director's Note." In *Ubu and the Truth Commission*, by Jane Taylor, viii–xv. Cape Town: University of Cape Town Press, 2007.

Khomeini, Ruhollah. *Sayings of the Ayatollah Khomeini*. Translated by Harold J. Salemson. New York: Bantam, 1979.

Kilmer, Beau, Nancy Nicosia, Paul Heaton, and Greg Midgette. "Efficacy of Frequent Monitoring with Swift, Certain, and Modest Sanctions for Violations: Insights from South Dakota's 24/7 Sobriety Project." *American Journal of Public Health* 103, no. 1 (2013): e37–e43.

Kirchner, Lauren. "The Elderly Prison Population Is Soaring and So Are Its Costs." *Pacific Standard*, April 2, 2015. https://psmag.com/the-elderly-prisoner-population-is-soaring-and-so-are-its-costs-24ddd8d28877#.fodtiaa4y.

Kittrie, Nicholas N. *The Right to Be Different: Deviance and Enforced Therapy*. New York: Pelican, 1973.

Klingensmith, Mark W. "Computers Laying Down the Law: Will Judges Become Obsolete?" *Florida Bar Journal* 90, no. 1 (2016), https://www.floridabar.org/divcom/jn/jnjournal01.nsf/8c9f13012b96736985256aa900624829/b31e0be4da96963485257f29005a0048!OpenDocument.

Kolber, Adam J. "The Subjective Experience of Punishment." *Colombia Law Review* 109, no. 1 (2009): 182–236.

Kosterlitz, Hans W., and Lars Y. Terenius, eds. *Pain and Society*. Berlin: Verlag Chemie, 1980.

Kress, Jack M., *Prescription for Justice: The Theory and Practice of Sentencing Guidelines*. Boston, MA: Ballinger, 1980.

Kropotkin, Petr. *Mutual Aid: A Factor of Evolution*. Boston: Extending Horizon Books, 1914.

Lafree, Gary, Laura Dugan, and Raven Korte. "The Impact of British Counterterrorist Strategies on Political Violence in Northern Ireland: Comparing Deterrence and Backlash Models." *Criminology* 47, no. 1 (2009): 17–45.

Lagemann, Ellen Condliffe. *Liberating Minds: The Case for College in Prison*. New York: New Press, 2016.

Lea, Henry Charles. *The Inquisition of the Middle Ages*. New York: Harper, 1979.

Lerman, Dorothea C., and Christina M. Vorndran. "On the Status of Knowledge for Using Punishment: Implications for Treating Behavior Disorders." *Journal of Applied Behavior Analysis* 35, no. 4 (2002): 431–64.

Levenson, Jill, and Richard Tewksbury. "Collateral Damage: Family Members of Registered Sex Offenders." *American Journal of Criminal Justice* 34, nos. 1–2 (2009): 54–68.

Levin, Michael. "The Case for Torture." *Newsweek*, June 7, 1982.

———. Interview. *Penthouse Magazine*, October 1982.

Levy, David. *Love and Sex with Robots: The Evolution of Human-Robot Relations*. New York: Harper-Collins, 2009.

Lewis, C. S. "The Humanitarian Theory of Punishment." In *Contemporary Punishment*, edited by Rudolph J. Gerber and Patrick D. McAnany. Notre Dame, IN: University of Notre Dame Press, 1972.

———. *The Problem of Pain*. London: Macmillan, 1973.

Lewis, Tanya. "Don't Let Artificial Intelligence Take Over, Top Scientists Warn." *Live Science*, January 12, 2015. https://www.livescience.com/49419-artificial-intelligence-dangers-letter.html.

Lichstein, Kenneth L., and Laura Schreibman. "Employing Electric Shock with Autistic Children: A Review of the Side Effects." *Journal of Autism and Childhood Schizophrenia* 6, no. 2 (1976): 163–73.

Lin, Shu S., Lauren Rich, Jay D. Pal, and Robert M. Sade. "Prisoners on Death Row Should Be Accepted as Organ Donors." *Annals of Thoracic Surgery* 93, no. 6 (2012): 773–79.

Lintott, Andrew. *The Constitution of the Roman Republic*. London: Oxford University Press, 2003.

Lockwood, Daniel. *Prison Sexual Violence*. New York: Elsevier, 1981.

Lockyer v. Andrade, 538 U.S. 63 (2003).

Logan, Charles H. *Criminal Justice Performance Measures for Prisons*. Washington, DC: National Institute of Justice, 1993.

Looman, Mary D., and John D. Carl. *A Country Called Prison: Mass Incarceration and the Making of a New Nation*. New York: Oxford University Press. 2015.

Lorenz, Konrad. *On Aggression*. Translated by Marjorie Kerr Wilson. New York: Bantam, 1967.

Lowenstein, L. F. "The Genetic Aspects of Criminality." *Journal of Human Behavior in the Social Environment* 8, no. 1 (2004): 63–78.

Luna, Erik. Review of *Inferno: An Anatomy of American Punishment*, by Robert A. Ferguson. *Criminal Justice Ethics* 34, no. 2 (2015): 210–47.

Mabbott, J. D. "Punishment." *Mind* 48, no. 190 (1939): 152–67.

MacDonald, Heather. "Obama's Tragic Let 'Em Out Fantasy." *Wall Street Journal*, October 23, 2015.

MacKenzie, Doris L., and Gaylene S. Armstrong, eds. *Correctional Boot Camps: Military Basic Training or a Model for Corrections?* Thousand Oaks, CA: Sage, 2004.

Maddan, Sean, and William Hallahan "Corporal Punishment in the 21st Century: An Examination of Supreme Court Decisions in the 1990s to Predict the Reemergence of Flagellance." *Journal of Crime and Justice* 25, no. 2 (2002): 97–120.

Maghan, Jess. "Long-Term and Dangerous Inmates: Maximum Security Incarceration in the United States." Working paper, Great Cities Institute, College of Urban Planning and Public Affairs, University of Illinois at Chicago, 1996.

Marcus, Steven. *Engels, Manchester, and the Working Class.* Piscataway, NJ: Transaction, 2015.

Marongiu, Pietro. *Criminalità e banditismo in Sardegna: Fra tradizione e innovazione.* Rome: Carocci, 2004.

Marongiu, Pietro, and Graeme R. Newman. *Vengeance: The Fight against Injustice.* Totowa, NJ: Littlefield Adams, 1986.

Martinson, Robert. "What Works? Questions and Answers about Prison Reform." *Public Interest* 35 (Spring 1974): 22–54.

Masters, Kim J. "Physical Restraint: A Historical Review and Current Practice." *Psychiatric Annals* 47, no. 1 (2017): 52–55.

Matson, Johnny L., and Thomas M. DiLorenzo. *Punishment and Its Alternatives: A New Perspective for Behavior Modification.* New York: Springer, 1984.

Matson, Johnny L., and Marie E. Taras. "A 20 Year Review of Punishment and Alternative Methods to Treat Problem Behaviors in Developmentally Delayed Persons." *Research in Developmental Disabilities* 10, no. 1 (1989): 85–104.

Matthews, Michael P. "Caning and the Constitution: Why the Backlash against Crime Won't Result in the Back-Lashing of Criminals." *New York Law School Journal of Human Rights* 14 (1998): 571–614.

Mazur, James E. *Learning and Behavior.* 3rd ed. Englewood Cliffs, NJ: Prentice Hall, 1994.

McAfee, James K., Christopher Schwilk, and Megan Mitruski. "Public Policy on Physical Restraint of Children with Disabilities in Public Schools." *Education and Treatment of Children* 29, no. 4 (2006): 711–28.

McCoy, Alfred W. *Torture and Impunity: The U.S. Doctrine of Coercive Interrogation.* Madison: University of Wisconsin Press, 2012.

McVay, Doug, Vincent Schiraldi, and Jason Ziedenberg. *Treatment or Incarceration? National and State Findings on the Efficacy and Cost Savings of Drug Treatment versus Imprisonment.* Washington, DC: Justice Policy Institute, 2004. http://www.justicepolicy.org/uploads/justicepolicy/documents/04-01_rep_mdtreatmentorincarceration_ac-dp.pdf.

Mears, Daniel P. *Evaluating the Effectiveness of Supermax Prisons.* Washington, DC: Urban Institute, 2006. https://www.urban.org/research/publication/evaluating-effectiveness-supermax-prisons.

Menninger, Karl. *The Crime of Punishment.* London: Penguin, 1977.

Meranze, Michael. *Laboratories of Virtue: Punishment, Revolution, and Authority in Philadelphia, 1760–1835.* 2nd ed. Chapel Hill: University of North Carolina Press, 1996.

Merskey, Harold. *Pain: Psychological and Psychiatric Aspects.* London: Baillière, Tindall and Cassell, 1967.

Midgely, James O. "Corporal Punishment and Penal Policy: Notes on the Continued Use of Corporal Punishment with Reference to South Africa." *Journal of Criminal Law and Criminology* 73, no. 1 (1982): 388–403.

Milgram, Stanley. "Behavioral Study of Obedience." *Journal of Abnormal and Social Psychology* 67, no. 4 (1963): 371–78.

Miller v. Alabama, 567 U.S. 460 (2012).

Montagu, Ashley. *The Nature of Human Aggression.* London: Oxford University Press, 1976.

Morash, Merry, and Lila Rucker. "A Critical Look at the Idea of Boot Camp as a Correctional Reform." *Crime and Delinquency* 36, no. 2 (1990): 204–22.

Morgan, Zachary R. *Legacy of the Lash: Race and Corporal Punishment in the Brazilian Navy and the Atlantic World.* Bloomington: Indiana University Press, 2014.

Morris, Norval, and Michael Tonry. *Between Prison and Probation: Intermediate Punishments in a Rational Sentencing System.* New York: Oxford University Press, 1991.

Muehlhauser, Luke, and Louie Helm. "Intelligence Explosion and Machine Ethics." In *Singularity Hypotheses: A Scientific and Philosophical Assessment,* edited by Amnon H. Eden, Johnny Søraker, James H. Moor, and Eric Steinhart. Berlin: Springer, 2012.

Mulder, Laetitia B. "The Difference between Punishments and Rewards in Fostering Moral Concerns in Social Decision Making." *Journal of Experimental Social Psychology* 44, no. 6 (2008): 1436–43.

Muller, Christopher, and Christopher Wildeman. "Punishment and Inequality." In *Handbook of Punishment and Society,* edited by Jonathan Simon and Richard Sparks, 169–85. Thousand Oaks, CA: Sage, 2012.

Murtagh, Kevin J. *Corporal Punishment: A Humane Alternative to Incarceration.* Cambridge, MA: LFB Scholarly, 2012.

———. "Is Corporally Punishing Criminals Degrading?" *Journal of Political Philosophy* 20, no. 4 (2012): 481–98.

Nagin, Daniel S. "Deterrence in the Twenty-First Century." *Crime and Justice* 42, no. 1 (2013): 199–263.

National Institute of Justice. *Electronic Monitoring Reduces Recidivism.* Washington, DC: US Department of Justice, Office of Justice Programs, 2011. https://www.ncjrs.gov/pdffiles1/nij/234460.pdf.

Newman, Graeme R. "Car Safety and Car Security: An Historical Comparison." *Crime Prevention Studies* 17 (2004): 217–48.

———. *Comparative Deviance: Perception and Law in Six Cultures.* 2nd ed. Patterson, NJ: Transaction, 2009.

———. *Just and Painful: A Case for the Corporal Punishment of Criminals.* New York: Macmillan, 1983.

———. *Just and Painful: A Case for the Corporal Punishment of Criminals.* 2nd ed. New York: Harrow and Heston, 1995.

———. "Khomeini and Criminal Justice: Notes on Crime and Culture." *Journal of Criminal Law and Criminology* 73, no. 2 (1982): 561–81.

———. "A Market Approach to Crime Prevention." In *Design against Crime: Crime Proofing Everyday Products,* edited by Paul Ekblom, 87–106. Boulder, CO: Lynne Reinner, 2012.

———. *The Problem of Identity Theft.* Guide no. 25. Washington, DC: Center for Problem Oriented Policing, 2004.

———. *The Punishment Response.* 2nd ed. New York: Routledge, 2017.

———. Review of *Conscience and Convenience: The Asylum and Its Alternatives in Progressive America,* by David J. Rothman. *Crime and Delinquency* 27, no. 3 (1981): 422–28.

———. "Theories of Punishment Reconsidered: Rationalizations for Removal." *International Journal of Criminology and Penology* 3, no. 2 (1975): 163–82.

———. "A Theory of Deviance Removal." *British Journal of Sociology* 26, no. 2(1975): 203–17.

Newman, Graeme R., and Pietro Marongiu. "Penological Reform and the Myth of Beccaria." *Criminology* 28, no. 2 (1990): 325–46.

Newman, Graeme R., and Mahesh K. Nalla, eds. *Crime and Punishment around the World.* Vol.1, *Africa and the Middle East.* Santa Barbara, CA: ABC-CLIO, 2010.

New York Times. "Solitary Confinement Is Cruel and All Too Common." Editorial, September 2, 2015.

Norton, Ben. "Scathing U.N. Report: 'Structural Racism' Endures in U.S., and the Government Has Failed to Protect African-Americans' Rights." *Salon,* October 7, 2016.

Nossiter, Adam. "Boko Haram Militants Raped Hundreds of Female Captives in Nigeria." *New York Times,* May 18, 2015.

Ormrod, Jeanne Ellis. "Applications of Instrumental Conditioning." In *Human Learning,* 6th ed., 113–25. New York: Pearson, 2012.

Pak, Jennifer. "How Does China's Social Credit System Work?" *Marketplace,* February 13, 2018. https://www.marketplace.org/2018/02/13/world/qa-china-s-social-credit-system.

Pate, Matthew, and Laurie A. Gould. *Corporal Punishment around the World.* Santa Barbara, CA: Praeger, 2012.

Payne, J. P., and R. A. P. Burt, eds. *Pain: Basic Principles, Pharmacology, Therapy.* Baltimore: Williams and Wilkins, 1972.

Penal Reform International. *Instruments of Restraint: Addressing Risk Factors to Prevent Torture and Ill-Treatment*. Factsheet. London: Penal Reform International, 2013. https://cdn.penalreform.org/wp-content/uploads/2016/01/factsheet-5-restraints-2nd-ed-v5.pdf.

People v. Mosley, 358 NYS2d 1004 (1974).

Pepinsky, Harold E. "This Can't Be Peace: A Pessimist Looks at Punishment." In *Punishment and Privilege*, edited by Graeme R. Newman, 2nd ed., 120–32. New York: Harrow and Heston, 2018.

Peters, Rudolph. *Crime and Punishment in Islamic Law: Theory and Practice from the Sixteenth to the Twenty-First Century*. Cambridge: Cambridge University Press, 2005.

Petersilia, Joan. *House Arrest*. Washington, DC: US Department of Justice, National Institute of Justice, 1988.

Pigliaru, Antonio. *Il codice della vendetta barbaricina*. Milan: Giuffrè, 1975.

Pizzato, Mark. *Theatres of Human Sacrifice: From Ancient Ritual to Screen Violence*. Psychoanalysis and Culture. New York: State University of New York Press. 2004.

Popp, Trey. "Black Box Justice." *Pennsylvania Gazette*, September/October 2017.

Porter, Rachel, Sophia Lee, and Mary Lutz. *Balancing Punishment and Treatment: Alternatives to Incarceration in New York City*. Washington, DC: Vera Institute of Justice, 2002.

Postman, Neil. *Technopoly: The Surrender of Culture to Technology*. New York: Vintage, 1993.

Radzinowicz, Leon. *A History of English Criminal Law and Its Administration from 1750*. Vol. 1, *The Movement for Reform 1750–1833*. London: Stevens and Sons, 1948.

Rattner, Arye. "Convicted but Innocent: Wrongful Conviction and the Criminal Justice System." *Law and Human Behavior* 12, no. 3 (1988): 283–93.

Reiman, Jeffrey. *The Rich Get Richer and the Poor Get Prison: Ideology, Class, and Criminal Justice*. 8th ed. Boston: Allyn and Bacon, 2006.

Rhodes v. Chapman, 452 U.S. 337 (1981).

Rieff, Philip. *The Triumph of the Therapeutic: Uses of Faith after Freud*. New York: Harper, 1966.

Risinger, D. Michael. "Innocents Convicted: An Empirical Justified Factual Wrongful Conviction Rate." *Journal of Criminal Law and Criminology* 97, no. 3 (2007): 761–806.

Roberts, Dorothy E. "The Social and Moral Cost of Mass Incarceration in African American Communities." *Stanford Law Review* 56, no. 5 (2004): 1271–1305.

Robertson, Campbell. "For Offenders Who Can't Pay, It's a Pint of Blood or Jail Time." *New York Times*, October 19, 2015.

Robertson, James E. "Conditions of Confinement in Lockups." *Correctional Law Reporter*, October/November, 2017.

———. "The Old and the New Prison Overcrowding: The Legacy of Rhodes v. Chapman." *Correctional Law Reporter*, December/January, 2017.

———. Review of *The Return of the Medical Model: Disease and the Meaning of Imprisonment from John Howard to Brown v. Plata*, by Jonathan Simon. *Correctional Law Reporter* October/November, 2013.

Robinson v. California, 370 U.S. 660 (1962).

Robinson, Paul H., and John M. Darley. "Does Criminal Law Deter? A Behavioural Science Investigation." *Oxford Journal of Legal Studies* 24, no. 2 (2004): 173–205.

Ronson, Jon. *So You've Been Publicly Shamed*. New York: Riverhead Books, 2015.

Roth, Patrick. "Va. Man Sentenced to 132 Years in Prison for Stealing Tires." *Washington's Top News*, July 18, 2017. http://wtop.com/loudoun-county/2017/07/loundoun-county-tire-thief-gets-137-years-prison/.

Rothman, David J. *Conscience and Convenience: The Asylum and Its Alternatives in Progressive America*. Boston: Little, Brown, 1980.

———. *The Discovery of the Asylum: Social Order and Disorder in the New Republic*. Rev. ed. New Brunswick, NJ: Aldine Transaction, 2002.

Rothman, David J., and Sheila M. Rothman. "The Organ Market." *New York Review of Books*, October 23, 2003. https://www.nybooks.com/articles/2003/10/23/the-organ-market/.

Rountree, Meredtith Martin. "Law and Loss: Notes on the Legal Construction of Pain." *American Journal of Criminal Law* 41, no. 2 (2014): 4–17.

Rummel v. Estelle, 498 F. Supp. 793 (WD Tex. 1980).

Rummel v. Estelle, 445 U.S. 263 (1980).

Ruthven, Malise. *Torture: The Grand Conspiracy*. London: Weidenfeld and Nicolson, 1978.

Sagan, Eli. *Cannibalism: Human Aggression and Cultural Form*. New York: Harper and Row, 1974.

Saleilles, Raymond. *The Individualization of Punishment*. Boston: Little, Brown, 1911.

Sarre, Rick. "Beyond 'What Works?' A 25 Year Jubilee Retrospective of Robert Martinson's Famous Article." *Australian and New Zealand Journal of Criminology* 34, no. 1 (2001): 38–46.

Scarre, Geoffrey. "Corporal Punishment." *Ethical Theory and Moral Practice* 6, no. 3 (2003): 295–316.

Schafer, Stephen. *Compensation and Restitution to Victims of Crime*. 2nd ed. Montclair, NJ: Patterson Smith, 1970.

Scheff, Thomas J. *Catharsis in Healing, Ritual and Drama*. Los Angeles: University of California Press, 2014.

Schneider, Carl E. "The Rise of Prisons and the Origins of the Rehabilitative Ideal." *Michigan Law Review* 77, no. 3 (1979): 707–46.

Schrader, Abby M. *Languages of the Lash: Corporal Punishment and Identity in Imperial Russia*. Dekalb: Northern Illinois University Press, 2002.

Schwartz, Deborah A., and Jay Wishingrad. "The Eighth Amendment, Beccaria, and the Enlightenment: An Historical Justification for the Weems v. U. S. Excessive Punishment Doctrine." *Buffalo Law Review* 24, no. 3 (1975): 783–838.

Schwirtz, Michael, and Michael Winerip. "Violence by Rikers Guards Grew under Bloomberg." *New York Times*, August 13, 2014. http://www.nytimes.com/2014/08/14/nyregion/why-violence-toward-inmates-at-rikers-grew.html?_r=0.

Schwirtz, Michael, Michael Winerip, and Robert Gebeloff. "The Scourge of Racial Bias in New York State's Prisons." *New York Times*, December 3, 2016.

Scolforo, Mark. "States Begin to Go After Restitution Owed by Criminals." *Times Union*, December 22, 2007. http://www.timesunion.com/news/nation-world/article/States-begin-to-go-after-restitution-owed-by-1837869.php.

Sellin, J. Thorsten. *Slavery and the Penal System*. New York: Elsevier, 1976.

Shakur, Sanyika. *Monster: The Autobiography of an L.A. Gang Member*. New York: Penguin, 1994.

Sharvit, Keren, Arie W. Kruglanski, Mo Wang, Xiaoyan Chen, Lauren M. Boyatzi, Boaz Ganor, and Eitan Azani. "The Effects of Israeli Use of Coercive and Conciliatory Tactics on Palestinian's Use of Terrorist Tactics: 2000–2006." *Dynamics of Asymmetric Conflict* 6, nos. 1–3 (2013): 22–44.

Shaw, George Bernard. *The Crime of Imprisonment*. New York: Philosophical Library, 1946.

Shehla, Farzana. "Behavior Modification through Punishment: Does It Work?" *Excellence* 2, no. 1 (2014): 42–51.

Shiono, Nanami. *Julius Caesar: To the Banks of the Rubicon*. Vol.4. of *The Story of the Roman People*, translated by Ronald Dore. N.p.: Shinchosha, 2014. Kindle edition.

Simester, A. P., and Andreas von Hirsch. *Crimes, Harms, and Wrongs: On the Principles of Criminalisation*. London: Hart, 2014.

Simon, Jonathan. "Mass Incarceration on Trial." *Punishment and Society* 13, no. 3 (2011): 251–55.

———. *Mass Incarceration on Trial: A Remarkable Court Decision and the Future of Prisons in America*. New York: New Press, 2014.

———. "Return of the Medical Model: Disease and the Meaning of Imprisonment from John Howard to *Brown v. Plata*." *Harvard Civil Rights-Civil Liberties Law Review* 48, no. 1 (2013): 217–56.

Smith, Cindy J., Jennifer Bechtel, Angie Patrick, Richard R. Smith, and Laura Wilson-Gentry. "Correctional Industries Preparing Inmates for Re-entry: Recidivism and Post-release Employment." Research report submitted to the US Department of Justice, May 2006. https://www.ncjrs.gov/pdffiles1/nij/grants/214608.pdf.

Smith, Kate, and José A. Cabranes. *Fear of Judging: Sentencing Guidelines in the Federal Courts*. Chicago: University of Chicago Press, 1998.

Smith, Roger. *Prison Conditions: Overcrowding, Disease, Violence, and Abuse.* Incarceration Issues. Washington, DC: Mason Crest, 2015.

Smith v. Doe, 538 U.S. 84 (2003).

Spohn, Cassia. *How Do Judges Decide? The Search for Fairness and Justice in Punishment.* 2nd ed. Thousand Oaks, CA: Sage, 2009.

Staples, William G. *The Culture of Surveillance: Discipline and Social Control in the United States.* New York: St. Martin's, 1997.

———. *Everyday Surveillance: Vigilance and Visibility in Postmodern Life.* New York: Rowman and Littlefield, 2000.

State v. Cannon, 55 Del. 587, 190 A.2d 514 (1963).

Stemen, Don. *Reconsidering Incarceration: New Directions for Reducing Crime.* New York: Vera Institute of Justice, 2007.

Stephenson v. State, 864 N.E.2d 1022 (Ind. 2007).

Stephenson v. Wilson, 629 F.3d 732 (7th Cir. 2011).

Sternback, Richard A. *Pain: A Psychophysiological Analysis.* New York: Academic Press, 1968.

Stinchcombe, Arthur L., Rebecca Adams, Carol A. Heimer, Kim Lane Scheppele, Tom W. Smith, and D. Garth Taylor. *Crime and Punishment: Changing Attitudes in America.* San Francisco: Jossey-Bass, 1980.

Stohr, Mary K., and Anthony Walsh. *Corrections: The Essentials.* Los Angeles: Sage, 2011.

Straub, Ervin. "The Psychology and Culture of Torture and Torturers." In *Psychology and Torture,* edited by Peter Suedfeld, 49–76. New York: Taylor and Francis, 1990.

Straus, Murray A. *Beating the Devil Out of Them: Corporal Punishment in American Families.* New York: Lexington, 1994.

Straus, Murray A., Emily M. Douglas, and Rose Anne Medeiros. *The Primordial Violence: Spanking Children, Psychological Development, Violence, and Crime.* Abingdon-on-Thames, UK: Routledge, 2014.

Streinhoff, Uwe. *On the Ethics of Torture.* Albany: State University of New York Press, 2013.

Ström, Folke. *On the Sacral Origin of the Germanic Death Penalties.* Stockholm: Wahlström and Widstrand, 1942.

Subcommittee on Federal Death Penalty Cases, Committee on Defender Services, Judicial Conference of the United States. *Federal Death Penalty Cases: Recommendations concerning the Cost and Quality of Defense Representation.* 1998. https://www.uscourts.gov/sites/default/files/original_spencer_report.pdf.

Suedfeld, Peter, ed. *Psychology and Torture.* New York: Taylor and Francis, 1990.

Szasz, Thomas. *The Myth of Mental Illness: Foundations of a Theory of Personal Conduct.* New York: Harper/Collins, 2011.

Tabarrok, Alex. "The Meat Market." *Wall Street Journal,* January 8, 2010. https://www.wsj.com/articles/SB10001424052748703481004574646233272990474.

Tagore, Rabindranath. "Civilization and Progress." Excerpt from a lecture delivered in China. Swaraj Foundation, 1924. http://www.swaraj.org/tagorecivilization.htm.

Taussig, Joseph K. *Military Law.* Annapolis, MD: United States Naval Institute, 1963.

Thaler, Richard H., and Cass R. Sunstein. *Nudge: Improving Decisions about Health, Wealth, and Happiness.* New Haven, CT: Yale University Press, 2008.

Thompson, Rachel H., Brian A. Iwata, Juliet Conners, and Eileen M. Roscoe. "Effects of Reinforcement for Alternative Behavior during Punishment of Selfinjury." *Journal of Applied Behavior Analysis* 32, no. 3 (1999): 317–28.

Timerman, Jacobo. *Prisoner without a Name, Cell without a Number.* Madison: University of Wisconsin Press, 2002.

Tonry, Michael. "Structured Sentencing." *Crime and Justice* 10 (1988): 267–337.

Torrey, E. Fuller, Aaron D. Kennard, Don Eslinger, Richard Lamb, and James Pavle. *More Mentally Ill Persons Are in Jails and Prisons Than Hospitals: A Survey of the States.* Arlington, VA: Treatment Advocacy Center, 2010. https://www.treatmentadvocacycenter.org/storage/documents/final_jails_v_hospitals_study.pdf.

Turney, Kristin. "Beyond Average Effects: Incorporating Heterogeneous Treatment Effects into Family Research." *Journal of Family Theory and Review* 7, no. 4 (2015): 468–81.

———. "Liminal Men: Incarceration and Relationship Dissolution." *Social Problems* 62, no. 4 (2015): 499–528.

Twenge, Jean M. *Generation Me: Why Today's Young Americans Are More Confident, Assertive, Entitled—and More Miserable Than Ever Before.* New York: Atria, 2014.

Twenge, Jean M., and W. Keith Campbell. *The Narcissism Epidemic: Living in the Age of Entitlement.* New York: Atria, 2010.

Ulmer, Jeffrey T., and Julia Laskorunsky. "Sentencing Disparities." In *Advancing Criminology and Criminal Justice Policy,* edited by Thomas G. Blomberg, Julie Mestre Brancale, Kevin M. Beaver, and William D. Bales, 170–86. London: Routledge, 2016.

UNICOR. *Federal Prison Industries, Inc.: Annual Management Report, Fiscal Year 2018.* https://www.unicor.gov/publications/reports/FY2018_AnnualMgmtReport.pdf.

US Probation and Pretrial Services. *Home Confinement.* Court and Community. N.p.: author, 2000. http://www.nhp.uscourts.gov/sites/default/files/pdf/cchome.pdf.

Vera Institute of Justice. *Recalibrating Justice: A Review of 2013 State Sentencing and Corrections Trends.* 2013. https://www.vera.org/newsroom/press-releases/thirty-five-states-enacted-reforms-to-reduce-prison-populations-lower-costs-and-improve-public-safety-in-2013-new-review-says.

Wacquant, Loïc. "The New 'Peculiar Institution': On the Prison as Surrogate Ghetto." *Theoretical Criminology* 4, no. 3 (2000): 377–89.

Walker, Nigel. *The Aims of the Penal System.* Edinburgh: Edinburgh University Press, 1966.

Wan, Tina. "The Unnecessary Evil of Plea Bargaining: An Unconstitutional Conditions Problem and a Not-So-Least Restrictive Alternative." *Southern California Review of Law and Social Justice* 17, no. 1 (2007): 33–61.

Warren, Ricks, and Robert T. Kurlychek. "Treatment of Maladaptive Anger and Aggression: Catharsis vs. Behavior Therapy." *Corrective and Social Psychiatry and Journal of Behavior Technology, Methods and Therapy* 27, no. 3 (1981): 35–139.

Warwick, Kevin. *March of the Machines: The Breakthrough in Artificial Intelligence.* Champaign: University of Illinois Press, 2004.

Weems v. United States, 217 U.S. 349 (1910).

Weissman, Marsha. "Aspiring to the Impracticable: Alternatives to Incarceration in the Era of Mass Incarceration." *New York University Review of Law and Social Change* 33 (2009): 235–69.

Widom, Cathy S. "Does Violence Beget Violence? A Critical Examination of the Literature." *Psychological Bulletin* 106, no. 1 (1989): 3–28.

Wildeman, Christopher, Kristin Turney, and Youngmin Yi. "Paternal Incarceration and Family Functioning: Variation across Federal, State, and Local Facilities." *Annals of the American Academy of Political and Social Science* 665, no. 1 (2016): 80–97.

Wilkins, Leslie T. *Principles of Guidelines for Sentencing: Methodological and Philosophical Issues in Their Development.* Washington, DC: National Institute of Justice, 1981.

Williams, Eric. *Capitalism and Slavery.* Chapel Hill: University of North Carolina Press, 1994.

Wiesenthal, Simon. *Murderers among Us.* New York: McGraw-Hill, 1967.

Wisnewski, J. Jeremy, and R. D. Emerick. *The Ethics of Torture.* London: Continuum, 2009.

Wolff, Harold G., and Stewart Wolff. *Pain.* 2nd ed. Springfield, IL: Charles Thomas, 1958.

Wool, Jon. "The Eighth Amendment: When Is a Sentence Disproportionate?" *Think Justice Blog*, May 24, 2010. Vera Institute of Justice. https://www.vera.org/blog/the-eighth-amendment-when-is-a-sentence-disproportionate.

World Prison Brief. "United States of America." http://www.prisonstudies.org/country/united-states-america.

Wright, Emily M., and Abigail A. Fagan. "The Cycle of Violence in Context: Exploring the Moderating Roles of Neighborhood Disadvantage and Cultural Norms." *Criminology* 51, no. 2 (2013): 217–49.

Zatzick, Douglas F., and Joel E. Dimsdale. "Cultural Variations in Response to Pain Stimuli." *Psychosomatic Medicine* 52 (1990): 544–57.

Zimbardo, Philip G. "The Human Choice: Individuation, Reason, and Order versus Deindividuation, Impulse, and Chaos." *Nebraska Symposium on Motivation* 17 (1969): 237–307.

Index

www.ingramcontent.com/pod-product-compliance
Lightning Source LLC
Chambersburg PA
CBHW030347270326
41926CB00009B/998